Saul Kripke

Philosophy Now

Series Editor: John Shand

This is a fresh and vital series of new introductions to today's most read, discussed and important philosophers. Combining rigorous analysis with authoritative exposition, each book gives a clear, comprehensive and enthralling access to the ideas of those philosophers who have made a truly fundamental and original contribution to the subject. Together the volumes comprise a remarkable gallery of the thinkers who have been at the forefront of philosophical ideas.

Published

Donald Davidson
Marc Joseph

W. V. Quine
Alex Orenstein

Michael Dummett
Bernhard Weiss

Richard Rorty
Alan Malachowski

Saul Kripke
G. W. Fitch

John Searle
Nick Fotion

Thomas Kuhn
Alexander Bird

Charles Taylor
Ruth Abbey

Robert Nozick
A. R. Lacey

Peter Winch
Colin Lyas

Forthcoming

Nelson Goodman
Daniel Cohnitz & Marcus Rossberg

Hilary Putnam
Max de Gaynesford

David Lewis
Daniel Nolan

John Rawls
Catherine Audard

John McDowell
Tim Thornton

Wilfrid Sellars
Willem de Vries

Thomas Nagel
Alan Thomas

Bernard Williams
Mark Jenkins

Saul Kripke

G. W. Fitch

First published in 2004 by Acumen

Acumen Publishing Limited
15a Lewins Yard
East Street
Chesham
Bucks HP5 1HQ
www.acumenpublishing.co.uk

ISBN: 1-902683-87-0 (hardcover)
ISBN: 1-902683-88-9 (paperback)

British Library Cataloguing-in-Publication Data
A catalogue record for this book is available
from the British Library.

Designed and typeset in Century Schoolbook
by Kate Williams, Swansea.
Printed and bound by Biddles, King's Lynn.

To Nancy

Contents

Abbreviations

IN "Identity and Necessity", in *Identity and Individuation*, M. K. Munitz (ed.), 135–64 (New York: New York University Press, 1971).

NN *Naming and Necessity* (Cambridge, MA: Harvard University Press, 1980).

OTT "Outline of a Theory of Truth", *The Journal of Philosophy* **72**(19) (November 1975), 690–716.

PB "A Puzzle About Belief", in *Meaning and Use,* A. Margalit (ed.), 239–83 (Dordrecht: Reidel, 1979). Reprinted in *Propositions and Attitudes*, S. Soames and N. Salmon (eds), 102–48 (Oxford: Oxford University Press, 1988); page references in the text are to this volume.

SCML "Semantical Considerations on Modal Logic", *Acta Philosophica Fennica* **16** (1963), 83–94. Reprinted in *Reference and Modality*, L. Linsky (ed.), 63–72 (Oxford: Oxford University Press, 1971).

WRPL *Wittgenstein on Rules and Private Language* (Oxford: Basil Blackwell, 1982).

SR "Speaker's Reference and Semantic Reference", *Midwest Studies in Philosophy* **2** (1977), 255–76.

Introduction

Saul A. Kripke is one of the most creative and influential philosophers of the twentieth century. It is not an exaggeration to say that he helped change the face of analytic philosophy in the last half of the century. He was born in New York on 13 November 1940. When he was a young child his family moved to Nebraska, where he was raised. Even as a child Kripke exhibited a great talent for mathematics together with an interest in philosophical questions. It is reported that he read the complete works of Shakespeare while in the fourth grade and he published a paper on the completeness of modal logic (which had a substantive impact on philosophy) when he was only 18 years old. He was appointed to the Harvard Society of Fellows in 1963, became an Associate Professor of Philosophy at Rockefeller University, New York in 1968, and was appointed the McCosh Professor of Philosophy at Princeton University in 1977. In 1973, he delivered the John Locke Lectures at Oxford and he was the subject of a *New York Times Magazine* article entitled "New Frontiers in American Philosophy" (1977). He became Professor Emeritus at Princeton in 1998.

One of the major changes of direction philosophy has taken in the latter third of the twentieth century is the revitalization of metaphysics as an area of research. As an area of interest in philosophy, metaphysics had just about died out under the constant attacks of the logical positivists, the ordinary language school of philosophy, and the nominalism of W. V. Quine and Nelson Goodman (although clearly Quine's work was concerned with metaphysical issues). Kripke, first with his formal interpretation of modal logic and later with his lectures on the nature of necessity and language, had a major role in changing the direction of contemporary philosophy. He argued that many of the "received" views in philosophy that had led to the rejection of metaphysics were not only mistaken, but deeply mistaken. Part of the problem, according to Kripke, was a faulty theory of reference. Kripke argued that if one rejected the traditional theory of reference in favour of a more direct theory, then the accepted view of the relationship between the epistemic status of a statement and its metaphysical status might be questioned. The framework that Kripke developed to consider these questions has expanded philosophical discussion and has led to some surprising results. It is a tribute to Kripke's genius that he has contributed groundbreaking results in both mathematical logic and philosophy.

For a number of reasons, it is still too early to say exactly what will be the effect of Kripke's philosophy on the history of philosophy. First, the issues and questions that Kripke raised with his philosophy are still being debated, with limited agreement on many of the problems. And, secondly, much of Kripke's work remains unpublished and is unavailable to the general philosophical public. I suspect that when this work is published it will have a strong influence on future discussions concerning the issues involved.

This book is intended to be an introduction to the philosophy of Saul Kripke as presented in his published work, with the exception of work that is highly formal and consequently of interest to only a limited number of philosophers (e.g. his work on intuitionistic logic). Even though Kripke's more formal contributions to logic will not be discussed here, it should be noted that his work in formal logic is significant. He has made contributions to tense logic, intuitionistic logic and mathematics, higher recursion theory and relevance logic, and his work in modal logic has had an impact on theoretical computer science. We have much of Kripke's philosophical work, including his most famous work, *Naming and Necessity*, in the form of published lectures. Kripke is well known for presenting detailed philosophical lectures with either no notes or only very limited notes. I attended a number of such lectures (on identity, the surprise exam, truth, Nozick's epistemology and others) and in every case the clarity and depth of Kripke's thought was impressive. He explained very complex and subtle issues in a way that it seemed that everyone could understand. This ease of presentation is reflected in the published transcripts of his lectures. As the secondary literature on Kripke reflects, this ease of presentation can also lead to diverse interpretations of Kripke's arguments and what he intended by certain passages. A perfect example of this is his introduction of the phrase 'rigid designator'. Roughly speaking, Kripke says that a rigid designator is an expression or phrase that designates the same thing in every possible world. Yet it turns out that there are distinct ways of understanding the basic idea. For a long time, for example, I understood Kripke to mean that a term α is a rigid designator provided that α designates the same object at each world whether or not that object exists in that world. This was the view that David Kaplan (1989a: 570, n.8) had thought to be Kripke's as well. But Kaplan reports that Kripke has written him to say that his view is neutral with respect to whether or not names designate objects at a world in which the object in question does not exist (see pp. 36–7). Hence we were wrong in our initial interpretations of what Kripke meant. No doubt this is true for other aspects of Kripke's work that are discussed in this book.

Kripke's work has produced a vast secondary literature of papers, dissertations and books. It would take many years to read all that has been written directly about Kripke's views, not to mention all the work that has been influenced by his contributions. This book is not intended as a survey of the secondary literature on Kripke. Nonetheless, a fair understanding of Kripke may be accomplished by considering some of the objections and replies that his work has produced. To this end I have included in each chapter a discussion of some of the main philosophical points of Kripke's philosophy covered in that chapter. This discussion often includes comments by others about his views. I do not claim that the views I discuss are the "best" comments about Kripke or the "most important". They are, I believe, either views that help illuminate Kripke's thought or exhibit what I take to be common misunderstandings concerning Kripke's argument or views.

Kripke cannot be said to be a system-building philosopher like Kant. His approach to philosophy seems to be to find a puzzle or problem to unravel and then follow the unravelled trail to wherever it leads. As we shall see, it often leads to rather surprising results. Certainly, a great deal of Kripke's philosophy has been inspired by his work on formal matters, particularly modal logic and his response to Quine's rejection of modality and similar issues (such as the need for identification conditions for objects). In reading Kripke, one finds deep and perplexing ideas presented with humour and wit, and examples that resonate with the reader. His love of logical and philosophical puzzles emanates throughout his work; often his exposition of a philosophical conundrum illuminates a whole range of philosophical issues.

Saul Kripke

As another well-known philosopher once said about Kripke, he is currently philosophy's true genius.

Acknowledgements

I wish to acknowledge the work and support of many other philosophers. Certainly the brilliant, insightful work of Kripke needs to be acknowledged. A number of other philosophers have also influenced my reading of Kripke and the issues with which Kripke is concerned. Naturally any misdescriptions or misunderstandings of their work are due entirely to me. I would like to recognize the work of George Bealer, Keith Donnellan, Michael Jubien, David Kaplan, David Lewis, Nathan Salmon, Scott Soames and Robert Stalnaker. I would also like to acknowledge the conversations and work of the following, who furthered my understanding of these issues: Bob Adams, Joseph Almog, David Armstrong, Kent Bach, David Braun, Richard Cartwright, David Chalmers, Stew Cohen, Earl Conee, David Cowles, John Devlin, Tom Downing, Fred Feldman, Richard Feldman, Kit Fine, Graeme Forbes, Ed Gettier, John Hawthorne, Robin Jeshion, Jeff King, Bernie Kobes, Ernie La Pore, Ruth Marcus, Mike Nelson, Terence Parsons, John Perry, Al Plantinga, Steve Reynolds, Mark Richard, Steve Schiffer, Ted Sider, Bob Sleigh, David Sosa and Takashi Yagisawa. I also owe a debt of gratitude, for their help and support (philosophically and otherwise), to Tom Blackson, Peter French, Ned Markosian, Jim Tomberlin, Ed Zalta and the two Dons: Don Senneville and Don Thayer. I also wish to thank Ted Guleserian. Not only is he a very good friend, but he is a terrific philosopher and everything I have written has benefited from his insightful comments. Finally, I would like to thank James Levine and an anonymous reader for helpful comments on an early version of this book, and I owe a very special thanks to Nancy Tribbensee and Kate Williams for help in preparing the final version of the manuscript.

Chapter 1
Necessity

Necessity has been called the mother of invention. In philosophy, however, the notion of necessity is viewed in a different and somewhat more controversial light. In certain philosophical circles necessity is viewed as the root of much, if not all, philosophical error. In the latter half of the twentieth century, W. V. Quine, one of America's most influential philosophers, claimed that the logic of necessity, now referred to as *modal logic*, was conceived in sin: the (logical) sin of confusing use with mention. In this philosophical environment, Saul Kripke published his earliest work on modal logic. Kripke's work in modal logic was to have a major influence on the development of modal logic and philosophy in the future. It also was the foundation of many of Kripke's later philosophical contributions. To understand Kripke's early work, it will be helpful to begin by briefly reviewing developments in logic through the twentieth century.

I

As a number of commentators have noted, philosophy at the beginning of the twentieth century took a decidedly linguistic turn, which led, among other things, to a greater interest in logic. The first comprehensive modern system of formal logic is Gottlob Frege's *Begriffsschrift*, published in 1879. Frege's work was not widely known at the time, however, and cannot be said to have had a great influence on the early development of modern logic. One notable exception is the influence it had on Bertrand Russell's own work in the field. Russell, along with A. N. Whitehead, published *Principia Mathematica*

(1910), which did reach a wide audience of philosophers and logicians.

Russell's logic contained the *propositional calculus*. It also contained a calculus for representing functions and properties (called the *functional calculus*, the *lower predicate calculus*, or the *first-order calculus*) that contained quantifiers. Quantifiers are operators that correspond to the functions of the words 'all' and 'some' in ordinary language. The propositional calculus represents important logical relations between propositions and operations that apply to propositions. For example, one of the simplest operations to apply to a proposition is the operation of negation. If p is the proposition that snow is white then the negation of p is the proposition that it is not the case that snow is white (or, less awkwardly, that snow is not white). Another propositional operation is conjunction. In this case the operation of conjunction applies to a pair of propositions to produce the conjunction of the propositions. If q is the proposition that grass is green (and p remains the same as before) then the conjunction of the pair of propositions p and q is the proposition that snow is white and grass is green. Russell and Whitehead (1910) used the symbols introduced by Giuseppe Peano for these various operations. Negation was represented by the symbol '~' and conjunction by the symbol '•'. Hence, the proposition that snow is not white is represented by '~p' and the proposition that snow is white and grass is green by '$p \bullet q$'.

Russell and Whitehead introduced the operation of implication, which they represented with the symbol '⊃'. A controversy arose, however, over whether the operation that '⊃' represented in the propositional calculus was indeed the operation of implication as Russell and Whitehead claimed. One of the main objections came from the philosopher and logician C. I. Lewis (Lewis & Langford 1959). Lewis claimed that 'p implies q' should be understood to mean 'q is deducible from p', but the operation of '⊃' that Russell and Whitehead introduced is too weak to represent the relation of deduction between propositions. The operation that '⊃' stands for, sometimes called the *material conditional*, has the feature that '$p \supset q$' is true if p is false. This cannot be correct according to Lewis because the mere fact that p is false will not entail that q is deducible from p.

To correct this problem, Lewis offered a propositional calculus that contains a stronger form of implication. Lewis called this stronger form of implication *strict implication*. He described various alternative logical systems using strict implication that he labelled

'S1' to 'S5' (the 'S' indicating strict, as opposed to material, implication). Although Lewis's reasons for introducing strict implication concerned the fact that '⊃' was too weak to capture the relation of deducibility or implication between propositions, he also defined the notion of strict implication in terms of the notion of possibility (Lewis & Langford 1959: 124). He defined '*p* strictly implies *q*' as 'the conjunction of *p* and not *q* is not possible', which in turn can be understood as 'it is necessary that *p* materially implies *q*'.

Lewis's introduction of the modal operator 'it is possible that' (symbolized as '◊') raised concerns among certain philosophers and logicians. Quine (1966a) claimed that Lewis's introduction of these modal notions to modern symbolic logic compounded a mistake made by Russell and Whitehead: the notion of implication that Russell and Whitehead appeared to be defining with their use of '⊃' actually described a feature of their formal system and not a feature contained within the system itself. Deducibility (which was taken to be equivalent to implication) mentions various formulas in the calculus but does not use them. But, Quine complained, rather than correcting the use–mention problem from *Principia Mathematica,* Lewis compounded the problem by introducing another relation into the system. The problem with which Lewis was concerned remained in Lewis's systems of strict implication. Although Quine admitted that one could introduce the modal operators without committing the sin of confusing use with mention, he and others found these operators unsatisfactory.

One problem with modal operators is that they are not truth-functional. Unlike negation, for example, the truth of a sentence formed using these operators is not always determined by the truth-value of the sub-sentence. 'It is not the case that snow is white' is true provided it is not true that snow is white. However, the truth of the claim that it is necessary that snow is white is not determined by the truth of the claim that snow is white. Similarly it may be true that it is possible that snow is blue even though it is false that snow is blue. The truth and falsity of modal claims seem to depend on items other than the simple facts of the world.

Quine and those he opposed were a part of a long tradition of identifying the notions of analyticity, necessity and the a priori (for more on this connection see Chs 4 and 5). Kant's synthetic a priori truths were an exception. Following that tradition, Quine says: "The general idea of strict modalities is based on the putative notion of *analyticity* as follows: a statement of the form 'Necessarily . . .' is true if and only if the

3

Saul Kripke

compound statement which 'necessarily' governs is analytic" (Quine 1943: 114). Hence, the only way modal claims could make any sense at all was if they were understood to be claims about our conventions of language use. They would say that the correct way to understand the claim that it is possible that snow is blue is to understand it as claiming that the sentence 'Snow is blue' is not analytically false. That is, it is not false in virtue of the way we use the words 'snow' and 'blue'. It is not possible that John be a married bachelor because we use the words 'bachelor' and 'married' in such a way that they cannot truly be jointly predicated of one individual. Hence, claims of necessity and possibility turn out not to be claims about the nature of the world but rather claims about how we talk about the world.

Another criticism of modal logic is that no obvious deductive system corresponds to Lewis's strict implication. As mentioned above, Lewis introduced five different deductive systems: that is, five different axiom systems that produce different classes of theorems. Lewis was not alone in considering various logical systems of possibility and necessity, resulting in a myriad of formal deductive modal systems. The number of different systems brought into question the coherence of the various propositional modal systems, systems that might be understood, according to Quine, in more or less conventional ways.

Quine thought that by confining the modal operators to operate on complete propositions (or sentences) we could correct for the use–mention confusion that Lewis continued in the presentation of his systems of strict implication (which did not make modal logic more palatable to him, however, because he famously rejected the analytic–synthetic distinction). Quine was concerned that eventually someone would combine the modal operators of Lewis's strict implication systems with quantification (i.e. with the functional calculus). Quine's fears were realized with the work of Ruth Barcan Marcus (1946, 1947) and Rudolf Carnap (1946, 1947). Marcus combined the quantification of *Principia Mathematica* with Lewis's strict implication systems, and Carnap developed a system of quantified modal logic, which he expanded in *Meaning and Necessity* (1947).

The systems of Marcus and Carnap exhibit the very features that concerned Quine. For example, Marcus's system allows the modal operators to apply directly to predicate expressions as opposed to the complete sentences of propositional logic. Unlike the propositional calculus, the predicate calculus represents simple subject–predicate sentences as complex. The sentence 'Socrates is human', for example,

4

contains the subject term 'Socrates' and the predicate expression 'is human'. If we let the letter 'H' represent the predicate 'is human' and 's' the term 'Socrates' we can symbolize our sentence as 'Hs'. The same sentence would simply be represented as 'p' in the propositional calculus. The extra complexity allows us to correctly represent certain arguments whose logical form cannot be correctly represented in the propositional calculus. It also allows us to symbolize quantified sentences such as 'Everything is human', which is symbolized as '$\forall x Hx$' (where '$\forall$' stands for the universal quantifier 'for all' and the 'x' is a variable that varies over things). This additional complexity also allows further complexity if one adds the modal operators to standard first-order logic. There are two places where the modal '$\Box$' can be put in our first-order sentence '$\forall x Hx$':

(i) $\Box \forall x Hx$

(ii) $\forall x \Box Hx$.

When she presented her formal system, Marcus argued that an axiom of quantified modal logic should be

(BF) $\forall x \Box \varphi \equiv \Box \forall x \varphi$.

This axiom, in effect, claimed that for the purposes of logic the placement of the modal operator with respect to the quantifier did not really matter. The axiom is rather famous in modal logic. It became known as the *Barcan formula* and has been the focus of philosophical issues in modal logic that connect to Kripke's contribution, as will be discussed below.

If we are to understand the modal operator '$\Box$' in terms of analyticity, as Carnap and Lewis suggested, it is easy to see why introducing it into first-order logic creates a problem. Sentence (i) can be understood to say 'It is necessary that everything is human' or, in translation, 'Everything is human' is analytic. What sentence (ii) is supposed to say is not as clear, however. Sentence (ii) appears to say 'For every thing x, necessarily x is human', which seems to be saying that for every thing x, it is analytic that 'x is human'. But this cannot be correct. The expression 'x is human' is a *predicate* expression and not a sentence, and hence the notion of analyticity does not apply to it. Another problem relates to Quine's use–mention concerns. We use quotations to name expressions and one cannot quantify into a name. So, if we are to understand sentence (ii) it cannot be in terms of the analyticity of a sentence. How are we to understand such sentences?

Understanding a sentence such as (ii) involves two questions. One concerns the formal interpretation of a formal system of quantified modal logic. The other is a philosophical question concerning the nature of necessity. What are we asserting when we claim that it is possible for Al Gore to have won the US presidential election in 2000 or when we assert that it is necessary that Al Gore is human? What is the correct philosophical interpretation of such claims? Kripke offered an answer to both questions.

II

In 1959, while still a teenager, Kripke published the *first* completeness proof for modal logic and a few years later he published his well known paper "Semantical Considerations on Modal Logic". While Kripke was not the only person to provide a semantical account of modal logic, his work has had a great influence on later developments both in modal logic and in philosophy. To understand the location of Kripke's work in the development of modal logic, we need to reconsider the situation in logic when Marcus and Carnap published their work on quantified modal logic.

In 1931, the logician Kurt Gödel published a completeness proof for the first-order logic of *Principia Mathematica*. A completeness proof connects the theorems with the logically true or valid formulas of the system. When one considers a system of logic that is defined by axioms and rules of inference (as is the case for the systems in *Principia Mathematica*), a number of questions arise *about* the system. For example, do the axioms and rules of inference of the propositional calculus allow us to deduce a proposition p and the negation of that proposition $\sim p$? A system that does not allow this deduction is said to be *consistent*. Another question that can be asked about a logical system is whether all the formulas that can be deduced in the system are logically true: whether the axioms of the system together with the rules of inference produce theorems that cannot fail to be true. If all the theorems of the system are logically true the system is said to be *sound*. Finally, a (consistent) system is said to be *complete* if all the logical truths of that system can be deduced using the axioms and rules of the system. In effect, this is what Gödel proved in 1931 for the first-order logical system of *Principia Mathematica*.

While Gödel's proof was the first of its kind, Alfred Tarski's work on the nature of truth had a profound influence on the development of what we now think of as formal semantics. A logical system such as the propositional calculus or the predicate calculus from *Principia Mathematica* is no more than a complex of symbols and rules for the manipulation of those symbols. If any meaning is to be given to the system of symbols it must be done through comments about the system. When we considered (above) the formula '∀xHx' we said that it meant 'Everything is human' and that is the intended interpretation. But how do we represent this or any intended interpretation in a formal way? Tarski offered a recursive definition of the value of a formula, which allowed a formal interpretation of the symbols of our logical systems. The key to Tarski's formal definition of truth for a formula of the predicate calculus is the notion of *satisfaction*.

In the predicate calculus or first-order logic (PL for short) even atomic propositions can be syntactically complex. We noticed this with the example 'Socrates is human', which was represented as '*Hs*'. To interpret the sentences of PL, we need to interpret the parts of the sentences. We start by considering a domain of individuals (labelled '*D*') that our language is to be "about". Every predicate in our language characterizes some subset of the individuals in D and so we interpret the predicates by assigning to each predicate some subset of D. An *interpretation* (<*D*, *f*>) of our language PL consists of a non-empty domain of individuals together with a function *f* such that for each one-place predicate F, $f(F)$ is a subset of D; for each two-place predicate R, $f(R)$ is a set of ordered pairs from D^2 and so on for all the predicates. If there are individual constants (names) in PL, *f* will assign some member of D to each name and will assign some member of D to each variable in PL as well. We will use the expression 'term' to mean either a variable or individual constant in PL. We can now recursively define the notion of *satisfaction*. That is, we shall first define the notion for the atomic formulas, and then define it for the complex formulas.

(1)   If A is an atomic formula of the form $Rt_1 \ldots t_n$ (i.e. an n-place predicate followed by n terms) then the interpretation <*D*, *f*> *satisfies A* if and only if the n-tuple $<f(t_1), \ldots, f(t_n)>$ is a member of $f(R)$.

(2)   If A is of the form ~*B* then <*D*, *f*> *satisfies A* if and only if <*D*, *f*> does not satisfy B.

(3)   If A is of the form (*B* & *C*) then <*D*, *f*> *satisfies A* if and only if <*D*, *f*> satisfies B and <*D*, *f*> satisfies C.

(4)   If A is of the form '∀x*B*' then <*D*, *f*> *satisfies A* if and only if

Saul Kripke

every interpretation <D, f^*> (where f^* is a *variant* (*with respect to x*) of f) satisfies B.

A *variant f^* (with respect to a variable* α) of an assignment f in < D, f > is a function that is exactly like f except possibly with respect to what it assigns to α. Or, more formally, $f^*_\alpha = f \sim \{<\alpha, f(\alpha)>\} \cup \{<\alpha, i>\}$ (where $i \in D$). A formula A is *true* with respect to an interpretation <D, f> just in case the formula is satisfied by the interpretation, and it is *logically true* (i.e. *valid*) just in case it is satisfied by all interpretations (of the language).

Using Tarski's techniques one can provide (using set theory) a formal interpretation to go along with the informal interpretation of the logical system in question. Gödel also provided a formal interpretation for the systems of *Principia Mathematica*, as mentioned above, but his interpretation was more narrowly focused, while Tarski offered a more general method. In providing a semantics for PL, Tarski did not change the definitions of the connectives in the propositional calculus (PC). Those definitions were the definitions that Russell and Whitehead used, including the definitions for '⊃'. So, while Tarski's account allowed a relatively straightforward interpretation or model for first-order logic, it did not provide an obvious way to interpret either Lewis's propositional systems of strict implication or quantified modal logic. Hence, there was no formal interpretation for modal logic at the time when quantifiers were combined with modal operators.

The problem for modal logic is that the truth of a modal formula is not a simple function of the truth of the parts of the formula. The formula '$\sim p$' is true provided that p is false. However, the formula '$\Diamond p$' can be true even if p is false (and is true if p is true) and the formula '$\Box p$' can be false even if p is true (and is false if p is false). One of the complaints raised against modal logic was that no formal semantics existed for modal logic as existed for non-modal predicate logic. Thus our interpretations of these systems were informal and (it was thought) not satisfactory. As we noted above, this led to a general dissatisfaction with the large number of different modal systems.

Kripke's papers on modal logic played a significant role in changing our attitudes towards modal logic. Kripke was the first to provide a completeness proof for quantified modal logic and in the process presented what are now known as *Kripke models* (or *Kripke model structures*) for the interpretation of modal logic. Kripke model structures are similar to the interpretations that we introduced in

Tarski's definition of satisfaction, but they differ from those sets in important ways. In the first place, we introduced interpretations so that we could provide a definition of truth for atomic and quantified sentences in the predicate calculus. These interpretations are not needed to define logical truth (tautology) for the propositional calculus. A tautology can be defined in terms of truth-tables alone.

We could introduce the notion of an interpretation for PC simply by introducing an assignment function, V, that assigns true or false to all the atomic formulas of some subset of the formulas of PC and then assigns true or false to the compound formulas formed from that subset on the basis of the definitions of the connectives. A formula would be logically true (i.e. valid) if it were assigned true for all such interpretations.

For reasons already mentioned, modal propositional logic is more complicated. Kripke suggested that, to help provide a semantics for propositional modal logic (MPC – *modal propositional calculus*), we introduce the notion of a *model structure*, <G, K, R>, where (intuitively) K is a set of *possible worlds*, G is the actual world ($G \in K$), and R is a relation that holds between worlds. Using the notion of a model structure, Kripke then defined the notion of *model* relative to a given model structure. Given a model structure <G, K, R>, a *model* φ assigns to each atomic formula a truth-value relative to each world $H \in K$. So for each atomic formula, p, in MPC, $\varphi(p, H)$ is either true or false.

Thus, formulas are not simply true or false, but true or false relative to a possible world. So, for example, let p be the proposition that Aristotle taught philosophy. We know that Aristotle taught philosophy so p is true relative to G (on this model $\varphi(p, G)$ is true). But it is reasonable to suppose that Aristotle might have done something else besides teaching philosophy: gone into banking, say. So there is a possible world H where p is false ($\varphi(p, H)$ is false). This idea that the truth-value of atomic formulas can vary with respect to possible worlds allows one to define truth for modal sentences in a way that was not available before. Intuitively, it is possible that p just in case p is true in some world. So one of the intuitive features of Kripke's models for modal logic was the introduction of a set of possible worlds in the model structure and another was the assignment of truth-values for formulas relative to those worlds. Hence, two important (and somewhat controversial) concepts that Kripke used in his models are *possible worlds* and the relation of truth *relative to a possible world*.

In Ch. 1.III we shall consider Kripke's philosophical conception of possible worlds in more detail, as well as some alternatives to

Kripke's position. Here I want to note a formal feature of Kripke's model structures. In addition to the set of possible worlds and the real world, Kripke introduced a relation R between the members of K: that is, a relation among the worlds. He describes this relation as a relation of relative possibility or what others have referred to as the *accessibility relation* among worlds. It is this idea – the idea that world w may be possible relative to another world w' but not possible relative to still another world w^* – that allows us to connect many of the different deductive modal systems (mentioned above) as part of a single semantical account. This provides, then, a kind of semantical explanation for the large number of different modal deductive systems. While Kripke was not the only logician to recognize the need for a notion of accessibility in our interpretations of modal logic, he was original in describing the relation of relative possibility as one among the worlds within the models as opposed to relations among the models themselves. So on Kripke's account the difference between, for example, Lewis's deductive system S4 and his strongest system S5 is a difference in the relation of relative possibility among the worlds. In S4 models, the relation is reflexive and transitive whereas it is an equivalence relation in S5 models. While not all the various deductive systems of modal logic can be accounted for in terms of standard differences in the relation of relative possibility, Kripke's work went a long way in helping our understanding of propositional modal logic.

It would be a mistake, however, to leave the impression that Kripke's work addressed only propositional modal logic. Kripke also offered a way to understand modal quantificational logic: the type of modal logic with which Quine was most concerned. To handle the problems that arose from the addition of quantification to modal logic, Kripke added to his model structures a function ψ that assigned to each world H in K a set called the *domain* of H. Intuitively, the domain of a world is the set of individuals that exist in that world. So, with the addition of ψ, the resulting sets were called *quantificational model structures* and using these, Kripke presented a model of quantification in modal logic. A number of questions arise, however, when we consider combining the ideas presented in Kripke's propositional modal logic with (say) Tarski's ideas on the treatment of quantifiers in classical logic.

Recall that predicates are assigned sets of n-tuples in the standard quantification models. Consider, for example, a simple one-place predicate 'P'. The sentence 'Px' is true if our assignment to $x(\varphi(x))$ is a member of the set assigned to P. In other words, a simple atomic formula is true if the object denoted by the singular term is a member of the set of objects assigned to the predicate. So the statement that Kripke is a philosopher is true provided that Kripke is a member of the set of individuals who are philosophers and the statement that George W. Bush is a philosopher is false provided Bush is *not* a member of the set of philosophers. What shall we say then about the claim that it is possible that Bush is a philosopher? We do not want the fact that Bush is not a member of the set of philosophers to rule out the *possibility*, however unlikely, of Bush's being a philosopher even though sets are *identified* by their members. So if S is the set of philosophers and Bush is not a member of S then Bush cannot be a member of S. So there is no possible world where Bush is a member of S and hence it appears that it is necessary that Bush is not a philosopher. It is necessary, that is, *if* we keep the standard interpretation for the predicates and simply assign each of them a set of objects.

To avoid this difficulty we relativize the assignments of the predicates to the possible worlds. Predicates are not assigned sets *simpliciter*, but are assigned sets relative to worlds. So Bush may be a member of the set assigned to the predicate 'is a philosopher' relative to world w and not a member of the set assigned to the predicate relative to another world. This allows that the statement that Bush is a philosopher is true at some world and thus it is indeed possibly true.

Still, more choices must be made. Each world has been assigned a domain of objects that intuitively represents the objects that exist in that world and each predicate is assigned a set of objects (n-tuples for n-place predicates where $n > 1$) relative to a world. So what is the relationship between the predicate assignments and the domains of the worlds? For a number of reasons, Kripke decided against any obvious formal relationship between the two assignments. This means that in Kripke's model structures, a given individual a from the universe of discourse might be a member of the set assigned to a predicate F relative to a world w, even though a is *not* a member of the domain of w. Intuitively, a can have a property at a world even though a fails to exist in that world. One of the reasons for allowing this is that every formula will receive a truth-value at every world even if the object mentioned in the formula is not a member of the domain of that world.

Since the quantifiers are tied to the domains of the worlds in that $\exists x F x$ is true at a world w provided that something in the domain of w is a member of the assignment to the predicate, Kripke's semantics for modal logic yields a "free" logic. One cannot infer from the truth of *Fa* at *w* that ∃*xFx* is true at *w* since the assignment to *a* may not be a member of the domain of *w*.

Kripke's semantics also allows that some of the objects in the universe of discourse (the union of all the domains of all the worlds) are not members of the domain of the actual world. The example that Kripke gives in his 1963 paper (*SCML* 1963) is Sherlock Holmes. Such an entity might be thought to be possible even if it is not actual. Kripke later retracts this example (in *Naming and Necessity*) because it involves a *fictional* object, but he holds to the idea he was attempting to present; namely, that there are some objects that are merely possible. Kripke says:

> The quoted assertion [about Sherlock Holmes] gives the erroneous impression that a fictional name such as 'Holmes' names a particular possible-but-not-actual individual. The substantive point I was trying to make, however, remains and is independent of any linguistic theory of the status of names in fiction. The point was that, in other possible worlds 'some existing individuals may be absent while new individuals ... may appear' ....
> (*NN*: 158)

Such individuals are not members of the domain of the actual world. While it is difficult to say exactly what Kripke's official position on such matters is since he has not published anything directly on the topic (although he has presented lectures on the topics of existence and empty names), it is fair to say that Kripke's early views on the subject tend towards what is often called 'possibilism'. Possibilism is the doctrine that there are merely possible objects and is contrasted with actualism: the view that holds that everything is actual, there are no merely possible objects. However, it is possible to read Kripke's comments concerning "new individuals" as only one way to use his formal account and not as any firm ontological commitment on his part to merely possible individuals. The possibilism–actualism debate is also related to the Barcan formula.

Recall that the Barcan formula says that everything is necessarily φ if and only if necessarily everything is φ. Using Kripke's model structures we can understand this claim to be saying everything in the (actual) world is φ in every world if and only if in every world everything is φ. For example, suppose we are essentialistic materialists and think that everything is essentially made up of matter. We think, then, that everything in this world is such that it is matter in every world where it exists. Hence we would hold that everything is necessarily matter. Does it then follow that in every world everything in that world is matter, that is, necessarily everything is matter? It does *if* the Barcan formula is correct. For the Barcan formula, in effect, requires (in S5) that the domains of all the worlds be the same.

It was thought for some time that if one accepted the strongest modal system that Lewis offered (S5), then when one added quantification to that system one had to accept the Barcan formula unless one made major changes in the rules for proofs. A. N. Prior (1956) had produced a proof that the Barcan formula followed from the usual rules of quantification together with the axioms of the S5 system. Kripke, however, showed that it was possible to present a system of quantified S5 logic without the Barcan formula with a slight change in the usual rules of proof for quantified logic. Standard rules of proof for quantification theory allow the following as a theorem:

$$\forall x A(x) \supset A(y)$$

This, together with the rule of necessitation (the rule that in effect states that all theorems are necessary) and the other standard rules for modal logic and quantification theory, allowed Prior to derive the Barcan formula in S5. Kripke pointed out that by requiring only closed formulas to be asserted one can avoid the proof of the Barcan formula without any loss to quantification theory. We replace the above with its closure:

$$\forall y (\forall x A(x) \supset A(y))$$

The semantics that Kripke presents corresponds to his rules of proof. Kripke allows the domains of worlds to vary. That is, if one allows that there are merely possible objects – objects that are not included in the domain of this world – then one can see how the Barcan formula can fail. In our example, we need only suppose that while there are no spirit objects, there could have been such objects. On the view in question this implies that there is a possible world whose domain contains objects that are not made of matter. These objects do not exist in our world since (given our assumption) everything that exists in our world is essentially made of matter. Still, they exist in some other worlds. Hence the claim that if everything (in the actual world) is material in every world, then in every world everything (in those worlds) is material is seen to be false. At this point, one might begin to wonder about the nature of these possible worlds. We turn to that issue next.

III

One of the novel features of Kripke's model structures was his intro-duction of the set of possible worlds to help define the truth-conditions for modal sentences. Kripke was not the first philosopher to use the notion of a *possible world* but the way he used possible worlds was unique. Most agree that Leibniz was the first to present and use the notion of a possible world to help explain modal notions. For various reasons, however, Leibniz's views fell out of favour and few discussed them until Kripke and his contemporaries reintroduced the notion as a way of understanding modal discourse. Precursors to Kripke's possi-ble worlds include theories by Carnap (1947) and Prior (1957), and oth-ers at the time saw that modality could be helped by something like a possible world. In any case, Kripke's model structures turned out to be very flexible and could be put to many uses. Also, possible worlds appeared to solve one of the early worries concerning modal logic; namely, that there was no formal way to make quantified modal logic coherent. Philosophers such as Quine, however, complained that quan-tified modal logic was understandable only to the extent that the no-tion of a possible world was understandable, and that Kripke's notion of a possible world was not understandable or at least not acceptable. In other words, much of the debate over modal logic shifted from formal questions and questions of interpretation of formal systems and axioms to questions about the nature of possible worlds themselves. Debate in philosophy certainly has taken a different form, if not sub-stance, as a result of the reintroduction of possible worlds.

When Kripke first presented his model structures, which included the notion of a possible world, he did not elaborate on them. In one sense, the items included in the formal account of Kripke's semantics for modal logic could have been almost anything. Intuitively, the set K is a set of possible worlds and G is the actual world but, formally, all that is required is that K be some non-empty set of objects. And although there are some hints in Kripke's papers on modal logic concerning the nature of possible worlds, no detailed theory or philo-sophical account is presented. But this is not surprising since Kripke's reason for introducing possible worlds into formal seman-tics in the first place was not so much philosophical as it was formal. As Kripke said some twenty years later:

> The main and original motivation for the 'possible worlds analysis' – and the way it clarified modal logic – was that it enabled modal logic to be treated by the same set theoretic

techniques of model theory that proved so successful when applied to extensional logic. It is also useful in making certain concepts clear. (*NN*: 19)

Philosophers could *not* look to Leibniz to find an account of possible worlds that was compatible with Kripke's account. Roughly speaking, Leibniz viewed a possible world as a complex idea in the mind of God involving many individual concepts: concepts of particulars. But Leibniz thought that the concept of an individual *mirrored* the world of which the concept was a member and hence no individual concept could be a member of more than a single world. But this way of looking at worlds is not compatible with Kripke's semantics. Recall that the domains of the possible worlds may overlap in a given model structure. That is, Kripke's quantificational model structures (*q.m.s.*) do not restrict the assignment of domains to worlds. Hence, given a particular triple (*G, K, R*) there will be one *q.m.s.* where the domain assignment function ψ assigns the same individuals to every world and one that assigns no overlap (i.e. no individual is in more than one world) and the rest will involve some overlap. Also it is clear that Kripke thinks that there is a particular assignment function ψ that is intuitively desired. It is one that assigns to *G* just those individuals that actually exist and to the other worlds just those individuals that exist in those worlds. Such an assignment will, on Kripke's view, involve overlap. So Kripke's view of worlds must be rather different from Leibniz's.

Kripke has never published a detailed theory of possible worlds, but he has remarked that certain views concerning the nature of worlds are mistaken while other views are on the right track. The best account we are given of his views comes in the preface to the publication of his lectures in the book *Naming and Necessity*. Here we are given an analogy. Consider a pair of dice. We might ask, before we throw the dice, what are the chances (assuming fair dice) that our throw of the dice will yield an eleven? The answer depends on what the possible outcomes of our throwing the dice are. There are 36 possible states that might be the outcome of our throw of the dice. Given that only two of those states have eleven as their result we can figure that the chance of getting eleven is 2 in 36 or 1 in 18. The 36 possible outcomes of our throw of the dice can be viewed as miniworlds. They are *abstract* states of the dice. Assuming that we throw the dice, one of those 36 states will be realized. But the physical entity that is the dice after the throw is not one of the 36 abstract states. As Kripke himself describes it:

15

> This complex physical entity ("the dice," thought of as a single object) is before me on the table, after the throw, and its actual position determines the actual state of the (two) dice. But when we talk in school of thirty-six possibilities, in no way do we need to posit that there are some thirty-five *other* entities, existent in some never-never land, corresponding to the physical object before me. Nor need we ask whether these phantom entities are composed of (phantom) "counterparts" of the actual individual dice, or are somehow composed of the same individual dice themselves but in "another dimension." The thirty-six possibilities, the one that is actual included, are (abstract) states of the dice, not complex physical entities. (*NN*:17)

While Kripke's analogy of the the dice helps to provide an intuitive idea or notion of a possible world it leaves many questions unanswered. For example, if possible worlds are abstract possible states of the world, then do possible worlds capture all the possibilities? The difficulty should be clear. While the number of possible states *of* the world may be infinite, it is reasonable to suppose that some possibilities are not possibilities for this world. That is, they are not ways *this* world might have been, but rather alternative possibilities that might have obtained. Kripke notes that in his dice analogy, the possibilities are "tightly controlled". We only consider possible states of the two dice. Leaving aside questions about how to consider a possible state of an entire world, is the world like the dice in that there are other possibilities that are not possible states of the dice?

Kripke's response to such questions seems to be that in practice we need not consider all possible states of the world, let alone all possibilities. Whether or not we can legitimately ignore certain possibilities depends on our purpose in using or discussing possible worlds. Kripke claims we need not answer detailed questions about the nature of possible worlds to provide an account of modal semantics or notions to be used in discussing theories of meaning such as the notion of a rigid designator. But philosophers disagree as to whether this is correct. Although Kripke does not provide a theory of the possible worlds that he helped to reintroduce and make so popular, he is clear in his rejection of certain views concerning possible worlds. In particular, Kripke rejects the modal realism of David Lewis (1986) and he offers a number of arguments against related views. Because a discussion of these arguments requires some understanding of Lewis's view, a brief description of that view and the reasons for it will follow.

In 1968, some five years after Kripke's paper "Semantical Considerations on Modal Logic", Lewis offered an alternative interpretation of quantified modal logic that he called *counterpart theory*. Lewis's basic idea was to formalize modal discourse in an extensional language (a goal he later said was not all that important). Lewis wanted to eliminate the modal operators of modal logic in favour of a modal theory that was expressible in the language of *Principia Mathematica*. One need not introduce modal operators to formalize modal discourse if one is willing to quantify over possible worlds themselves. For example, consider the sentence

(1)   There could have been immortal human beings.

This sentence can be read as saying

(1a)   It is possible that there is a human being who is not mortal,

which in turn is represented in standard modal logic as

(1b) $\Diamond \exists x \, (Hx \, \& \, {\sim}Mx)$.

That is, it is represented as a formula that contains the modal operator '$\Diamond$'. As we noted in previous sections, a number of issues arise when we mix the modal operators with the quantifiers. Lewis suggested that we eliminate the operator in favour of quantifiers over possible worlds. Sentence (1) can be represented in Lewis's theory along the following lines:

(1c) $\exists w \exists x (w$ is a world $\& \, x$ is in $w \, \& \, Hx \, \& \, {\sim}Mx)$.

The modal operator of (1b) is replaced with the worlds quantifier in (1c). This seems straightforward when the scope of the modal operator is primary. But how are we to treat cases when the scope of the modal operator is secondary? To answer this question consider a simple case first.

(2)   Socrates might have been a banker.

Sentence (2) can be understood to mean (ignoring questions of tense)

(2a)   It is possible that Socrates is a banker,

which in turn is represented in our standard operator logic as

(2b) $\Diamond Bs$

Given our interpretation above, it would seem natural to represent (2a) as

(2c) $\exists w(w$ is a world & s is in w & s is a banker).

Assuming that (2) is true, which world or worlds can be used in the interpretation that satisfies (2c)? The actual world is no help here because in the actual world Socrates is not a banker. So, for (2c) to be true, Socrates will have to be a banker in some other world. The view that Socrates himself could be in more than a single world is unacceptable for someone who is a realist about worlds according to Lewis. The problem is that this view appears to lead to the view that Socrates both has and lacks certain intrinsic properties and that is not possible. Lewis calls this *the problem of accidential intrinsics*. An example of an accidential intrinsic property is the colour of one's hair. Assuming that Socrates actually has black hair, it does not seem impossible for Socrates to have had blond hair. Because the colour of one's hair is a property that is not dependent on objects other than oneself (including which world one happens to inhabit) there can be no world where *Socrates* has blond hair. For this reason and others, Lewis holds that the objects that are the parts of worlds, such as Socrates in this world, are only parts of a single world. So we return to our orginal question. What worlds can be used in the interpretation to satisfy (2c)?

According to Lewis, the worlds in question are those worlds that contain *counterparts* of Socrates. A *counterpart* of Socrates is an individual that Socrates would have been had the world been different from the way it is. A world that has a counterpart of Socrates can be said to *represent* Socrates. In one of the worlds that contains a counterpart of Socrates we find that counterpart to be a banker and hence (2) is made true by that world. So the correct paraphrase of (2) in Lewis's counterpart theory is not (2c) but

(2d) $\exists w \exists x(w$ is a world & x is in w & x is a counterpart of s & Bx).

As Lewis tells us, he is offering a theory of modality, not an alternative logic. He uses the standard predicate logic with identity and then limits the models by providing axioms for the interpretation of the predicates of counterpart theory. Although Lewis first presented this view as an alternative account for the logical treatment of modal discourse, it is part of a complete metaphysical framework that provides an account of a myriad of issues in philosophy. Kripke rejects Lewis's realism about worlds together with his counterparts. Kripke's remark quoted above ("Nor need we ask whether these phantom entities are composed of (phantom) 'counterparts' of the actual individual dice") is clearly directed at Lewis's view.

Kripke raises three problems or issues as objections to Lewis's counterpart theory. First, he claims that there is a formal problem in the interpretation that Lewis provides for quantified modal logic. Secondly, he suggests that Lewis's view of worlds is based on a false presupposition concerning how we individuate worlds and, thirdly, he objects to Lewis's understanding of sentences such as (2). Kripke presents the formal complaint as follows:

> on his [Lewis's] interpretation of quantified modality, the familiar law $(y)((x)A(x) \supset A(y))$ fails if A is allowed to contain modal operators ... Since Lewis's formal model follows rather naturally from his philosophical views on counterparts, and since the failure of universal instantiation for modal properties is intuitively bizarre, it seems to me that this failure constitutes an additional argument against the plausibility of his philosophical views. (*NN*: 45)

To understand the objection, consider what appears to be the following instance of universal instantiation

(I) $(x)\Diamond(x \neq y) \supset \Diamond(y \neq y)$

It turns out that '$(x)\Diamond(x \neq y)$' is satisfiable in Lewis's system, but '$\Diamond(y \neq y)$' is not. This seems to be a serious problem for Lewis. However, in response to this objection Lewis points out that (I) is not really an instance of universal instantiation in his theory. While it is true that '$(x)\Diamond(x \neq y)$' is satisfiable in counterpart theory and '$\Diamond(y \neq y)$' is not, the reason for this concerns the interpretation of the formulas. In effect, '$\Diamond(y \neq y)$' says that there is a world with a counterpart z of y where z is not identical with itself, which is nonsense. On the other hand '$(x)\Diamond(x \neq y)$' says that every actual thing lacks a counterpart in some world, which might very well be the case. Yet (I) seems to be an instance of a general logical truth. So what has gone wrong here?

Two things can help to explain the situation. Lewis's actual system has no modal operators, so strictly speaking (I) cannot be an instance of universal instantiation in Lewis's system. Lewis does, however, provide a translation between standard modal syntax and his counterpart theory. In the translation the modal operators are treated as quantifiers both over worlds and (when open sentences are involved) over counterparts. So according to Lewis, use of modal operators often conceals the quantification over counterparts that is occurring. As Lewis puts it: "So counterpart theory is no threat to standard logic. It is only a threat to simplistic methods of keeping

19

track of variable-binding and instancehood when we are dealing with the perversely abbreviated language of quantified modal logic" (1983: 46). Kripke describes his complaint about Lewis's logical system as a "failure of universal instantiation for modal properties". But what are modal *properties* according to Lewis? It is clear that open sentences with modal operators, for example, '$\Diamond Fx$', express relations among counterparts. Roughly speaking, '$\Diamond Fx$' says that there is a world that contains as a part a counterpart of x and it has F. And this is the basis for the disagreement. Thus, Kripke's formal complaint is related to his complaint about Lewis's understanding of (2). We shall return to this below, but first let us consider Kripke's more general objection.

Kripke's general objection to treating possible worlds in a certain way is not directed at Lewis's view specifically, but at a whole range of views that includes Lewis's. Here is an abbreviated version of the general view that Kripke rejects. Kripke presents this view in the form of an objection to his own use of possible worlds.

> And the objection that people make may be stated as follows: Look, you're talking about situations which are counterfactual, that is to say, you're talking about other possible worlds. Now these worlds are completely disjoint, after all, from the actual world which is not just another possible world; it is the actual world. So, before you talk about, let us say, such an object as Richard Nixon in another possible world at all, you have to say which object in this other possible world would *be* Richard Nixon ... An extreme view has even held that, since possible worlds are so disjoint from our own, it cannot really say that any object in them is the *same* as an object existing now but only that there are some objects which resemble things in the actual world, more or less. We, therefore, should not really speak of what would have been true of Nixon in another possible world but, only of what "counterparts" (the term David Lewis uses) of Nixon there would have been.   (*IN*: 146–7)

Now here is Kripke's response to such complaints:

> All of this seems to me to be a totally misguided way of looking at things. What it amounts to is the view that counterfactual situations have to be described purely qualitatively ... This seems to me to be wrong. Who is to prevent us from saying "Nixon might have gotten Carswell through had he done

certain things?" We are speaking of *Nixon* and asking what, in certain counterfactual situations, would have been true of *him*.

(*IN*: 147–8)

And, in *Naming and Necessity:*

> Of course, if someone makes the demand that every possible world has to be described in a purely qualitative way, we can't say "Suppose Nixon had lost the election," we must say, instead, something like "Suppose a man with a dog named Checkers, who looks like a certain David Frye impersonation, is in a certain possible world and loses the election." Well, does he resemble Nixon enough to be identified with Nixon? A very explicit and blatant example of this way of looking at things is David Lewis's counterpart theory but the literature on quantified modality is replete with it. Why need we make this demand? That is not the way we ordinarily think of counterfactual situations. We just say "suppose this man had lost." It is *given* that the possible world contains *this man,* and that in that world, he lost. (*NN*: 44–6)

The objection that Kripke appears to be presenting in these passages and other similar passages goes as follows. Lewis and others hold that possible worlds are disjoint and hence we need to introduce counterparts to be able to talk about objects in these other worlds. The reason for thinking worlds are so disjoint as to require us to introduce counterparts is that worlds need to be described purely qualitatively. But this is not how we talk about worlds, so we don't need to introduce counterparts or view worlds as disjoint. Another aspect to Kripke's objection is a caution to philosophers not to get carried away with talk about possible worlds and build wild and elaborate metaphysical systems using notions designed only to do a limited job: "Certainly the philosopher of 'possible worlds' must take ⅄ care that his technical apparatus not push him to ask questions whose meaningfulness is not supported by our original intuitions of possibility that gave the apparatus its point" (*NN*: 18). I suspect that Lewis's concrete possible worlds are the very sort of "grand worlds" that Kripke is cautioning us about.

Lewis responds to the first part of the objection by rejecting Kripke's claim that his theory of disjoint worlds amounts to the view that counterfactual situations need to be described purely qualitatively:

> So when Kripke emphatically insists that it is entirely legiti-
> mate and proper to specify worlds by making reference to indi-
> viduals – call this *Kripkean specification* – he is not entering
> into any debate over (what I call) haecceitism, and no anti-
> haecceitist need hesitate to agree with him. (1986: 222)

Roughly speaking, haecceitism, as Lewis views it, is the view that
worlds may differ with respect to who is in the world without differing
qualitatively. Some qualification of this description of haecceitism is,
however, required. Remember that on Lewis's view worlds are disjoint
and so nothing that is a part of one world is a part of another. It follows
that on his view all worlds differ with respect to who is a part of them
whether or not they differ qualitatively. So a better description of
haecceitism from Lewis's point of view is that it is the view that worlds
may differ in what things they represent (what Lewis calls *representation de re*) without differing qualitatively. Lewis is, of course, an anti-
haecceitist, but he does not view Kripke's complaint as really an objection to anti-haecceitism. Lewis claims that he can agree with Kripke
that worlds may be specified in the way Kripke suggests.

Kripke does say, in a footnote: "What I defend is the *propriety* of
giving possible worlds in terms of certain particulars as well as qualitatively, whether or not there are in fact qualitatively identical but
distinct worlds" (*NN*: 18, n.17). Lewis takes this to mean that Kripke
remains neutral with respect to the haecceitism issue as Lewis defines it, and hence Kripke's comments about how we ordinarily think
about counterfactual situations do not bear on the main metaphysical issue concerning the nature of worlds.

Is Lewis correct that he and Kripke do not disagree on this issue? I
think that they do disagree and the disagreement can be found in what
is being specified when one gives a Kripkean specification. It may be
that any possible world in which, say, Nixon exists is a world where a
certain bundle or collection of properties is exemplified. If so, then
there may be no worlds that are qualitatively identical, and yet Nixon
exists in one and not the other. Similarly for all other objects. If this is
the case then it is likely there are no qualitatively identical but distinct
worlds and Lewis and Kripke can agree on this. But Kripke appears to
make a stronger claim. Kripke claims that Nixon exists in many possible worlds and not that he is just "represented" (by counterparts) in
different worlds. To this, of course, Lewis cannot agree.

Lewis describes the above issue in a famous passage as follows
(using the example of the loser of the 1968 US presidential election,
Hubert Humphrey):

Kripke's point seems to be that we are supposed to respect Humphrey's intuition that it is *he himself* who would have been victorious in another world, and we are suppose [*sic*] to do this by declining to think of that other world as the sort of thing that he himself could even be a part of! What is going on?

I think counterpart theorists and ersatzers [this includes Kripke] are in perfect agreement that there are other worlds (genuine or ersatz) *according to* which Humphrey – he himself! (stamp the foot, bang the table) – wins the election. And we are in equal agreement that Humphrey – he himself – is not *part* of these worlds.
(1986: 196)

When one compares Lewis and Kripke on this issue, one has the distinct impression that Kripke's complaint is not exactly the one to which Lewis is responding, although the difference (if there is one) is subtle. One issue involves what it means to be *part* of a world that does not presuppose any particular view concerning the nature of possible worlds. On Kripke's view (however the details are worked out) possible worlds are abstract states. So consider the abstract state of Nixon's winning the1968 US presidential election. Is Nixon a part of that state? Well, if by 'part' we mean part of a concrete object, then Nixon is not a part of that state. But Nixon is certainly included in that state in the sense that the state cannot obtain unless Nixon exists. So the relationship between Nixon and the state of affairs of Nixon's winning is like the relationship between Nixon and the set of US presidents. Of course, Nixon did win so there is a concrete item – some part of the "enormous scattered object that surrounds us" – of which Nixon is a part and which may also be described as the event of Nixon's winning. But the existence of such an object is really beside the point here. Consider the state of affairs of Humphrey's winning the election. Since he lost, the state of affairs is not actual and there is no concrete event of which Humphrey is a part. But Humphrey is included in the state of affairs that he hoped would have been realized. Lewis says that he and Kripke (and others) agree that there is a world according to which Humphrey won the election, and neither he nor Kripke holds that the way the possible world makes it true that Humphrey won is by Humphrey's being a *part* of the world. That may be true, but on a Kripke-like view Humphrey is included in the state of affairs in question and this is not true on Lewis's view. According to Lewis, it is the existence of a counterpart of Humphrey who wins that assures the truth of the claim that Humphrey might have won the election. Some may take this to be a rather odd consequence. This way of looking at things is part of the third objection that Kripke raises against Lewis.

In "Identity and Necessity" Kripke says:

> Even more objectionable is the view of David Lewis. According to Lewis, when we say "Under certain circumstances Nixon would have gotten Carswell through," we really mean "Some man, other than Nixon but closely resembling Nixon could have gotten some man closely resembling Carswell through." . . . But *that* would not comfort either Nixon or Carswell, nor would it make Nixon kick himself and say "*I* should have done such and such to get Carswell through." The question is whether under certain circumstances Nixon *himself* could have gotten *Carswell* through.
>
> (*IN*: 148)

In *Naming and Necessity*, he repeats the same charge using the Humphrey example:

> Probably, however, Humphrey could not care less whether someone *else*, no matter how much resembling him, would have been victorious in another possible world. Thus, Lewis's view seems to me even more bizarre than the usual notions of transworld identification that it replaces. (*NN*: 45, n.13)

However, Lewis quite correctly points out that on his view Humphrey *himself* has the property of being such that he might have won and Nixon *himself* has the property of being such that he might have got Carswell through. Surely, what Humphrey and Nixon care about is whether or not they have the modal property of being such that they might have done such and such. Lewis and Kripke agree that they do in fact have this property. Or do they? There is the question that Kripke raised in his technical point about Lewis's system mentioned above. Exactly how does Lewis express modal properties? Lewis has no modal operators in his system, so is it true that Lewis's system really does express the fact that Humphrey himself has a certain modal property? In one sense it does if, as Lewis claims, Humphrey's having the modal property in question just *is* Humphrey's standing in some counterpart relation to some individual in another world who wins an election. Does Humphrey care if someone resembling him won a different election? Probably not if presented that way, but an analysis of the claim that Humphrey might have won the election is not likely to interest politicians.

On the other hand, it is difficult to see how the fact that some individual (not Humphrey) in some other possible world who resembles Humphrey has the property of winning the election (in that world) grounds the truth of the claim that Humphrey could have won. One reason why this is so odd is that there could be another election at a later time in our world that resembles the Nixon–Humphrey election, where the Humphrey resembler wins, and that election is (qualitatively) indistinguishable from the election in the other world that is supposed to assure the truth of 'Humphrey might have won'. It seems completely arbitrary or mysterious that the other-worldly fact is what determines the truth of the claim that Humphrey might have won.

Lewis does allow that in certain contexts our own worldly facts can represent certain possibilities. In one example he imagines our world as one of eternal recurrence where we exist in the seventeenth epoch and says:

> The possibility which represents me *de re* as living instead in the 137th epoch is not the some other world that differs haecceitistically from ours; it is my this-worldly duplicate in the 137th epoch. Insofar as he is my counterpart (that is, on those resolutions of vagueness that make him my counterpart despite the fact that we are worldmates) he is a possibility for me; that is all I mean when I say that I might have been him.
>
> (1986: 232)

Yet it is unclear how this helps with our problem. Suppose our world is not a world of exact recurrence but only similar recurrence (perhaps due to random events at the quantum level) and in the 138th epoch there is a Lewis-like person who is a banker. Should we then conclude that what assures us of the truth of the claim that Lewis might have been a banker is the fact that the Lewis-like person in the 138th epoch is a banker? And if this is the case, why bother looking at other epochs or other worlds? If what makes it true that Lewis might have been a banker is that a counterpart of Lewis's is a banker, and context determines the features that one must have to count as a counterpart of Lewis's, and worldmates of Lewis can qualify as counterparts, surely there is someone in our own epoch who is similar enough to Lewis to count as a counterpart for the purposes of determining the truth of the claim that Lewis might have been a banker. There is no need to bring other worlds into the picture; just look to the counterpart relation for questions of *de re* modality. Such an approach will not work for all possibilities if one includes, as Lewis

Saul Kripke

does, those possibilities that involve states or individuals that have no counterparts (under any contextual resolution of the counterpart relation). But the question remains with respect to *de re* modal attribution: how does the fact that someone other than Humphrey won an election make it true that Humphrey might have won the election?

Chapter 2

Names

The linguistic turn that philosophy took at the beginning of the twentieth century was not only exhibited as a concern with formal logic, but also manifested itself by an intense enquiry into the nature of linguistic meaning. One of the functions of language is representation or reference. We use linguistic symbols to stand for or represent some item or entity in the world such as a person or an event. While the theories of meaning that were developed in conjunction with formal logic by Frege and Russell differed significantly in their approach to language generally, they took similar approaches to explaining designation with respect to ordinary proper names. Their views, or versions of them, dominated the theory of naming in the philosophy of language in the twentieth century prior to Kripke. Kripke was not alone in rasing problems with the orthodox view of the naming relation, but his work has had a great influence on both the subsequent developments in the philosophy of language and the theory of naming. To help understand Kripke's contribution, we first present the philosophical context in which it occurred.

I

One natural account of the meaning of a word or phrase is that a word or phrase means what it stands for or refers to. This was Mill's view for naming expressions. The meaning of a naming phrase such as 'the current prime minister' or 'Tony Blair' is simply the person to whom the expression refers. But by the end of the nineteenth century, Frege saw a difficulty for a theory of meaning for naming expressions if the meaning of such an expression is simply the object named. Frege noted that the expressions 'the morning star' and 'the evening star' both named the same object, Venus. Yet the sentences 'The morning star is the evening star' and 'The morning star is the morning star' have different meanings because one is informative and the other is not. This led Frege to reject the idea that the meaning of a designating expression is the object named and to introduce a distinction between what he called the *sense* of an expression and what the expression designates.

Exactly what Frege had in mind by a *sense* is not completely clear and different philosophers have offered different theories. Roughly speaking, the *sense* of an expression α is the information contained or associated with α. So the *sense* of the expression 'the morning star' is something like being the star of the morning (where 'star' is used simply to mean 'bright heavenly body'). Some philosophers have identified *senses* with properties and hence the *sense* of 'the morning star' just is the property of being the star of the morning.

Senses solve the problem that the simple theory of naming encountered. The sentence 'The morning star is the evening star' is informative because it expresses some content, what Frege called a *thought*, that involves the *senses* of the naming expressions in the sentence. This is not, of course, the whole story. After all, the sentence is about Venus and not some *sense* of an expression. Frege accounted for this fact by claiming that naming expressions, along with all other expressions, functioned by having both a *sense* and a referent. The *referent* of a naming expression is that item that is uniquely characterized by the *sense* of the expression. In the case at hand, Venus is the item that had the property of being the star of the morning and hence the sentence is about Venus. Still, it is important to note that the sentence is about Venus in an indirect way. The sentence expresses the thought, or *proposition* as it is commonly called, and that proposition involves the *senses* of expressions in the sentence, *not* the referents. The sentence is *about* Venus because the proposition expressed by the sentence involves *senses* that characterize Venus. A fundamental element of Frege's theory of language is the distinction between the *sense* of an expression and the referent. This feature allows us to avoid Frege's problem concerning the information contained in true identity statements between distinct naming expressions.

A slightly different problem for naming expressions led Russell to develop his theory of naming expressions. Russell realized that naming expressions could sometimes fail to name anything. As an example, Russell offered the sentence

(1)   The golden mountain does not exist.

On the simple theory of naming expressions, the content or information expressed or contained in a sentence is a simple function of the items named. But if there is no item named, as in the case of (1), then the sentence itself could not express a complete thought or proposition. Russell thought that if a sentence did not express a proposition then that sentence had to be nonsense, but clearly (1) is not nonsense; it is true. One solution to this problem is to hold that all naming expressions name something, even if what they name does not exist or is not real. This was the view adopted by Alexius Meinong. Russell, who once agreed with Meinong, abandoned this view because he claimed that it required one to accept that there are objects that are not real which, he argued, led to contradictions; not to mention offending our "robust sense of reality".

This left Russell with the problem of what to do with sentences such as (1). His answer was a theory of language based on the idea of logical analysis. According to Russell, Mill's idea that the meaning of a naming expression is what the expression stands for or names is correct, *provided* that one first applies the technique of logical analysis to the sentence to identify the logical parts of the sentence. One can then apply the simple theory of meaning to the logical parts to produce the proposition expressed by the sentence. When one does the logical analysis on such sentences as (1), what appears as a naming expression in the ordinary language sentence becomes a complex functional expression in the logical language. This is a result of Russell's famous theory of descriptions. Roughly speaking, sentence (1) is understood as:

(1*)   It is not the case that there is one and only one golden mountain.

Notice that in (1*) there is no singular naming expression, only general terms. On Russell's analysis, all definite descriptions (expressions of the form 'the so-and-so') are analysed in terms of general terms and quantifiers.

One of the important features of Russell's analysis is that it allowed for what are called *scope ambiguities*. Consider the following sentence:

(2)   The present King of France is not bald.

Because there is no King of France we are inclined to think that (2) is false. But if (2) is false then it would seem to follow that the opposite of (2)

(3)   The present King of France is bald

is true. Yet, the truth of (3) appears to commit us to the existence of the present King of France. So what are we to do?

According to Russell, the answer lies in the fact that (2) is ambiguous. It can be read either as:

(2a)   It is not case that there is one and only one King of France and he is bald,

or as

(2b)   There is one and only one King of France and he is not bald.

Only (2a) is the opposite of (3), but (2a) is not false. The false proposition is (2b), which does not contradict (3). Hence (3) and (2b) can both be false without fear of violating the logical law of the excluded middle (each proposition is true or its denial is true).

Notice that Russell's analysis can also solve Frege's problem without the introduction of *senses*. Russell argued that Frege's *senses* led to a contradiction when one directly *named* a *sense*. His argument against Frege is very obscure and assumes that it is possible to name an object directly, which Frege appears to reject. So we will not pursue the matter here. The solution that Russell's view offers to Frege's problem is straightforward. Recall that the sentence 'The morning star is the evening star' appears to be informative, yet the naming expressions name the same object. On Russell's view the naming expressions are analysed via his theory of descriptions with the result that the sentence expresses the proposition (roughly put as):

(4)   There is one and only one star of the morning, x, and there is one and only one star of the evening, y, and x is y.

Clearly this proposition is informative as it involves identifying something that has very different characteristics.

So far we have considered naming expressions generally and the particular problems that motivated Frege and Russell, and it should be noted in this connection, lest there be some misunderstanding, that while Russell was concerned with the question of nonexistent objects when he wrote "On Denoting" in 1905, he was also concerned with the very problems that motivated Frege. Still, we have not discussed naming expressions that are not complex expressions or descriptive by nature, such as ordinary proper names. Frege presented his problem in very abstract terms, asking how a sentence of the form

(5) $a = b$

could be informative. He took the sentence 'The morning star is the evening star' to be an instance of the abstract form given in (5). Sentences of the form of (5), but in which the expressions are ordinary proper names as in the often used example

(6)   Hesperus is Phosphorus,

present the problem that these naming expressions do not appear to have the sort of descriptive content we found in 'the evening star'. Here is a similarity between Russell's and Frege's views. Both thought that *ordinary* proper names do have the same sort of descriptive content as do definite descriptions. For Russell, almost all ordinary proper names are *abbreviations* of definite descriptions. The name 'Hesperus' is an abbreviation of the description 'the evening star' and the name 'Phosphorus' of the description 'the morning star'. Thus, (6) expresses the proposition roughly put in (4). For Frege, the descriptive content comes in the form of the *sense* associated with the name. But the *sense* associated with an ordinary proper name is the *sense* of an associated definite description. So the *sense* of 'Hesperus' is the *sense* of the description 'the evening star'. Russell and Frege disagree over whether or not ordinary names have *senses*, but they agree that the content of a name comes from the content of an associated definite description.

Russell also thought that *logically speaking* a name was something that directly designated a particular object. Since most uses of ordinary names (e.g. 'Socrates') are abbreviations of descriptions, they are not strictly speaking names for Russell. Hence Russell says: "That makes it very difficult to get any instance of a name at all in the proper strict logical sense of the word. The only words one does use as names in the logical sense are words like 'this' or 'that'" (1956: 201). Certain special cases, however, allow an ordinary name to be a logically proper name. Russell says:

> Assuming that there is such a thing as direct acquaintance with oneself, Bismarck himself might have used his name directly to designate the particular with whom he was acquainted. In this

case if he made a judgement about himself, he himself might be a constitutent of the judgement. Here the proper name has the direct use which it always wishes to have, as simply standing for a certain object, and not for a description of the object.

(1959: 54)

So in very special cases, according to Russell, certain uses of ordinary proper names directly designate particulars, although in general they are abbreviations for descriptions. Frege rejected any such uses of names. On his view all uses of names involved a *sense* that could be identified with the *sense* of some associated definite description.

II

Many have disagreed over whether Frege's theory of *senses* or Russell's theory of logical analysis as given by his theory of descriptions is the correct view of ordinary proper names. Virtually everyone has agreed, however, that naming expressions designate the items that they designate by describing those items in some way. Still, in the years between Russell's introduction of his theory of descriptions and Kripke's attack on this fundamental feature of the two views, a number of philosophers thought that the details of both Frege's and Russell's view needed to be corrected. One problem with the description view of names as presented by Frege and Russell is that according to that view each use of a name has a single description associated with it. John Searle, for example, raises the following problem for the view as presented by Frege and Russell:

> Suppose we agree to drop 'Aristotle' and use, say, 'the teacher of Alexander', then it is a necessary truth that the man referred to is Alexander's teacher – but it is a contingent fact that Aristotle ever went into pedagogy (though I am suggesting that it is a necessary fact that Aristotle has the logical sum, inclusive disjunction, of properties commonly attributed to him).

(1958: 170)

If we associate only one description 'the φ' with a name 'α' then the claim that 'α is the φ' becomes a necessary truth and that cannot be correct. So to avoid this problem and some related difficulties, the *description theory of names* (as Kripke came to call it) was modified in various ways from the original formulations of Frege and Russell.

Kripke distinguishes two versions of the modified description theory: a meaning version and a reference version.

> The substitute is that, although a name is not a disguised description it either abbreviates, or anyway its reference is determined by, some cluster of descriptions ... The stronger version would say that the name is simply *defined*, synonymously, as the cluster of descriptions. (*NN*: 61)

The "cluster of descriptions" that Kripke refers to is that collection of descriptions that Searle describes as being commonly attributed to the referent of the name. According to the meaning version of descriptivism, the meaning (in the sense of Frege's *sense*) of a proper name is given by an associated cluster of descriptions. According to the reference version, however, only the reference of the name is determined by the associated cluster of descriptions. Since most (but not all) of Kripke's arguments apply to both versions, we shall, for the moment, ignore this distinction in presenting Kripke's objections. We shall return to the distinction in Ch. 2.III.

Kripke explicitly rejects descriptivism as it applies to ordinary proper names, arguing that it is based on a number of faulty premises or presuppositions. He nonetheless also explicitly notes the power and elegance of the view:

> Let me not pay inadequate tribute to the power of the then prevailing complex of ideas, emanating from Frege and from Russell, that I then abandoned. The natural and uniform manner by which these ideas appear to account for a variety of philosophical problems – their marvelous internal coherence – is adequate explanation for their long appeal. (*NN*: 5)

While definite descriptions, certain pronouns and adverbs (e.g. 'he' and 'today') and ordinary proper names such as 'Saul Kripke' and 'Al Gore' are naming expressions, we usually reserve the expression 'name' for proper names, including those names that resemble descriptions (e.g. 'the Empire State Building'). Kripke focused on names in the sense of ordinary proper names in his objections to the description theory.

Kripke presented the description theory in the form of four theses: (i) for every name N there is a cluster of properties φ such that a speaker who uses N believes that the referent of N has the properties in φ; (ii) one of the properties or some collection of the properties in φ is believed by the speaker to designate someone uniquely; (iii) if most of the properties in φ are had by some thing *x* then *x* is the referent of *N*; and (iv) if no object has enough of the properties in φ then *N* lacks a referent. (In the lectures, Kripke mentions six theses, but two of them are really consequences of the other four as Kripke himself notes (*NN*: 73).) In addition to the theses, Kripke added a condition that any theory of naming must satisfy if it is to count as a theory of naming. This condition (usually called the *circularity condition*) requires that the properties contained in the cluster of properties associated with a given use of a name *N* do not include, in some uneliminable way, the relation of reference or naming itself. For example, suppose someone suggests that included in the cluster of properties associated with the name *N* is the property of being the person called *N* and this property is the one that secures the reference of *N*. But if being the person called *N* is what secures the reference of the name *N*, then just what is required for this property to be exemplified? If the answer is that someone has the property of being called *N* just in case that person is the referent of the name *N*, we have not presented much in the way of an account of the reference of proper names. For such a theory in effect claims that the referent of the name *N* is the referent of the name *N*. So it is no help to replace the relation of *referring* with the relation of *calling* if the relation of *calling* is defined in terms of the relation of *referring*. As we shall see in Ch. 2.III, there are some questions about how the circularity constraint should be used, but for the moment we shall turn our attention to Kripke's main objections to the description theory.

While Kripke offers a number of different objections to the description theory, we can roughly group the objections into three categories: modal arguments, semantic arguments and epistemic arguments. In each case Kripke argues that the description theory misdescribes the facts, be they modal facts, semantic facts or epistemic facts. If most or all of Kripke's objections to the description theory are successful, then Kripke will have shown not only that the theory is mistaken, but that it is deeply mistaken and no single addition or change to the theory is likely to save the view. What is needed, if Kripke's objections are successful, is a new approach to a theory of reference or naming.

According to Kripke, the description theory of names gets the modal facts wrong. The theory holds that the meaning of the name *N* is given by the properties in the associated cluster φ. So, for example, the meaning of the name 'Aristotle' may be 'the person who taught Alexander, who was the most famous student of Plato, . . .' where the ellipsis is filled in with properties associated with a use of the name

'Aristotle'. Since the relationship being considered here between the name and the associated cluster is one of meaning, it will follow that some subset of the properties included in the cluster is essential to Aristotle. That is, according to this view, it is necessary that if Aristotle exists then Aristotle taught Alexander or became the most famous student of Plato or whatever. Yet Kripke argues that this cannot be correct:

> Most of the things commonly attributed to Aristotle are things that Aristotle might not have done at all. In a situation in which he didn't do them, we would describe that as a situation in which *Aristotle* didn't do them. ... Not only is it true *of* the man Aristotle that he might not have gone into pedagogy; it is also true that we use the term 'Aristotle' in such a way that, in thinking of a counterfactual situation in which Aristotle didn't go into any of the fields and do any of the achievements we commonly attribute to him, still we would say that was a situation in which *Aristotle* did not do these things. (*NN*: 62)

Kripke points out that many of properties that we commonly associate with people are properties that are not essential to the person. Although it is true that Aristotle taught Alexander the Great, he might not have taught him. So the property of having taught Alexander the Great is a contingent property of Aristotle's. Moreover, most of the other properties we commonly attribute to Aristotle such as being Plato's most famous student are also contingent properties of Aristotle. This being the case, there seems to be no reason for holding that the cluster itself is essential to Aristotle. Not only is it possible that Aristotle not have taught Alexander, it is possible that he not have taught Alexander and not have been a student of Plato's and so on. The fact that the properties in the cluster are contingent properties of Aristotle leads to a problem for the description theory of names. The description theory holds that the meaning of the name 'Aristotle' is given by the cluster of associated properties in much the same way that the noun 'bachelor' is defined by the phrase 'adult unmarried male'. It follows from the meaning of the term 'bachelor' that no one *can* be a bachelor unless he is unmarried. So similarly no one *can* be Aristotle unless he taught Alexander or was a student of Plato's and so on. Yet we agree that Aristotle might not have done any of those things.

Kripke takes pains to point out that a description theorist cannot avoid the problem by claiming that while it is true that the man we call 'Aristotle' might not have had these properties, still we use the name to mean one who has these properties. Kripke argues that we use the name 'Aristotle' to describe the counterfactual situation in which Aristotle did not do the things that we commonly attribute to him, and in that instance we are using the name 'Aristotle' to designate the same person that we use the name to designate in describing a factual situation. This is an important difference between our use of names and our use of descriptions.

To help clarify the different ways that we may use expressions, Kripke introduced the notion of a *rigid designator*. He introduces this notion within the framework of the possible worlds that he used in providing a semantics for modal logic: "Let us use some terms quasi-technically. Let's call something a *rigid designator* if in every possible world it designates the same object, a *nonrigid* or *accidental designator* if that is not the case" (*NN*: 48). Although it is natural for Kripke to present the notion of rigid designation in terms of the possible worlds framework, one should not conclude that the notion is dependent upon Kripke's metaphysical views concerning possible worlds. The basic idea of rigid designation is one where the expression in question has a fixed designation (given the context of use) when considering various counterfactual situations. So, if we describe a counterfactual situation where Aristotle did not teach Alexander, and if 'Aristotle' is a rigid designator, then we use the name to designate the same person in the counterfactual situation that we designate when we use it to describe a factual situation. In other words, 'Aristotle' designates the same person in every possible world (in which Aristotle exists).

When Kripke first introduced the notion of a rigid designator, the question arose as to Kripke's intent with respect to 'Aristotle' when considering possible worlds in which Aristotle does not exist. Some thought Kripke intended 'Aristotle' to designate Aristotle even when considering a possible world in which Aristotle does not exist. This view receives some support from a claim Kripke makes in the preface to *Naming and Necessity*, which was written some years after the lectures were given: "I say that a proper name rigidly designates its referent even when we speak of counterfactual situations where that referent would not have existed" (*NN*: 21). David Kaplan (1989a) has reported, however, that in correspondence, Kripke has indicated that his intent was to remain neutral with respect to what if anything names designate when considering worlds where the object in question fails to exist. So Kripke in-

tended that the notion of a rigid designator as it applies to proper
names be understood as follows:

> A term *d* is a rigid designator of an object *x* if and only if *d* desig-
> nates *x* at every possible world where *x* exists and does not
> designate anything other than *x* at any possible world.

These conditions for a rigid designator leave open the question of
whether the name 'Aristotle' (for example) designates anything at all
at worlds where Aristotle does not exist.

Kripke's comments in the preface appear to be incompatible with
his later description of the notion of a rigid designator, but they can
be reconciled. When one considers what a name designates *with
respect to* or *at* a possible world, it is natural to understand that question to mean what object *in* the world is designated. Roughly speaking, to say an object is *in* a possible world is to say that the object is a
member of the domain of objects associated with the world. We are in
a world where Aristotle does exist and we can use the name 'Aristotle'
to refer to someone who does not exist in the counterfactual situation
(as Kripke indicates in his comments in the preface quote above); but
in such a case 'Aristotle' *may* fail to designate anything at all *at* the
possible world in question. That is, the name may fail to designate
anything in the domain associated with the world. My view is that
the name 'Aristotle' does not designate anything in a world where
Aristotle fails to exist even though we can describe such a world
using the name 'Aristotle'. Kripke indicates that he remains neutral
on this question, leaving open the possibility that the name designates a merely possible object at that world.

Returning now to the main argument against the description
view, consider the definite description formed from the properties
included in the cluster associated with 'Aristotle'; namely, 'the
teacher of Alexander, who is the most famous student of Plato, ...'
(which we shall abbreviate as 'the teacher of Alexander, etc.'). Unlike
the name, the definite description is not a rigid designator. If, for
example, we consider a situation where the teacher of Alexander is
not a philosopher, we are not thereby considering a situation where
Aristotle is not a philosopher. When we describe counterfactual situations using descriptions, we refer to whomever satisfies the description in the situation regardless of whether that person satisfies the
description in the actual world. A situation in which the teacher of
Alexander is not a philosopher may not be a situation in which Aristotle is not a philosopher and hence the description can designate

someone other than Aristotle in certain counterfactual situations. Because the descriptions can designate someone other than Aristotle in different counterfactual situations, descriptions are not rigid designators. If ordinary proper names are rigid designators and definite descriptions are not, it follows that the names are not descriptions. Also, definite descriptions admit various scope readings, as we noted in connection with our discussion of Russell's theory of descriptions. Names on the other hand do not have such scope readings and this is another indication that names are not disguised descriptions.

We can sum up the modal argument as follows. Consider the sentences:

(1)   Aristotle was a teacher.

(2)   The teacher of Alexander, etc. was a teacher.

Sentences (1) and (2) can have different truth-values in the same counterfactual situation. Consider a situation where Aristotle did not go into teaching but someone did teach Alexander the Great. In such a situation, (1) is false but (2) is true. If 'Aristotle' means 'the teacher of Alexander, etc.' then (1) and (2) could not differ in truth-value in any counterfactual situation. Hence, the description theory gets the modal facts wrong.

What about the epistemic facts? According to the description theory, a speaker using a proper name associates a cluster of properties such that some combination of these properties is believed by the speaker to be had uniquely by the bearer of the name. This is thesis (ii) of Kripke's four theses noted above. Yet this cannot be correct. We often use names without having at our command any such cluster of properties. Kripke presents the example of the well-known physicist Richard Feynman, and notes that most people who have heard of him do not associate a unique property of his when using the name. Of the man in the street, Kripke says: "When asked he will say: well he's a physicist or something. He may not think that this picks out anyone uniquely. I still think he uses the name 'Feynman' as a name for Feynman" (*NN*: 81). Kripke's point is that we often use names to refer to certain persons without believing that we have unique descriptions of those persons. Hence, thesis (ii) is false.

There is another epistemic problem with the description theory. According to the theory, the meaning of a proper name is given by the associated cluster of properties. So just as one knows a priori that a bachelor is unmarried, it follows that if 'the teacher of Alexander, etc.' is the meaning of 'Aristotle' then we know a priori that Aristotle is the teacher of Alexander. Yet, we cannot know a priori that Aristotle taught Alexander. We need some empirical evidence that he in fact did the teaching. Hence, the description theory gets the epistemic facts wrong as well.

Kripke also offers arguments against the description view based on semantic facts. Remember that according to the description view, if some collection of the properties in the cluster are uniquely had by an object then that object is designated by the name (thesis (iii)). Kripke offers a now famous example to argue that this view gets the semantic facts wrong. Gödel is a well-known logician who proved the incompleteness of arithmetic. This theorem of logic, roughly stated, is that one cannot provide a finite list of axioms of arithmetic that together with the laws of logic will allow a deduction of all the truths of arithmetic. Most people who know of Gödel know him as the man who proved the incompleteness of arithmetic. Kripke, in his example, asks his audience to suppose that Gödel did not prove the incompleteness of arithmetic, but that someone else – Schmidt – did the proof and somehow Gödel got his hands on it and published it as his own. These facts (fictions really) are unknown to all but Gödel. Kripke asks whether, in this case, when we use the name 'Gödel' we are really referring to Schmidt: the person who proved the incompleteness of arithmetic unbeknownst to us. Clearly not. Even if we are wrong about who proved which theorem, we are using the name 'Gödel' to refer to Gödel. Moreover, we need not present a fictional case in order to see the problem. Many people mistakenly think that Einstein invented the atomic bomb, but it does not follow that when they use the name 'Einstein' they are not referring to Einstein. One can be mistaken about who did such and such and still use the names correctly. So thesis (iii) is mistaken.

Thesis (iv) suffers from similar problems. No one person invented the atomic bomb; it was a team of people. But according to thesis (iv), if no one uniquely has some collection of the properties in the cluster then the name has no referent. So, if someone uses the name 'Einstein' thinking that he invented the atomic bomb, then, according to description theory, the name fails to refer to anyone. Yet clearly this is wrong. One can be mistaken about who, if anyone, invented the atomic bomb without failing to refer to Einstein when using his name. So theses (iv) and (iii) are mistaken and the description theory gets the semantic facts wrong as well as getting the epistemic and modal facts wrong.

If Kripke's arguments against descriptivism are correct, then neither the meaning of a proper name nor its reference is determined by a cluster of properties or descriptions associated with a given name. Yet we do refer to people by using their names. So just how does reference take place? Kripke first describes the issue as follows:

> What is the true picture of what's going on? Maybe reference doesn't really take place at all! After all, we don't really know that any of the properties we use to identify the man are right. We don't know that they pick out a unique object. So what *does* make my use of 'Cicero' into a name of *him*? ... Someone, let's say, a baby, is born; his parents call him by a certain name. They talk about him to their friends. Other people meet him. Through various sorts of talk the name is spread from link to link as if by a chain. (*NN*: 90–91)

He continues:

> A rough statement of a theory might be the following: An initial "baptism" takes place. Here the object may be named by ostension, or reference of the name may be fixed by a description. When the name is "passed from link to link," the receiver of the name must, I think, intend when he learns it to use it with the same reference as the man from whom he heard it. (*NN*: 96)

Kripke's basic idea is relatively simple, although the details will be complicated. A given use u of a proper name N refers to a given entity x provided two conditions obtain: (a) at some time x was *baptized N,* and (b) there is a chain of reference-dependent uses of N leading from u to the baptism. The phrase *reference-dependent use* is not Kripke's. It captures Kripke's idea, however, that when we go from link to link in the chain of uses of a given name, the user intends to use the name to refer to what the prior use referred to. This idea of reference-dependent use is complicated. Still, Kripke needs some constraint like reference-dependent use in any view that depends on a historical chain for reference. Otherwise, as Kripke notes, he would be unable to name his pet aardvark 'Napoleon', which is something he can clearly do. Also the notion of 'baptism' that Kripke is employing is a semi-technical one. In the brief description of the view, Kripke notes two forms of "baptism". One sort of baptism takes place when one exhibits or demonstrates an object such as by pointing to it or holding it up and then dubs that object with a name. The other form of baptism is when one fixes on an object by description and then dubs the object with a name. For example, suppose we find an ancient written work detailing various adventures of various persons but the work has no author identified. Because we have the work before us, however, we name the work '*Nomus*' (a lead character in the work). We thus exhibit the work and name it by baptism. We cannot however exhibit the author of *Nomus*. This person is long gone. We can, nonetheless, refer to the author by describing him as the author of *Nomus* (we may assume that experts in these matters have informed us that it is the work of a single male author). Using the description 'the author of *Nomus*' we may thereby baptize its author as 'Persis'. We have thereby fixed the designation of the name 'Persis' via the description 'the author of *Nomus*'. So in this example we have both an example of baptism by ostension (the work in question) and baptism by fixing by description.

In a footnote to the passage just quoted above Kripke adds the following comments concerning introducing names via baptism:

> The case of a baptism by ostension can perhaps be subsumed under the description concept as well ... Two things should be emphasized concerning the case of introducing a name via a description in an initial baptism. First, the description used is not synonymous with the name it introduces but rather fixes its reference. Here we differ from the usual description theorists. Second, most cases of initial baptism are far from those which inspired the description theory. Usually a baptizer is acquainted in some sense with the object he names and is able to name it ostensively. (*NN*: 96, n.42)

Kripke clearly distinguishes his view of baptism by description from the view of descriptivism that he is arguing against. First, Kripke claims that few names are actually introduced purely descriptively, as opposed to introductions involving pointings and/or demonstratives such as 'this child before us', and so on, and hence unlike descriptivism, not all names have an associated definite description or even some cluster of descriptions. But even if Kripke were wrong about this and many names are fixed purely descriptively (this is a linguistic empirical claim after all), this would not be a form of descriptivism. Kripke's notion of "fixing by description" is a kind of baptism of objects for names, not for subsequent uses of the names. Once an object has been baptized with a given name, whether the baptism was by ostension or description or some other way, subsequent uses of the name designate the baptized object even in counterfactual contexts. So, there are counterfactual situations in which it is true to say that Persis is not the author of *Nomus*. But there are no counterfactual situations in which it is true to say that the author of *Nomus* is not the author of *Nomus* (leaving aside questions of existence).

The difference between descriptivism and Kripke's approach is that according to descriptivism, the designation of a name in a context of use depends on what satisfies some description relative to that context, while on Kripke's approach it is the object that was baptized with that name (as determined via the reference-dependent links). Also Kripke makes it absolutely clear that the relation of reference is *not* eliminated in favour of some other relation or relations. Hence, his approach is not intended as a theory of reference or meaning for names. He says with respect to his remarks on his approach:

> Notice that the preceding outline hardly *eliminates* the notion of reference; on the contrary, it takes the notion of intending to use the same reference as a given. There is also an appeal to an initial baptism which is explained in terms of fixing a reference by description or ostension (if ostension is not to be subsumed under the other category). (*NN*: 97)

His approach is intended to provide an account of how names function as designators in general. Although Kripke never claims this, it appears that Kripke has serious doubts about our ability to eliminate the notion of reference in favour of other better understood notions.

III

One of the main responses to Kripke's proposals has been that the idea that names lacked descriptive content leads to difficulties when we consider those problems that led Frege and Russell to develop their views in the first place. As mentioned in Ch. 2.I, Frege postulated the existence of senses for names to account for the informativeness of true identity sentences containing distinct names. If names lack descriptive content then how can such sentences be informative? This is a complex problem for anyone who accepts a theory of reference similar to Kripke's. We shall discuss Kripke's response to this objection in Chapter 3, where we also address Keith Donnellan's (1966) distinction between referential uses and attributive uses of descriptions.

Another common response to Kripke's claim that names are rigid designators is that Kripke must be wrong because many people have the same name. Hence, names are not even fixed in their designation in our world, let alone other possible worlds. It is true, of course, that there are many different people named 'John Smith'. One is an American adventurer and another an English composer. Does the fact that in one context I use the name 'John Smith' to refer to the composer and in another context I use it to refer to the adventurer show that names are not rigid designators as Kripke claims? Here two issues must be separated.

We need to distinguish the relation of reference that obtains between language users and items in the world and the relationship between expressions in a language and items in the world. Most philosophers use the same expression, 'reference', for both relations, often holding that one of the relations is definable or dependent upon the other. Kripke uses the term 'reference' for both relations but he explicitly distinguishes them in *Naming and Necessity* and discusses them in some detail in his paper "Speaker's Reference and Semantic Reference" (1977). Here we need only put aside the issues that arise when someone uses a name N to refer to a person x even though in the linguistic community the name N is used to refer to a different individual y. So we shall assume for the moment that the intended objection to Kripke's claim concerning rigid designators involving many individuals with the same name does not depend on the distinction between speaker's reference and semantic reference. So how does Kripke avoid the objection?

In the preface to *Naming and Necessity,* Kripke takes up this issue directly. He asks us to consider (in a given context) the sentence:

(1)   Aristotle was fond of dogs.

He then comments:

> In the present instance, that context made it clear that it was the conventional use of 'Aristotle' for the great philosopher that was in question. Then, *given* this fixed understanding of (1), the question of rigidity is: Is the correctness of (1), *thus understood,* determined with respect to each counterfactual situation by whether a certain single person would have liked dogs (had that situation obtained)?   (*NN*: 9)

If the answer to this question is yes, as Kripke claims, then the use of 'Aristotle' in (1) is rigid.

Kripke indicates that a test for whether an expression is rigid or not is best conducted by considering particular uses of the expression in statements (and presumably other linguistic forms such as questions and commands). Because we are to consider particular statements, the expressions in those statements are being used with a determinate meaning. Hence (1) understood in its context is not about the shipping magnate, but about the philosopher. This is true even though a different token in a different context of a similar sentence could be about the shipping magnate and not the philosopher. So the fact that a given expression can have many bearers does not imply that the expression is not rigid (nor does it imply that it is rigid). The question of rigidity comes after the question of determinate meaning. This is true for both Kripke's view and descriptivism.

Consider now the sentence:

(2)   The teacher of Alexander was fond of dogs.

Again, the question of whether or not the expression 'the teacher of Alexander' is rigid is determined after questions about the use of the expression are answered. Perhaps some question about the exact meaning of 'teacher' needs to be answered before we can determine whether (2) is true or not. Once those issues are settled, we can ask whether the statement made by (2) in its context of use would be true or false in various counterfactual situations and what determines the truth of the statement in those situations. Given this, the description is not rigid, because the truth of (2) in various counterfactual situations depends on who is the teacher of Alexander in the situation and whether that person is fond of dogs.

But is it fair for Kripke to point to particular *uses* of a name like 'Aristotle' when considering the question of whether a name is a rigid designator? Does this not make the claim trivial? After all, a given use of a description denotes a particular object and not another object. Why not say, then, that a particular use of a description is rigid?

A few points need to be mentioned here. The question of rigidity for a given expression can only arise *after* we have determined which expression we are considering. For example, is the description 'the smallest odd one' a rigid designator? You cannot answer the question until you determine the meaning of it. If by 'odd' we mean not evenly divisible by 2 and the context is about the natural numbers then the answer is yes, it is a rigid designator. If, on the other hand, 'odd' is understood to mean 'unusual' and the context concerns living philosophers, then the answer is no, it is not a rigid designator. So we first must determine the meaning of the expression and then we can ask about rigidity.

So if we use 'Aristotle' (in sentence (1)) to refer to the philosopher in one context and the shipping magnate in another, (i) are we using different names, (ii) are we using the same name with different meanings, or (iii) are we using the same name with the same meaning? For Kripke's point concerning rigidity to hold, it does not matter if one accepts (i) or (ii) as the correct account of the fact that two people share the name 'Aristotle'. Only if (iii) is correct will Kripke's claim be in doubt. For if (iii) is the correct answer, then clearly 'Aristotle' as it occurs in (1) is not rigid since in some contexts the issue will be if the philosopher is fond of dogs while in others it will turn on the affections of the shipping magnate.

Some philosophers accept (iii) as the correct answer, under one of two different views. On one view, the name in all of its contexts of use has a single meaning and that meaning is 'the bearer of "Aristotle"'. Russell once held this view and it is currently defended by Kent Bach (1994). This is also a version of the descriptive theory of names and is subject to the objections that Kripke presented against descriptivism. We will consider this view in more detail when we consider the responses to Kripke's arguments against descriptivism.

The other view holds that names are indexical-like expressions and are to be understood along the lines of 'this n' where n is the name in question. Tyler Burge (1973) offers a version of this view. A reason often given for this view is that we can account for the fact that names can be shared by many people without postulating semantic ambiguity as Kripke and others do. First, even if this is the correct view, it does not count against Kripke's claim of rigidity:

> For example, some philosophers would assimilate proper names to demonstratives. Their reference varies from utterance to utterance the way that of a demonstrative does. This does not affect the issues discussed [rigid designation], since the reference of a demonstrative must be given for a definite proposition to be expressed. (*NN*: 10, n.12)

Secondly, there are reasons to think that such a theory of *names* is not correct. Imagine a small linguistic community that had the restriction that in the introduction of any label of anything (person, place, time), the label had to be new. In such a community persons would be labelled. But no two persons would have the same label. Are there any names in this community? It would seem that there are names and it would be very implausible to think of those names as indexicals or demonstratives. This shows that the function of a name in the language is rather different from the function of a demonstrative or indexical. Because a detailed discussion of this position goes beyond a discussion of Kripke and his views, we leave this issue to consider a different complaint.

One argument that Kripke offers in support of his claim that proper names are not descriptions is the modal argument. Names designate the same individual in various counterfactual situations, but descriptions do not. A common response to this argument is that descriptions admit scope distinctions in modal statements and hence are rigid in one sense. Consider the following two sentences:

(3)   The teacher of Alexander might not have taught Alexander.

(4)   Aristotle might not have taught Alexander.

Sentence (4) seems clearly true, but (3) appears doubtful. After all, even if Aristotle did not teach Alexander, the teacher of Alexander certainly taught Alexander. But those who defend the view that names are descriptions argue that there are two readings of (3): one where the description has primary scope and one where the description has secondary scope. We can exhibit these in the following way:

(3a)   It might have been the case that: the teacher of Alexander did not teach Alexander.

(3b)   The teacher of Alexander is such that: he might not have taught Alexander.

Sentence (3a) is false (leaving aside issues of existence). There are no possibilities where the teacher of Alexander did not teach Alexander. Sentence (3b) is another matter altogether. It states that whoever taught Alexander might not have. And this seems clearly true. Being a teacher of Alexander is not an essential property of whoever happens to have it. So, it is said, all Kripke has shown is that the descriptions involved in the use of a proper name need always take primary scope (as in (3b)), but this does not show that names are not descriptions.

In the preface to *Naming and Necessity*, Kripke argues that this use of scope does not address his arguments. Kripke agrees that (3) has two distinct readings and that (3b) is true and hence some of our intuitions with respect to the truth of (4) may be explained by reference to (3b). Reference to (3b), however, really misunderstands the original modal argument. The original modal argument was based on a distinction in truth-values between the statements made by (1) and (2) (above) relative to different possibilities. These sentences do not raise questions of scope because no operators occur in the sentences (we are ignoring temporal operators here because they are not at issue). Since no question of scope arises, one cannot use the difference in scope with respect to (3a) and (3b) to explain the truth-values of (1) and (2) in different counterfactual circumstances. Hence, while in some sentences differences in scope can be used to account for apparent differences of truth-values, such differences are not universal and cannot be used to show that names are (have the same meaning as) definite descriptions. One common response to Kripke is that the truth-value of a simple statement *at* a possible world is not something that is determined prior to theorizing. That is, it is not part of the data concerning our modal views that the statements made by (1) and (2) differ in truth-value at a given possible world. The claim that (4) is true is part of the data that our theorizing must account for, but it can be accounted for by noting the scope distinctions in (3).

This response to Kripke's claims is not convincing. After all, considering whether a given statement is true in a described possibility does not seem to involve much theorizing and it is something we do all the time and not just when we happen to be in the philosophy room (i.e., doing philosophy). For those philosophers who still may be persuaded by these considerations, Scott Soames (1998c) argues that scope distinctions cannot replace the rigidity of names and that Kripke's modal argument cannot be avoided by appeal to scope distinctions. Soames asks us to consider the following argument:

(P1) The proposition that if n is F, then something is both F and G = the proposition that if the G is F, then something is both F and G.

(P2) The proposition that if the G is F, then something is both F and G is a necessary truth.

(C) The proposition that if n is F, then something is both F and G is a necessary truth.

This argument ought to be a valid one since it is simply of the form: $p = q$ and p is a necessary truth, therefore q is a necessary truth. But, in fact, (C) does not follow from (P1) and (P2) if (C) is understood according to a primary scope description analysis. This is because *n* is understood as the description 'the *G*' where the description has primary scope. That is, the statement that the *G* is such that necessarily if it is *F* then something is both *F* and *G* is not true. Yet, the argument should be valid. Thus, scope distinctions cannot be used to avoid Kripke's argument against identifying names with descriptions.

Another common response to Kripke's modal argument against descriptivism is to claim that Kripke has simply chosen the wrong descriptions. The descriptions that Kripke uses to argue against descriptivism are descriptions that contingently apply to the object in question. What about those descriptions that necessarily apply to the object in question: so-called rigid descriptions? Consider, for example, a revised version of (2):

(2a) The actual teacher of Alexander was fond of dogs.

The description 'the actual teacher of Alexander' is a rigid description since the expression 'actual' is being used as an indexical and hence denotes that possible world that corresponds to our world since the sentence is being used in our world. This means that the truth-values of (1) and (2a) when uttered in the context of this world will be the same. The reason that they will be the same is that when we consider the truth of the statement made by (2a) we look to see who was the *actual* teacher of Alexander (namely Aristotle) and ask whether that person was fond of dogs at the counterfactual circumstance under consideration.

This view also has difficulties. The description is rigidified by introducing the indexical 'actual', which functions in such a way as to remove other counterfactual circumstances as possibilities for the satisfaction of the description. One standard view on how 'actual' does this is that it designates the actual world itself. Thus, we understand (2a) to be about the actual world as well as dogs, teachers and the relation of fondness. But the actual world is not really a part of what is said by (1). Sentence (1) is not about the actual world in the sense that it is part of the subject of what is being claimed. Of course, one would not utter (1) in the usual situation unless one thought that it was true in the actual world, but that fact does not imply that the statement one makes has the world (as well as Aristotle and dogs) as part of its subject matter. On this view, if (1) is uttered in a context that differs with respect to worlds then a different statement is made from the statement made in the actual context. Soames (1998c) has also argued that this form of descriptivism will not work.

Even if one could avoid Kripke's modal argument against descriptivism with rigid descriptions, there remain the semantic and epistemic arguments that do not involve rigidity *per se*. For example, suppose the description that is associated with the name N is *the actual* φ (where φ may be a complex disjunction of predicates) and N and *the actual* φ designate x. Even if N and *the actual* φ designate x in exactly the same counterfactual situations, the statement:

(5) N is *the actual* φ

is not known a priori. Yet the theory seems to demand that it is so known. So it does not seem that rigidifying the descriptive content can really produce the results for descriptivism.

Now, some philosophers have claimed that the problem with Kripke's view is that he ignored the most obvious description that is associated with a given proper name. Russell once claimed that the meaning of all names is the description given by the phrase the object called by that name. More recently, Bach has developed and defended the view that the meaning of a name N is the description *the bearer of N*. While such a view has a certain amount of plausibility, if it is to be understood as an account of the semantic content of a name in the way that other versions of descriptivism are intended, it must face the arguments that Kripke has offered against descriptivism generally. On the surface Kripke's modal argument shows that such a view is flawed. According to this view (1) has the same semantic content as:

(6)   The bearer of 'Aristotle' was fond of dogs.

Yet the two sentences have different truth-values in the same counterfactual circumstance. Consider a possibility where Aristotle was named 'Aeschylus' and was fond of dogs, and someone else who was not fond of dogs was named 'Aristotle'. In such a circumstance, (1) is true and (6) is false. Thus, (1) and (6) do not have the same content.

Unfortunately, Bach considers Kripke's modal objection in a slightly different form from Kripke's version of the argument. Bach's version of the objection involves the scope distinction issue discussed above. We may ignore this aspect of Bach's remarks because we have already considered such complaints. Basically, Bach responds by saying that all Kripke's examples show is that it is *uses* of names, not names themselves, that are rigid. So the fact that (1) and (6) seem to have different truth-values in the same circumstance is based on the fact that one has a particular use of 'Aristotle' in mind when uttering (1). As Bach puts it, "Kripke is *stipulating* that utterances of a name count as instances of the same name use only if the reference is the same" (1994: 152).

Kripke is not, however, *stipulating* that different utterances of a given name (type) count as utterances of the same name if the reference of the name is the same. Rather, Kripke thinks that the individuation conditions for names (usually) satisfy the above constraint. Still, Bach thinks that such a view of names is clearly mistaken and this is the key to his defence against the modal argument.

Names, according to Bach, are not ambiguous. The meaning of any name *N* is simply *the bearer of N*. Different *uses* of a name can result in different referents, but this fact about the use of a name is a pragmatic fact, not a semantic one. Suppose, for the moment, that Bach is correct. How does this avoid the modal objection? It appears to avoid the objection by claiming that (1) (by itself) is not "about" Aristotle the philosopher. On some *uses* (1) will be true just in case the philosopher is fond of dogs while on other uses we need to consider if the shipping magnate is fond of dogs and on still others something else named 'Aristotle' (my dog, for example) will be involved. The context of the utterance determines which proposition is involved. Moreover, in those contexts in which the philosopher figures in what is expressed by an utterance of (1), the philosopher will also figure in what is expressed by an utterance of (6). Thus, the modal argument fails because it fails to differentiate between uses of the description and uses of the name. That is, the mistake in the argument above was to suppose that in a context in which we considered the counterfactual possibility in which Aristotle (the philosopher) was named 'Aeschylus', the truth of (1) depended on the philosopher and not on whoever happened to be named 'Aristotle' in the counterfactual circumstance, or the mistake was in thinking that the truth of (6) depended upon whoever happened to be named 'Aristotle' as opposed to just considering the philosopher's affection for dogs. Which mistake is being made depends on the details of the context, or so Bach argues. But is this correct?

The answer depends in large part on how we treat quotation. If the expression inside the quotation marks is interpreted *à la* Kripke, then only the philosopher can be the bearer of 'Aristotle' just as only unmarried men can satisfy the predicate 'bachelor' as we use the term. What is being named is an interpreted expression and not just the symbol or sign design. This is one way that the use of quotation can be understood. If, on the other hand, what is named by using quotation is an uninterpreted symbol or sign design, then just about anything can be the bearer of 'Aristotle'. Of course, because (1) is a sentence of our language, it cannot be understood to mean that redness is fond of dogs, even though we might have used 'Aristotle' to name redness.

So, understood in one way, Bach is correct that the truth of (1) and (6) is connected and the modal argument fails to show that (1) and (6) differ in content. But that requires us to understand quotation in such a way that what is quoted in (6) is a *particular* name as Kripke individuates names. This way of viewing the situation, however, is far from an objection to Kripke's view of names because it presupposes it. So for Bach this is presumably not the way we are to understand quotation.

But on the other standard way of understanding quotation, Bach's response simply fails since (1) is a sentence of our language and cannot be used (without changing the standard meanings of the parts) to mean something like redness is fond of dogs even though (6) can be so used.

It appears that Bach intends to be naming (with quotation) an interpreted expression. The disagreement is over the interpretation. Bach denies that part of the individuating conditions for a particular name is what the name designates. Yet Bach does not provide individuating conditions; he simply rejects Kripke's necessary condition. Moreover, it is not easy to provide conditions that do not involve what is designated. Clearly it is not appearance or sound that individuates names. Consider the following tokens: 'Aristotle' and 'Aristotle'. They look very different, yet it is hard to deny that they are tokens of a single name type (and in this context a single name). Or consider a discussion of the philosopher Aristotle between someone from England and someone from the deep south of the United States. Occurrences of the same name would sound very different. Given that we do not have the details from Bach, we do not have a way to avoid Kripke's modal argument.

Many issues concerning the nature of names and the naming relation have not been discussed in this chapter. For example, a common objection to Kripke's positive view of reference for names is the problem of reference shifts. A name that refers to one object when introduced into the language can at a later time refer to a completely different object. According to Kripke (*NN*: 163), Gareth Evans offers the example of 'Madagascar'. According to Evans, when Marco Polo first learned the name he thought that it was being used to refer to the island off the mainland of Africa, but in fact it was used to refer to part of the mainland. If what the name referred to when it was introduced determines what it refers to now, as Kripke's view seems to claim, then our use of 'Madagascar' refers to part of the mainland and not the island. This is implausible and hence some have concluded that Kripke's positive account of how reference takes place must be mistaken. We do not take up this issue here as it is best discussed in the context of some more general issues concerning reference that are discussed in Chapter 3. Other problems concerning names that are not discussed in this chapter will be discussed at various points throughout the book. But one problem will be noticeably absent: the problem of providing an account of names that fail to designate. Kripke has not published anything directly on this topic although he has lectured on these issues. In 1973, Kripke presented the John Locke Lectures at the University of Oxford on the topics of reference and existence. These lectures were recorded and transcribed, and, one may presume, they were to be published, but for some reason they never were. Some philosophers have copies of these lectures, however, and from time to time various comments concerning Kripke's views on these topics have appeared in the literature. Perhaps these lectures represented a work in progress and Kripke was not completely satisfied with the final result or perhaps he became interested in other projects and never finished the work to his satisfaction. Because the work has never been published, any comments based on these lectures would, of course, be highly speculative.

Chapter 3
Reference and belief

In presenting his objections to descriptivism, Kripke assumes that both descriptions and names satisfy the general scheme that:

(R)   The referent of 'X' is X

where 'X' is to be replaced by a name or a definite description. Kripke sees this as a point of agreement between himself and those (such as Russell) who adopt some version of descriptivism. But although it is likely that Russell would have accepted Kripke's (R), Donnellan (1966) had objected to Russell's theory of descriptions on the grounds that his theory incorrectly assumes (R) for definite descriptions. This led some philosophers to think that if Donnellan was correct in his objections to Russell's theory, which assumes (R), then Kripke's objections to descriptivism, which also assume (R), may fail to show that descriptivism is mistaken when Donnellan's position is taken into account. Donnellan did not view his objections to Russell's theory of descriptions as a reason for adopting descriptivism since he had independently offered a theory of names that is very similar to Kripke's (Donnellan 1972). So it is something of an irony that some would use Donnellan's distinction as an objection to Kripke.

Kripke does note this issue at the very beginning of *Naming and Necessity*, but claims that the points that Donnellan makes against Russell "have little to do with semantics or truth conditions" (*NN*: 25, n.3). In a later paper, "Speaker's Reference and Semantic Reference", Kripke *defends* Russell's theory of descriptions against the objections of Donnellan and in the process draws certain methodological conclusions about certain types of questions and theories in the philosophy of language.

53

Another common objection to Kripke's view that names are rigid designators is not related to Donnellan's complaint. This objection is that on Kripke's view, it appears that accepted differences between ordinary ascriptions of attitudes are lost. The idea is this: the theory of names that Kripke offers in *Naming and Necessity* is Millian in spirit. As Kripke says, "The present view, directly reversing Frege and Russell, (more or less) *endorses* Mill's view of *singular* terms, but *disputes* his view of *general* terms" (*NN*: 135). (Kripke's account of general terms is discussed in Chapter 5.) According to Mill, ordinary proper names simply designate what they designate without any accompanying sense or description. Since the sole semantic function of a name is to designate its object, co-designative names should be interchangeable in sentences without loss of either truth or significance. If there is a sentence '... α ...' in which the name α is used, and if α and β are names of the same object then we should be able to replace α with β in the sentence, '... β ...', with the result that the same statement is made. Hence, if Jones believes that Hesperus is Hesperus, some argue that it follows that Jones believes that Hesperus is Phosphorus. Yet, it is claimed, the inference is not valid and so Kripke's view of names must be mistaken and some form of descriptivism must be correct. In a classic paper, Kripke responds to these objections by pointing out the difficulties involved in trying to provide an account of our practice of ascribing beliefs for any theory of names. In this chapter we take up this objection as well as the objection Kripke based on Donnellan's view of descriptions. In presenting Kripke's responses to both of these objections, we shall see that what, on the surface, may appear to be relatively simple issues emerge, in the hands of Kripke, in their true complexity. We begin with a brief review of Russell's theory of descriptions (see Ch. 2.I) and Donnellan's objections.

I

In "On Denoting", one of the classic papers in analytic philosophy in the twentieth century, Russell (1905) presented and defended his theory of denoting phrases. What Russell seemed to mean by a *denoting phrase* is now called a *quantifier phrase*, as described in Ch. 1.I. While providing a general account of such phrases as 'all', 'some' and 'none', Russell also claimed that definite descriptions, such as 'the present Queen of England', should be included as examples of denoting phrases. Including definite descriptions among quantifier phrases may seem somewhat odd because definite descriptions function as singular terms and not as quantifiers. Russell argued that the surface or syntactical structure of the language is deceiving. He claimed that upon analysis definite descriptions are seen to be complex denoting phrases and not singular terms.

The idea is relatively simple. Consider a simple sentence of the form:

(1)   The *F* is *G*.

Now this sentence is true provided that there is something that is an *F* and only one thing is an *F* and that thing is a *G*. So Russell claimed that (1) means the same as:

(2)   There is a unique *F* and it is *G*.

> DONNELLAN → 'attributive use'
> KRIPKE 'relies' on (2) to argue against definite description theory of names.

Sentence (2) does not have the appearance of expressing a singular statement. It begins 'There is a ...'. Such sentences are general and not singular in the sense that the expression 'there is' is a quantifier ranging over a vast array of objects. So it has the form of a general claim as opposed to a sentence of the form:

(3)   *a* is *G*

where *a* is a singular term such as a name or a pronoun. Now Russell says the fact that (1) means the same as (2) allows us to explain a host of philosophical puzzles that otherwise present problems for any theory of meaning.

For Russell's theory of descriptions to be successful, it must be the case that the truth-conditions for (1) are indeed the truth-conditions for (2). According to Donnellan, this is the problem. Donnellan argued that while the truth-conditions for (2) apply to some uses of (1), different truth-conditions apply for different uses. Donnellan claimed that there are two distinct truth-conditions for sentences containing definite descriptions depending on how the description is being used: the *attributive use* and the *referential use*. The truth-conditions associated with (2) are the truth-conditions for the attributive use and they are the conditions on which Kripke relies when arguing against identifying the meaning of a name with the meaning of a definite description. So Donnellan agrees with Russell that there are uses of definite descriptions that accord with Russell's theory. But, according to Donnellan, Russell's view is incomplete. It does not account for the referential uses of descriptions in which the truth-conditions for the statement made with such uses differ from the conditions for (2): "A speaker who uses a definite description referentially in an assertion, on the other hand, uses the description to enable his audience to pick out whom or what he is talking about and states something about that person or thing" (Donnellan 1966: 285). Hence, the truth-conditions for referential uses of descriptions, according to Donnellan, are more similar to the truth-conditions for (3) than the truth-conditions for (2). The difference is that for (2) to be true there must be a unique *F*, but this is not required for (3) to be true.

To support the two uses of descriptions, Donnellan presents a number of very plausible cases indicating that we can refer to someone using a definite description even if that person fails to satisfy the description. Consider this example. Suppose a man, Jones, is on trial for the murder of Smith. The evidence of Jones's guilt is very strong and everyone believes that Jones murdered Smith. Further, suppose that Jones has been acting very strangely during the trial. The person next to you at the trial leans over to you and says:

(4)   Smith's murderer is insane.

In this case Donnellan thinks that what is being asserted is that Jones is insane even if Jones is not the murderer. The circumstances in which (4) is true, according to Donnellan, are not the same as those in which (2) is true, but are the same as those in which (3) is true. This is an example of the *referential* use of descriptions. Another example would be if I were to say to you at a party:

(5)   The woman over there drinking a martini is a famous philosopher.

Suppose someone is indeed drinking out of a martini glass across the room and she is a famous philosopher. Yet, it turns out that the philosopher is drinking water, not martini. Is what I said to you true or false? Donnellan thinks that it is obviously true because I used the phrase 'the woman over there drinking a martini' not to describe her, but simply to designate her so that I can comment that she is a famous philosopher. What she is actually drinking is not important. So, I am using the description to refer to this woman and to say *of* her that she is a famous philosopher. Yet Russell's truth-conditions are such that on them (5) is false in the circumstances described since she is not drinking a martini. (For a similar argument see Prior (1963).)

Finally consider the case where you are observing a couple and remark to a friend:

(6)   Her husband is kind to her.

But suppose that the person that is being referred to is not her husband at all, but is instead her lover with whom she has taken up to escape her cruel husband. In these circumstances, what you say is false according to Russell's analysis, but it seems that in the context in which you make the statement what you say is true. The man to whom you are referring is kind to her. Again, the circumstances in which your statement is true are the same as those of (3) as opposed to (2).

On Donnellan's view, it can be said that when the description is used referentially the circumstance in which (1) is true is more similar to the circumstance in which (3) is true than it is for the truth of (1). This makes the issue between Donnellan and Russell relatively clear. Kripke argues, however, that Donnellan's distinction also applies to proper names and hence (3) itself may be thought to have two distinct uses. This is discussed below. Still, the use of (1) in the referential sense is similar to the use of (3) in that both will be singular statements whose truth depends solely on whether or not a specific object has the property *G* and not a general statement to the effect that whoever satisfies the description has *G*.

II

Donnellan's distinction is important in its own right but some have thought that it shows that Kripke's arguments against descriptivism do not work. If Donnellan is correct that there are referential uses of definite descriptions, then some of Kripke's arguments against descriptivism may fail.

Donnellan's distinction might help descriptivism in two ways. It might be used to avoid some of Kripke's semantic arguments against descriptivism and it might be used to avoid some of Kripke's modal arguments. Consider, for example, the semantic argument presented in Ch. 2.II concerning Gödel. In that case we were imagining a situation where associated with the name 'Gödel' is the description 'the person who proved the incompleteness of arithmetic'. Yet it turned out that Schmidt, and not Gödel, had done the proof. Still, Kripke argued, we would not say, as descriptivism does, that the name 'Gödel' refers to Schmidt. One might think that Donnellan's distinction can help the descriptivist here. We can still refer to Gödel even though Gödel fails to satisfy the description. Kripke explicitly considers this possibility and says:

> If the hypothetical fraud were discovered, however, the description is no longer usable as a device to refer to Gödel; henceforth it can be used only to refer to Schmidt. We would withdraw any previous assertions using the description to refer to Gödel (unless they were also true of Schmidt). We would *not* similarly withdraw the *name* "Gödel," even after the fraud was discovered; "Gödel" would still be used to name Gödel, not Schmidt. The name and the description, therefore, are not synonymous.
>
> (*SR*: 261)

Kripke's point is that even if one accepts Donnellan's distinction at face value, it cannot save descriptivism from Kripke's semantical arguments. Even if one could use the associated description to refer to Gödel before the "truth" were known, once it was discovered that Schmidt had done the proof we would no longer be able to use that description to refer to Gödel, but we would still be able to use his name to refer to him.

One might respond to Kripke's point by saying that once the "truth" was known a different description would then be associated with the name 'Gödel' and that is why we would be able to use the name to refer to Gödel even though the original description could no longer be used to refer to him even on Donnellan's referential use (unless it is used in an ironic way).

This response to Kripke has two problems. First, according to the response, the name 'Gödel' changes its meaning after the "truth" is discovered even though we still used it to refer to Gödel. It is implausible to think that the meaning of the name has changed just by our discovery. And, secondly, and perhaps more importantly, as Kripke notes in the above passage, once the "truth" is known, not only is the description no longer used to refer to Gödel, but we would withdraw our *previous* statements using the description. For example, if we had said "The person who discovered the incompleteness of arithmetic lives in Princeton", but Schmidt lives in Idaho, we would correct our past usage. But we would not withdraw the statement that Gödel lives in Princeton.

The question of whether invoking Donnellan's referential use can avoid Kripke's modal arguments against descriptivism is more complicated. Referential uses of descriptions are plausibly taken to designate their referents rigidly. Hence, the arguments concerning the non-rigidity of descriptions will not apply to referential uses of descriptions. So, one might avoid Kripke's modal arguments *if* statements made with proper names can reasonably be thought to have the same meaning as statements made with definite descriptions where the descriptions are understood referentially. The question of whether or not one can avoid Kripke's modal arguments against descriptivism using Donnellan's distinction depends in large part on exactly how one understands the distinction. Kripke argues that the distinction does not have the semantic force that some have thought. It cannot, according to Kripke, be used to show that Russell was mistaken in his analysis of definite descriptions.

In "Speaker's Reference and Semantic Reference", Kripke reviews an important distinction in the theory of language, namely the distinction between speaker's meaning and semantic meaning. Kripke describes the notion of semantic meaning as follows:

> The notion of what words can mean, in the language, is semantical: it is given by the conventions of our language. What they mean, on a given occasion, is determined, on a given occasion, by these conventions, together with the intentions of the speaker and various contextual features. (*SR*: 263)

The notion of meaning that Kripke presents here seems to be that of semantic *content* or *information* present in a word or sentence *on a given occasion of use*. The idea is that the rules of language, plus the context of use, plus the speaker's intentions, fix the content or information conveyed by the expression or sentence. Kripke's notion of semantic meaning presents additional issues, but it will be helpful *not* to make this notion more precise at this time. Instead, let us compare Kripke's account of the notion of speaker meaning. The contrast between the two notions will help in understanding each of them.

> Finally, what the speaker meant, on a given occasion, in saying certain words, derives from various further special intentions of the speaker, together with various general principles , applicable to all human languages regardless of their special conventions. (*SR*: 263)

Consider the following example (from Kripke). Suppose one burglar says to another "The cops are around the corner." What the burglar may well have meant is "Our time is up; let's get out of here", but this is not what the sentence means even on this occasion of use. Hence what the speaker meant on this occasion is not what her words meant. The sentence meant that the police are around the corner, not "Let's get out of here". Or consider another example. Suppose your car runs out of petrol. Someone pulls over and asks what the problem is. When you tell her, she says, "There is a garage around the corner." What she means is that you can get petrol at the garage around the corner, but the sentence she uses to express that thought only means that there is a garage around the corner and it says nothing at all about petrol. Again, what the speaker means is not the same as what the sentence means.

Within this very rough and broad distinction between semantic meaning and speaker meaning is a sub-distinction (or special case, as Kripke calls it) between speaker reference and semantic reference. The semantic referent of a designator in a given idiolect (which usually includes a large linguistic community) is that object or item that is determined by the conventions of the idiolect together with facts about the world (e.g. who satisfies the descriptive property in question) on the occasion of use of the designator. The occasion of use is required to account for ambiguous and indexical expressions.

The speaker's referent, on the other hand, is closely associated with what the speaker wants to talk about: "We may tentatively define the speaker's referent of a designator to be that object which the speaker wishes to talk about, on a given occasion, and believes fulfills the conditions for being the semantic referent of the designator" (*SR*: 264). As an example of the distinction between speaker's reference and semantic reference Kripke offers the following case. Suppose you are standing in your living room with a friend and through your window you see someone in the distance doing something in your neighbour's garden. It looks like your neighbour, Jones, and you say to your friend, "What is Jones doing over there?" He responds, "Raking the leaves". It turns out that it is not Jones, but Smith that you see raking the leaves. The semantic referent of 'Jones' is Jones in your idiolect, yet in *some sense* you referred to Smith when you asked "What is Jones doing over there?" You referred to Smith even though the expression you used designated Jones. This is an example of speaker's referent. In this case, you believed that the person you were looking at was the semantic referent of the term 'Jones', and was the object about which you wished to talk. Hence, Smith satisfies the conditions for speaker's reference. But Smith is not the semantic referent of 'Jones' even on that occasion of use since Jones, and not Smith, satisfies the conditions for the semantic referent of the name. Kripke further elaborates this distinction by noting two different intentions speakers have when using language. Kripke says:

> In a given idiolect, the semantic referent of a designator (without indexicals) is given by a *general* intention of the speaker to refer to a certain object whenever the designator is used. The speaker's referent is given by a *specific* intention, on a given occasion to refer to a certain object. (*SR*: 264)

As I understand Kripke here, the expression 'general intention' is intended to refer to the intention of a speaker to use an expression according to the general rules of use for that expression within the speaker's linguistic community. So if the name 'Jones' is used as a name for Jones in Brown's linguistic community, Brown intends to use the name to designate Jones whenever he uses the name. This is Brown's general intention. On a given occasion (as in the raking the leaves case), Brown has the specific intention to refer to a particular person whom he thinks satisfies the semantic conditions for the designator. If the specific intention is simply to designate whatever the semantic referent is, then the speaker's referent *is* the semantic referent. Kripke calls this the *simple* case. If the specific intention is to designate some particular person who may or may not be the semantic referent, then this is what Kripke calls a *complex* case. Still, if all goes well in the complex case, and both intentions are satisfied by the same object, then the speaker's referent still is the semantic referent. But this more complex case allows for the possibility of divergence between speaker's referent and semantic referent. Kripke argues that Donnellan's distinction between attributive and referential uses of descriptions is simply an example of the distinction between speaker's reference and semantic reference. In particular, it is the distinction between the simple case, Donnellan's attributive use, and the complex case, Donnellan's referential use. Moreover, this distinction also applies to proper names. If Kripke is correct and Donnellan's distinction is part of the semantic–pragmatic distinction, then it cannot be used to show that Russell's theory is mistaken because Russell was only attempting to provide an account of the semantics of definite descriptions. Moreover, it also cannot be used to defend descriptivism against Kripke's arguments since descriptivism is intended as a semantic theory of meaning. But is Kripke correct?

Part of the question here involves deciding between alternative analyses of a given linguistic phenomenon. Both Donnellan and Kripke agree that a given speaker may refer to a given object using a description that is not satisfied by the object. That is, both Donnellan and Kripke agree that a speaker might say "Her husband is kind to her" and refer to a particular man and yet that man might not be the husband of the woman. The issue between them is whether the expression 'her husband' as used by that speaker on that occasion refers to her lover or whether the speaker refers only to her lover even though the description denotes her husband and hence, strictly speaking, the sentence is false.

To decide this issue, Kripke offers a general methodological principle for deciding between opposing analyses of a linguistic phenomenon.

> If someone alleges that a certain linguistic phenomenon in English is a counterexample to a given analysis, consider a hypothetical language which (as much as possible) is like English except that the analysis is *stipulated* to be correct. Imagine such a hypothetical language introduced into a community and spoken by it. *If the phenomenon in question would still arise in a community that spoke such a hypothetical language (which may not be English), then the fact that it arises in English cannot disprove the hypothesis that the analysis is correct for English.*
> (*SR*: 265)

Kripke's idea is this. Suppose *A* proposes a view about the semantics of English, *T*, and *B* claims that *A*'s proposal cannot work because a certain linguistic occurrence *e* is present in English and *T* does not account for *e*. So consider a language that may not be English, but that is similar to English except that *T* is explicitly true for this other language (call it 'ET'). If *e* is still present in ET, then the presence of *e* in English cannot show that *T* is not true about English. As an example of the use of this principle, Kripke refers us to a question concerning the use of identity in English he discusses in *Naming and Necessity*. Because it is not trivial that Cicero is Tully, some have argued that "identity" statements of the form:

(7) $a = b$ (or a is b)

where a and b are names, have to be understood as expressing a relation between the names themselves and not the entities referred to by the names. On one analysis of the English 'is' of identity, it is taken to mean strict identity. An objection to that analysis is that 'Cicero is Tully' is not trivial, so the strict identity analysis of the English 'is' of identity is mistaken. Who is right? Kripke's principle offers a way to decide or at least provide some evidence for our decision. Consider a language that is just like English (call it 'Strict English') except possibly in its interpretation of the 'is' of identity. In Strict English, 'is' is explicitly defined as strict identity. But notice that even in Strict English the non-triviality phenomenon occurs, as can be seen by the fact that 'Cicero is$_{SE}$ Tully' is non-trivial. It is not obviously true even when 'is' is explicitly defined as strict identity. Hence, the reason why such sentences are not trivial is not dependent upon the particular interpretation of 'is'. Some other factor must be involved. So this non-triviality phenomenon in English cannot help us decide whether or not English is Strict English.

So what does Kripke's principle say with respect to the debate between Russell and Donnellan? Kripke asks us to consider three possible languages that are Russellian in spirit. He labels these the *weak Russellian* language (wR), the *intermediate Russellian* language (iR) and the *strong Russellian* language (sR). The differences among the three languages are as follows: wR is just like English except that definite descriptions are explicitly viewed as primitive designators whose conditions for designation are the conditions that Russell gives for denotation of descriptions; iR is like English except that definite descriptions are explicitly viewed as abbreviations for the Russellian analysis (i.e. sentences of the form of (1) are explicitly taken to be abbreviations for sentences of the form of (2)); and, finally, sR is a language that does not contain any sentence of the form of (1) but only sentences of the form of (2). So instead of saying (6), in sR one would have to say:

(8)   There is a unique man that she is married to and he is kind to her.

Would the phenomenon that Donnellan points out occur in a linguistic community that spoke any of the Russellian languages?

It seems reasonable to suppose that people who spoke either wR or iR could find themselves in a situation exactly like the situation described above with respect to (4), (5) or (6). Assuming that one thought that the man that is being kind to her is her husband, one could certainly utter (6) in such circumstances even if one spoke iR or wR. Moreover, even in sR one could assert (8) intending to talk about a particular man (who just happens to be her lover and not her husband).

Because the same situations that led Donnellan to postulate that Russell's account was incomplete could arise in a language that was expressly Russellian, Kripke argues that the distinction Donnellan is drawing is not one that shows that Russell's theory is incomplete. English could be a Russellian language and we would still find the linguistic phenomenon that Donnellan identifies.

Even if Kripke is correct that Donnellan's examples do not, in themselves, show that English is not a Russellian language, it is also true that the linguistic phenomenon Donnellan identifies is consistent with the hypothesis that descriptions in English have two semantic uses. If both views are equally good in accounting for the linguistic facts, then one might offer Donnellan's distinction as a way to avoid Kripke's modal argument. But Kripke argues that strong methodological reasons support adopting a unitary account of language, such as Russell's semantic account of descriptions, rather than one that postulates ambiguity. Unitary accounts appeal to general principles and practices to explain similar cases. We can use this approach to explain Donnellan's phenomenon with respect to definite descriptions by reference to the distinction between speaker's reference and semantic reference, and to explain the example of Jones's raking the leaves, which is an example that does not appear to involve any semantic ambiguity. So we do not need to introduce a special ambiguity to account for the case of descriptions.

Moreover, Kripke adds, if we do consider postulating a semantic ambiguity to explain some linguistic phenomenon, it should pass a linguistic ambiguity test. This test is made up of two parts:

> First, then, we can consult our linguistic intuitions, independently of any empirical investigation. Would we be surprised to find languages that used two separate words for the two alleged senses of a given word? ... Second, we can ask empirically whether languages are in fact found that contain distinct words expressing the allegedly distinct senses. (*SR*: 286)

Kripke is careful to note that the test needs to be applied with some caution. It is not the case, for example, that if one language has two words indicating different sub-classes of a given sort, then it follows that a language with a single word that covers both sub-classes is ambiguous. For example, imagine a language that contains a word that corresponds to our use of 'mammal' and a single word, α, for all other kinds of animals. It does not follow that α is ambiguous even though *we* have distinct words for fish, insects and birds. One needs to look at the relationships between the various postulated senses of the words in question to see if true ambiguity arises.

Finally, Kripke offers an example designed to show that English is more likely to be Russellian than to involve a semantic ambiguity among descriptions. Consider the following brief exchange:

A: Her husband is kind to her.

B: No, he isn't. The man you are referring to isn't her husband.

How does Donnellan's distinction handle this case? It is a problem. If A uses the description 'her husband' referentially then B's first comment, "No, he isn't", makes no sense since the expression 'he' would designate the lover following A's referential use of the description. On the other hand, if A is using the description attributively, then B's second comment would make no sense since A would not be referring to her lover. Hence, it is difficult to see how a Donnellan-like distinction between two uses of descriptions can provide an accurate account. Such a case, however, produces no problems for Kripke's account. There is both a semantic referent (her husband) and a speaker referent (her lover) in the context and B can refer to either of them since both have become salient as a result of A's remark. B's first comment refers to the semantic referent of 'her husband' and B's second comment to the speaker referent of 'her husband' (in this context).

Kripke does not think that the issue of whether or not English is a Russellian language can be decided solely by considering the examples offered above. He notes that a certain kind of definite description, namely incomplete definite descriptions such as 'the table', causes some difficulties for Russell's analysis. He does not offer an analysis of such examples but others have defended Russell's analysis. David Lewis (1979a), for example, suggests that indefinite definite descriptions should be completed along the lines of "the most salient φ". Whatever one thinks of Lewis's suggestion, it does seem clear that what one finally says about such descriptions is unlikely to help those who would use Donnellan's attributive–referential distinction as a way of avoiding Kripke's modal arguments with respect to names.

Before we turn to our discussion of Kripke's defence of Russell and his arguments concerning names and descriptions, this is a good place to answer one of the objections to Kripke's account of how names can refer to objects if descriptivism is incorrect. The objection is that reference shifting seems impossible on Kripke's view. Recall Evans's Madagascar example mentioned in Chapter 2. In this case, when Marco Polo learned the name 'Madagascar' he thought that the natives were referring to the island when in fact the natives were referring to a part of the mainland. Kripke notes in his discussion of the distinctions between speaker reference and semantic reference that this distinction can help explain how a shift of reference can take place. Kripke leaves the details of exactly how this is supposed to work to the reader. The idea, I suspect, is something like the following. It is a feature of Kripke's account of the function of names (what we have labelled *reference-dependent use*, see p. 40) that speakers intend to refer to the object that was referred to by those from whom the name was learned. This intention roughly corresponds to what Kripke calls the *general* intention on the part of speakers that produces the semantic referent for designators. That is, when using an expression of a given language, special cases aside, speakers intend to mean by that expression what other speakers in the same linguistic community mean. When learning a new name one intends to refer to what is referred to by the community that uses the name and from whom one learns the name. This can be viewed as an instance of the general intention to speak as others in our community speak.

In addition to the general intention to speak as others do, one also has a specific intention to mean x when using expression α. For designators this means that one has the specific intention to refer to a certain object when using a designator. As Kripke notes, the specific intention might simply be the intention to refer to whomever is referred to by others with the use of the designator or one might have a particular object in mind, such as a particular island or person.

The objection concerning 'Madagascar' was that if we traced back the use of the name we would find that the name originally referred to a part of the mainland and not the island, but clearly we refer to the island when we use the name now. So Kripke's account in terms of an initial baptism must be mistaken.

In the addenda to *Naming and Necessity,* Kripke notes that the use of an initial baptism in the sense of a public or identifiable baptism is something of an oversimplification of how things always work. True, in many cases there is an identifiable baptism to which a given use of a name can be traced. But not all cases have this feature and examples of reference shifting are examples where identifiable baptisms may not be available. This seems to be the case for 'Madagascar'. Polo intends to refer to the place to which the natives refer when he uses the name 'Madagascar', but he also intends to refer to the island. Thus, we have an example of what Kripke called the complex case where speaker referent (the island) and semantic referent (a part of the mainland) diverge in Polo's early use of the name. No doubt there came a point in time when Polo explicitly and in a public way named the island 'Madagascar', perhaps by labelling the island on a map with that name or perhaps when sailing past the island and pointing it out to others while using the name 'Madagascar'. So the island was baptized with the name, but the baptism is not easily identified since it occurred under a misunderstanding. If the misunderstanding had been corrected soon enough, then perhaps the island would not today have the name that it does. But the error was not corrected, and the common usage became linked to Polo's baptism of the island and not the native baptism, even though Polo himself thought he was referring to what the natives referred to with his use of the name.

What this example and others like it show is that the notion of a baptism is a complicated one and it cannot be assumed that only identifiable baptisms count. Moreover, one can baptize an object with a name unintentionally (as it appears Polo did). Polo did not intend to baptize the island: he thought the island was already named 'Madagascar'. Yet when he began using the name as a name for the island, he unknowingly baptized the island and his usage became the common one for his linguistic community. In certain respects this case is similar to the case where one uses the name of a famous person (real or fictional) to name a pet. If you name your pet aardvark 'Napoleon', you can then use the name either to refer to the French general or to your pet. In fact, it seems reasonable to suppose in this case that you introduced a new name and after you named your pet there were (at least) two homonymous names. The difference between naming your pet 'Napoleon' and Polo's naming the island 'Madagascar' is that Polo had no intention of not using the name to refer to the place to which those from whom he learned the name referred. Yet, due to a misunderstanding, he in fact used the name to refer to an island. Hence, a divergence between the speaker's referent and the semantic referent can lead to a reference shift even when that shift is a result of some misunderstanding.

III

While most philosophers of language recognize the distinction between speaker's meaning and semantic meaning that forms the basis for Kripke's development of the distinction between speaker's referent and semantic referent, not all agree with Kripke that this distinction shows that Donnellan's distinction is not truly a semantic one. The responses to Kripke vary in their focus. Some, such as Michael Devitt's (1981a), discussed below, focus directly on Kripke's objections to Donnellan. Others, such as Howard Wettstein's (1981), also discussed below, focus on an area in which Kripke does not offer an account. We shall discuss the latter only briefly to give the reader the sense of the ongoing debate surrounding these issues.

Consider Kripke's analogy in the Smith–Jones raking the leaves case (see Ch. 3.II). Kripke claimed that the linguistic phenomenon that Donnellan identifies in making the attributive–referential distinction for descriptions also appears in the use of proper names when certain assumptions of the speaker fail. This suggests that the phenomenon is general and we do not need to posit a semantic ambiguity with respect to descriptions to account for it. Devitt disputes Kripke's argument. He says the following about Kripke's example:

> My intuitions about what the speaker of [(9) Jones is raking the leaves] meant are as follows. He did not straightforwardly mean Smith, as Kripke claims he did, but neither did he straightforwardly mean Jones. The belief the speaker expressed by [(9)] comes with two others, the true one that that man (pointing to Smith) is raking the leaves and the false one that that man (pointing to Smith) is Jones. *The speaker is confusing two people.* As a result, we have no clear intuition that he meant one and not the other. There is no determinate matter of fact which he meant to refer to. (1981a: 514)

It is unfortunate that Devitt presents the issue in terms of the *beliefs* of the speaker. The issue is not about the beliefs of the speaker, but rather about to what if anything the speaker referred. Of course, the beliefs of the speaker will play a role in determining the speaker's referent (given Kripke's account of speaker reference), but they are not at issue. I think that Kripke would agree with Devitt that the speaker believes that the person he is looking at is raking the leaves and that person is Jones. In fact, it is in virtue of the speaker's mis-identification that the speaker claims that Jones is raking the leaves. Recall that, in Kripke's example, one person says, "What is Jones doing?" while looking at someone in the distance and his companion says "Raking the leaves". Devitt asks us to suppose for convenience that the final comment is (9). Thus, the speaker we are considering is the second speaker of Kripke's example. Is there really any doubt that the second speaker meant to refer to the person raking the leaves when he said "Raking the leaves" in answer to the question "What is Jones doing?" True, he has the mistaken belief that the person raking the leaves is Jones, just as the first speaker has the mistaken belief that the person he is looking at is Jones. But these mistaken beliefs cannot seriously cast into doubt of whom these two speakers wish to talk. They mean to be referring to the person they are looking at. But Devitt says that the speaker "would also agree the he 'referred to' Jones. If we have evidence of anything here it is that the speaker meant *more* than what he said, a view that supports my intuitions rather than Kripke's" (1981a: 514). Yet Kripke's view is that in addition to the semantic statement that was made (which is that Jones is raking the leaves), at least one pragmatic statement is also being expressed, which is that Smith is raking the leaves. So it is part of Kripke's view that the speaker meant more than what he said. This fact hardly supports Devitt's intuitions over Kripke's. And exactly what intuitions does Devitt find supported here? His intuitions seem to be that in this case there is no clear speaker referent and hence this case is very different from the cases that Donnellan presents as evidence for his distinction. In Donnellan's cases it is clear to whom the speaker is referring to.

Devitt thinks that there is no clear speaker referent because on *his own* theory of reference two objects have claim to being the speaker's referent in Kripke's example, but not in Donnellan's example. On his theory of reference, x is the speaker referent, provided x stands in a certain causal relation to the speaker (in the context in question). Here, both Jones and Smith satisfy the conditions for being the speaker's referent. So Devitt says that each of them is a *partial* referent of the speaker and the statement the speaker meant is partially true and partially false.

Yet it seems to me that the Kripkean explanation of what is going on in this case is far more satisfying than Devitt's account. As far as Donnellan's distinction is concerned, we have other reasons for thinking that the linguistic phenomenon is best captured by the semantic–pragmatic distinction.

Devitt also challenges some of Kripke's other arguments such as the argument concerning Russellian languages. Devitt says:

> Speakers of Russell English will behave differently from speakers of English. Donnellan's phenomena could not arise in Russell English. Kripke's claim to the contrary can seem obvious only if we tacitly treat the speaker as if he were like us, able to use descriptions referentially; i.e., as if he spoke English.
>
> (1981a: 520)

Of course, speaking a Russellian language does not make one omniscient. One could very well say, "Her husband is kind to her" in circumstances in which one believes that the person, x, one is looking at is her husband and he is kind to her. Devitt would have us believe that if x *is* her husband then the speaker did refer to x (when speaking the Russellian language). But what if x is not her husband? Is this not the very case that Donnellan and others have identified? It seems then that the examples that Donnellan offers arise, even when one speaks an explicitly Russellian language. Devitt's claim, therefore, is simply false.

Devitt also offers some positive reasons for accepting Donnellan's distinction as a semantic distinction and not simply as a semantic–pragmatic distinction. The positive reasons are based on an account of what Donnellan called *indefinite definite descriptions*. Wettstein (1981) also raises concerns for Russell's unitary position on descriptions based on indefinite definite descriptions. Kripke makes it clear that his main purpose is not to defend Russell's unitary account of descriptions, but rather to present certain methodological principles that can be used in considering different theories of language. He holds that the arguments and examples that Donnellan presented in his original paper do not provide any reason for abandoning Russell's account. Still, he admits that it *may* be that the use of certain definite descriptions, namely indefinite definite descriptions (such as 'the table'), provide evidence for the view that some descriptions are indeed semantically referential in Donnellan's sense. I emphasize the "may" here because Kripke is very cautious in stating his conclusions, particularly those related to indefinite definite descriptions. Because Kripke does not offer an official account of indefinite definite descriptions, however, any extended discussion of this matter as it applies to Kripke's view will be somewhat speculative. Still, since some have used these descriptions as an objection to Kripke's position, we will consider the matter, if only briefly.

The argument against Kripke's defence of Russell's unitary account of descriptions is roughly this: Russell's account of indefinite definite descriptions fails and the correct account of such descriptions is the referential account that Donnellan offered. Given this account for these descriptions, a referential account applies generally. Furthermore, because descriptions are sometimes used attributively we can conclude that Donnellan was correct after all and there is a semantic ambiguity with respect to descriptions generally, contrary to what Kripke cautiously claims.

Obviously, for the above argument to be successful it must be shown that Donnellan's referential account is the correct account for incomplete definite descriptions. The problem with incomplete definite descriptions is that they are never satisfied by a unique object. So on a strict reading of Russell's account they would all be false. Much, if not most, of our use of definite descriptions falls into this group. Yet it seems implausible to think that the speaker's meaning and the semantic meaning of our uses of such descriptions never coincide. So, it seems that an account of the semantic meaning of such descriptions must not be Russellian.

The standard Russellian response to such cases is to view the descriptions as elliptical. But it is claimed, by Wettstein for example, that the elliptical view will not work because no additional content can be added to the incomplete description such that it is clear that the result is the statement semantically expressed by the sentence. Although Wettstein does not consider David Lewis's general suggestion mentioned above, I think that he would not see Lewis's suggestion as supportive of Kripke's position. Consider, for example, the following sentence:

(10) The table is covered with books.

Clearly, there are many tables. So, on a strict Russellian account, (10) is false because there is no unique table. On the view that some definite descriptions are elliptical, the phrase 'the table' is elliptical for a more complete description such as 'the table in the living room next to the fireplace'. But Wettstein points out that there are lots of ways one can complete the description. Why not 'the red table on the left side of the living room', or 'the table on top of the green rug', or 'my favourite table', or 'the table that is worth the most money' and so on. There are, it is claimed, far too many ways to complete the description in a given context. Each way of completing the description results in a different semantically expressed proposition on the Russellian analysis. It cannot be that all of them are the semantically expressed proposition. The solution to the problem, according to Wettstein, is to treat the expression 'the table' as a linguistic device of direct reference, as Donnellan suggests, and 'the table' should be viewed referentially.

One problem with Wettstein's proposed solution is that the problem of indefiniteness that plagues indefinite definite descriptions also plagues other denoting phrases such as 'every' and 'most'. Suppose you come over to my house and indicate that you are thirsty, and I say to you, "All the beer is in the fridge." No one thinks that the phrase 'all the beer' in this context denotes all the beer that exists. Clearly, some restriction is intended. But there are many ways that one can restrict the phrase that have the result that the same class is denoted. Perhaps it is 'all the beer in the house' or 'all the beer that I presently own' or 'all the beer that you are allowed to drink', or 'all the beer that you would be interested in' or 'all the beer that I made last week' and so on.

The point is that the problem is a general problem for all denoting phrases (in Russell's sense of denoting) and hence we should expect that the solution will be a general solution. Yet, Wettstein's solution can only apply to the definite article. There is no referential use of 'every'. Also, some ways of completing the definite description are more natural than others. Stephen Neale (1990) points out that Wilfred Sellars has suggested we treat 'the table' as meaning 'the table over there' or 'the table over here'. This might work for some cases but other cases might suggest 'the table we were just talking about' or even 'the table I am thinking of' or even Lewis's more general 'the most salient table' (1979a). A close examination of the facts in these cases simply does not lead to the conclusion that definite descriptions are semantically ambiguous in the way that Donnellan suggests. For more on this issue I suggest Neale's book *Descriptions* (1990).

IV

In *Naming and Necessity* Kripke explicitly endorses exchanging coextensive names if the sentence is either simple in nature or involves one or more modal operators. So consider the sentence

(1)   Necessarily Cicero is Cicero.

Since 'Cicero' and 'Tully' are names for the same person we can, on Kripke's view, replace 'Cicero' in (1) with 'Tully', yielding

(2)   Necessarily Cicero is Tully.

This result has led some to object to Kripke's view on the grounds that while (1) is true, (2) is not. Kripke defends the interchange of names in modal contexts (see Chapter 4) and many have found his arguments convincing with respect to (1) and (2). But Millianism also appears to allow for the inference from:

(3)   Jones believes that Cicero is bald

to

(4)   Jones believes that Tully is bald.

This inference is less plausible than the inference from (1) to (2). In *Naming and Necessity* Kripke explicitly rejects interchanging codesignating names in sentences that express attitudes such as belief, knowledge, wonder and so on.

Still, some philosophers have used the failure of the inference from (3) to (4) as an objection to Kripke's position on the grounds that if names are rigid designators without descriptive content, then such inferences should be allowed on his view. The fact that Kripke himself rejects the inferences does not remove the burden of explaining why such inferences fail. Some have concluded that Kripke might have been a bit hasty in his rejection of the Russell–Frege theory of names, which does provide an explanation of the failure of these inferences.

Although Kripke does not discuss this matter in *Naming and Necessity* (aside from a brief remark in the preface), he does consider the matter in some detail in his paper, "A Puzzle About Belief". In this paper, Kripke argues first that the failure of substitution of codesignating names in belief reports does not support a Russell–Frege view of names and, secondly, that the problems that arise with respect to belief reports are general problems. They arise not from any principle of substitutation based on a Millian theory of names but rather from our common practices in attributing beliefs.

According to the Fregean view of names, each name has a sense and that sense determines the referent of the name. Different names of the same object, such as 'Cicero' and 'Tully', can have different senses and this difference in the senses of the names can explain why the inference from (3) to (4) is unacceptable. The proposition that Jones believes if (3) is true is distinct from the proposition that Jones believes if (4) is true, due to the difference in the sense of the names. Hence, it does not follow that Jones believes that Tully is bald from the fact that he believes that Cicero is bald, because these are two different propositions and it is possible that someone can believe one proposition without believing the other. So it appears that the failure of substitution of names in belief reports provides evidence for the Fregean view of names.

Yet, according to Kripke, when we consider the matter carefully, we realize that Frege's view cannot really be helpful here. First, there is no single sense that we can attach to 'Cicero' such that everyone who uses that name uses it with that sense. At least there is no sense of the name such that all who use the name understand that they are expressing that sense with their use. This is, of course, something that both Russell and Frege noted in their discussions of names. Different users of a name may use the name with different senses (or different descriptions in Russell's view). This leads to surprising results. For example, we cannot say, "Some people are unaware that Cicero is Tully", for there is no single proposition expressed by the sentence "Cicero is Tully." So, as Kripke says, "There is no single fact 'that Cicero is Tully' known by some, but not all members of the community" (*PB*: 109).

Kripke argues that the Fregean view cannot even explain the very phenomenon that was the prime motivation for the view in the first place. As Kripke notes in *Naming and Necessity*, many users of a name do not have anything like a complete description backing their use of the name. Thus, many users of the name 'Cicero' only associate the sense of the indefinite description 'a Roman orator' or even 'some Roman'. They may associate exactly the same sense for 'Tully' as well as other such names, for example, 'Catiline'. But even if they have the same sense associated with the name, the inference from (3) to (4) will not be acceptable. So the view cannot really explain the failure of the inference.

The problem both views must explain is that we think that (3) and (4) can differ in their truth-values. But why do we think this? Certainly one of the main reasons we think this is that Jones can assert the sentence "Cicero is bald" while not assenting to the sentence "Tully is bald." So Jones's own utterances on the topic can convince us of the truth of (3) and the falsity of (4), assuming, of course, that these utterances take place in standard conditions and that Jones's behaviour is consistent with what he says. Still, a presupposition is at work here. When someone utters a given sentence *S*, then under usual conditions we will ascribe to that person the belief that *S*. Kripke calls this the *disquotational principle* and states the principle as follows:

(DP) If a normal English speaker, on reflection, sincerely assents to '*p*', then he/she believes that *p*.

In DP, '*p*' is replaced throughout with an appropriate English sentence that is free from ambiguities, and indexical and pronominal expressions. Obviously, adjustments need to be made when reporting on what someone believes when such expressions are used. But when no such expressions are present we typically use (DP). For example, if someone sincerely says "London is pretty" we can, and do, report them as believing that London is pretty.

This principle is a principle of English disquotation, but of course similar principles apply to different languages. There is a French disquotation principle, a Spanish disquotation principle, one for German and so on for each language. It is also true, of course, that we can report in one language the beliefs of someone who speaks a different language (from the language of the report). So if a French speaker says *"Dieu existe"* we can report that that speaker believes that God exists. Kripke offers the following as a principle of translation:

(TP) If a sentence of one language expresses a truth in that language, then any translation of it into any other language also expresses a truth (in that other language).

In TP the word 'translation' means an accurate or correct translation. One might perhaps hold that a bad translation is still a translation, although this matter is not completely clear since it might be better to describe such an example as an attempted translation and reserve the word 'translation' for successful attempts. In any case, the word is used in TP to mean accurate translation.

Using these two principles, Kripke argues that we can generate the very difficulties that are often used against the Millian theory of names. But these are general principles that say nothing about the interchangeability of names in ascriptions of attitudes. So, Kripke argues, whatever problems arise in connection with (3) and (4), they are not due to the principle of the interchangeability of names in attitude ascriptions.

Kripke generates the puzzle for belief reports with the following example. Suppose Pierre is a normal French speaker who has heard of a beautiful city in England. Perhaps he has even seen some postcards exhibiting the city's beauty. On the basis of what he has heard and the pictures he has seen he comes to sincerely assent to the French sentence *"Londres est jolie"* and we can then report Pierre's belief as

(5)   Pierre believes that London is pretty.

At some later time Pierre is taken to London, but to a particularly unattractive part of London. He almost never leaves the part of the city he has come to and since no one there speaks any French he must learn English directly from the local inhabitants. He learns from them that the city he is living in is called 'London' and he comes to assent to the English sentence "London is not pretty" and he is not at all inclined to assent to the English sentence "London is pretty".

Given that he has become a normal speaker of English we can infer from what he says that:

(6) Pierre believes that London is not pretty.

But now we have a problem, because (5) and (6) appear to imply that Pierre has contradictory beliefs. If need be, we can also assume that Pierre is a leading logician and would never accept contradictory beliefs. But as Kripke notes, this will not help us:

> But it is clear that Pierre, as long as he is unaware that the cities he calls 'London' and '*Londres*' are one and the same, is in no position to see by logic alone, that at least one of his beliefs must be false. He lacks information, not logical acumen. He cannot be convicted of inconsistency: to do so is incorrect.

(PB: 122)

Notice that the problem is generated by using DP and TP alone; we need introduce no additional principle concerning the interchangeability of names in attitude reports.

Kripke considers four responses that naturally come to mind when considering this example. First, we might say that when Pierre learns English and comes to assent to "London is not pretty", he no longer retains his previous belief expressed by him as "*Londres est jolie*". This is to say that Pierre has *changed* his beliefs, yet we have no reason to say so. Indeed, we can suppose that Pierre writes (in French) to his friends in Paris that he wishes he could visit '*Londres*' because 'London' is so unattractive while '*Londres est jolie*' (looking at the pictures he owns).

Secondly, we could fail to respect his English utterances. But again we have no reason to do this because we would accept his other English utterances.

Thirdly, we could deny both his English and French utterance or, fourthly, we could accept both. Accepting both leads to the problem of convicting Pierre of logical inconsistency and denying both leads to both of the difficulties mentioned in denying either.

Another response that one might make here is to claim that this example shows that the names '*Londres*' and 'London' have different senses for Pierre (*à la* Frege). And because they do have different senses for Pierre we cannot translate Pierre's use of '*Londres*' as 'London' and hence we cannot deduce (5) using DP and TP as claimed by Kripke. The idea is that this sort of example shows that descriptivism was correct all along and different descriptions are associated with '*Londres*' and 'London' by Pierre.

But suppose that Pierre associates the same descriptions, albeit in different languages, with the names. That is, suppose that Pierre associates the property of being the largest city in England with 'London' and the same property expressed in French for '*Londres*'. In this latter case, of course, the term '*Angleterre*' would occur in the French expression of the property in place of the English 'England'. Kripke notes that the same problem can arise for '*Angleterre*' and 'England' that arose for '*Londres*' and 'London':

> Of course the description theorist could hope to eliminate the problem by 'defining' '*Angleterre*', 'England', and so on by appropriate descriptions also. Since in principle the problem may rear its head at the next 'level' and at each subsequent level, the description theorist would have to believe that an 'ultimate' level can eventually be reached where the defining properties are 'pure' properties not involving proper names (nor natural kind terms or related terms . . .) . . . Such speculation aside, the fact remains that Pierre, judged by the *ordinary* criteria for such judgements, *did* learn both '*Londres*' and 'London' by *exactly* the same set of identifying properties; yet the puzzle remains even in this case. (*BP*: 127)

Kripke questions whether any ultimate level can be reached, and even if it could the problem for Pierre would remain because Pierre does not associate the names with descriptions at that level (if anyone does).

Another way to avoid the problem is to restrict the translation principle with respect to proper names. As we have noted before, some philosophers hold that proper names are not really a part of any language and hence we cannot translate such terms from one language to another. Yet, as Kripke remarks, such a view is drastic. It assumes that we cannot translate many sentences from one language into another, despite our routine practice of doing so. Also, the problem is not just with names. Similar problems to Pierre's case with '*Londres*' and 'London' can arise for various kinds of expressions such as '*lapin*' and 'rabbit'. Moreover, as Kripke shows with a slightly different example, the same puzzles arise without the use of TP.

Suppose that Peter learns the name 'Paderewski' as someone who is a famous pianist. Peter assents to the sentence "Paderewski had musical talent" and thus we can infer using DP:

(7)   Peter believes that Paderewski had musical talent.

Later Peter learns of the Polish statesman named 'Paderewski'. Peter believes, not surprisingly, that politicians have little talent for music and so assents to the sentence "Paderewski had no musical talent" and hence, we infer

(8)   Peter believes that Paderewski had no musical talent.

But now, on the basis of just DP alone, we have inferred that Peter has contradictory beliefs.

The conclusion to be drawn, according to Kripke, is that there is a basic puzzle concerning our attributions of beliefs. The puzzle can be put in the form of a question about Pierre. Does he or does he not believe that London is pretty? The puzzle is that no answer to the question seems acceptable and yet it seems as though there should be an answer. This is not a case of vagueness such as where we might ask "Is Jones bald?" and there be no clear answer. If we say that Pierre believes that London is pretty then we are ignoring his explicit claims to the contrary. If we say that he does not believe that London is pretty, then again we have to ignore his comment "*Londres est jolie*". If we claim that he believes both, then we have to claim that he has contradictory beliefs and so is not rational (appearances to the contrary). And if we claim that he neither believes that London is pretty nor believes that London is not pretty, we have to discount his claims about London in French and his claims about London in English. None of these alternatives seems satisfactory, yet it seems there should be an answer to our question about what Pierre believes.

Kripke does not offer a solution to the puzzle. He takes the primary point of the puzzle to be that it is a puzzle and any theory that provides an account of belief reports will need to consider it. Kripke draws other morals from this puzzle, however, including issues concerning Millianism and its alternatives. Consider again the objection to Kripke's view of names based on the problem presented by (3) and (4) above. Kripke comments on that case in the context of the puzzle about Pierre:

> Philosophers, using the disquotation principle, have concluded that Jones believes that Cicero was bald but that Tully was not. Hence, they have concluded, since Jones does not have contradictory beliefs, beliefs contexts are not 'Shakespearean' in Geach's sense: co-designative proper names are not interchangeable in these contexts *salva veritate* ... It is wrong to blame unpalatable conclusions about Jones on substitutivity. The reason does not lie in any specific fallacy in the argument but rather in the nature

of the realm being entered. Jones's case is just like Pierre's: both are in an area where our normal practices of attributing belief, based on principles of disquotation and translation or on similar principles, are questionable ... The point is *not*, of course, that co-designative proper names *are* interchangeable in belief contexts *salva veritate*, or even that they *are* interchangeable in simple contexts even *salva significatione*. The point is that the absurdities that disquotation plus substitutivity would generate are exactly paralleled by absurdities generated by disquotation plus translation, or even 'disquotation alone' (or: disquotation plus homophonic translation). (*PB*: 133–4)

So although the primary point of the puzzle is to show the difficulties of providing an account of belief attribution, a secondary point is the defence of Kripke's own theory of names. The defence is simply that no theory of names can avoid the puzzles and problems that a consideration of belief attribution brings. Descriptivism suffers from the same unwanted consequences with respect to belief attribution that Millianism does. It is not the case that descriptivism and Millianism are on an equal footing, one providing the best account of the rigid designation (and other features) of proper names, and the other providing the best account of how names function in belief attributions. Descriptivism suffers the same difficulties as Millianism does with respect to belief attributions and also has all the problems mentioned in Chapter 2.

V

While Kripke does not offer a solution to the puzzle about belief, he is perhaps the only philosopher who works on these topics not to have done so. Even before Kripke's paper, there was considerable interest in the problems surrounding an acceptable account of belief attribution; Kripke's paper helped produce a virtual philosophical industry in the discussions concerning the puzzles of belief.

One way to reject the puzzle is to reject one of the two principles that Kripke used in presenting the puzzle. As we saw above, one can generate the puzzle without the use of the translation principle, so rejection of that principle really will not be of much help. Robert Fogelin (1995) is an example of a philosopher who rejects the disquotation principle as it is presented by Kripke. Fogelin argues that many persons are *divided believers* and the DP does not apply to them without qualification. According to Fogelin: "A person has a divided belief system if he believes something in one subsystem that he does not believe in another" (1995: 205).

So a divided believer is someone with a divided belief system and we cannot answer directly the question "Does S believe that p?" if S is a divided believer with respect to p. According to Fogelin, DP will not apply to believers divided with respect to p (the sentence in question). Fogelin provides an example of a divided believer. We are to consider Martin, who, when drunk, claims to be a great lover, yet when sober denies he is a great lover. If we try to ask the simple question "Does Martin believe he is a great lover?" we cannot give a simple answer since he appears to believe it when drunk but not when sober. A restricted version of DP – one restricted to believers that are not divided with respect to p – is acceptable (Fogelin 1995: 206). But with this restriction and given that Pierre is a divided believer (which Fogelin claims follows from Kripke's story) one cannot produce the puzzle.

One obvious question arises given Fogelin's restriction on DP: how do we determine whether someone is a divided believer with respect to some claim p? It is not obvious how to answer this question since if someone is a divided believer we cannot use disquotation with respect to what he says. Hence, if we assume Martin is a divided believer we cannot use what he says, drunk or sober, about his being a great lover to determine if he is a divided believer. We cannot use what Martin says about being a great lover as evidence that he believes what he says *if* he is a divided believer, yet the only evidence we have that he is a divided believer is what he says. What this shows is that, even in the case of Martin, we need to use the disquotation principle for our conclusion that Martin is a divided believer.

In any case, the disquotation principle is not intended to imply that if someone sincerely asserts that p that person believes that p under any and all circumstances. People change their minds. One simple way to explain Martin is that, when drunk, he does believe that he is a great lover and does not believe that he is not a great lover. When he sobers up he comes to believe that he is not a great lover and does not believe that he is a great lover. Pierre is not like this. The problem with Pierre is that, after he lives in London and learns English, it appears he both believes that London is pretty and that London is not pretty at the same time and in the same circumstances. So it is not clear that we can avoid Kripke's puzzle simply by noting that people believe different things in different circumstances at different times.

Fogelin is not the only philosopher to reject DP. One of the problems in rejecting DP, however, is that we routinely use it in our belief attributions and without it (or something very much like it) we are forced to reject our ordinary practices. Additionally, as a number of philosophers have noted, we can generate the puzzles without the use of DP. We can describe Peter as believing that Paderewski had musical talent and believing that Paderewski had no musical talent without using DP. The puzzle is still here.

Another way to avoid Kripke's puzzle is to accept DP and TP but argue that they alone will not produce the puzzle. To produce the contradiction that Pierre is and is not rational we need to use another principle hidden in Kripke's presentation of the problem. David Sosa (1996) took this approach in his paper "The Import of the Puzzle About Belief". Consider the argument concerning Peter and Paderewski. We can present the argument without the use of DP as follows (this is a version of Sosa's description of the argument):

(i)   Peter is rational.
(ii)   Peter believes that Paderewski had musical talent.
(iii)   Peter believes that Paderewski had no musical talent.
(iv)   If (ii) and (iii), then Peter has contradictory beliefs.
(v)   Peter has contradictory beliefs.
(vi)   If Peter has contradictory beliefs, then Peter is not rational.
(vii)   Hence, Peter is not rational.

Because (vii) conflicts with (i), we seem to have produced a contradiction with perfectly acceptable premises and hence the puzzle or paradox. But Sosa points out that (iv) is true only if 'Paderewski' is not ambiguous in (ii) and (iii). Sosa asks us to consider the cities of Paris, Texas and Paris, France. Rocky may believe that Paris is pretty and that Paris is not pretty. But Rocky's beliefs here do not provide any concern since the name 'Paris' is ambiguous between the two cities and hence it is perfectly consistent for Rocky to believe that Paris (Texas) is not pretty and believe that Paris (France) is pretty.

The point is that (iv) by itself is not true. The truth of (iv) depends on some further principle that rules out the 'Paris' example as a counter-example. Sosa suggests that the principle that Kripke is indirectly using to justify his claim of (iv) is the following:

> H(ermeneutic): If a name in an ordinary language has a single *referent* then it may correctly be represented logically by a single constant. (1996: 388)

81

Sosa's idea is that behind Kripke's informal account of the puzzle is a semi-formal argument and that the formal account employs principle H. The conclusion we can now draw from the example is not that Peter is not rational, but rather that principle H is false. It is principle H that is causing all the problems, according to Sosa. Moreover, H is supported by Millianism and hence if H is false then Millianism must be false as well. Consequently, one of the main reasons Kripke had for presenting the puzzle, namely in showing that Millianism is no better or worse than descriptivism when it comes to an account of belief ascriptions, is seen to be mistaken.

It is not clear how Kripke would respond. Still, certain things can be said in support of Kripke's puzzle as a puzzle. It seems that the issue is not really H, but rather (iv). Sosa is certainly correct to point out that (iv) can be true only if there is no ambiguity in the terms that are used in (ii) and (iii). In presenting his disquotation principle, Kripke explicitly rules that ambiguous expressions must first be disambiguated and the same sense used in the disquoted sentence as in the quoted sentence. So (ii) and (iii) should not contain ambiguous expressions in the correct rendering of Kripke's argument. And Sosa might agree that (iv) is true *if* there are no ambiguous expressions in (ii) and (iii). If (ii) and (iii) contain no ambiguous expressions, then Sosa either has to reject one of the premises or accept the puzzle.

Sosa considers this response to his argument and claims that (ii) and (iii) (assuming no ambiguity) do not correctly describe Peter's beliefs:

> If Peter did not attach different senses to 'Paderewski,' he would not assent to both "Paderewski has musical talent" and to "Paderewski does not have musical talent." But if he does attach different senses to that word, then to disquote him properly, we must preserve that ambiguity in a corresponding way in our belief attributions. (1996: 396)

Sosa assumes that Peter cannot (rationally) assent to the two sentences unless he has attached different senses to the name. Yet, this seems incorrect if we accept the fact that many speakers have indefinite senses for names, as Kripke explicitly argued. Peter, for example, may simply attach the sense of 'a famous Polish person' to the name and still have the beliefs expressed by (ii) and (iii). Moreover the issue does not depend on the fact that the description in question is indefinite. It could be definite.

For example, suppose Jones comes to believe that there are two physicists named 'David Green'. He heard about them at different times and thought that the person being discussed at one time was *not* the person being discussed at another time. This is fixed in his mind but he cannot now recall any other information that might distinguish them. Later he comes to believe that one David Green lives in the East and that the other David Green lives in the West. Thus, Jones believes that David Green lives in the East and he believes that David Green does not live in the East. The only sense he attaches to the names is the sense of 'being a living famous physicist named "David Green"'. If, in fact, there are two physicists named 'David Green' then we see no problem with Jones's beliefs. Jones can have these beliefs even if the only sense he attaches to the names is the indefinite one. But if Jones can have the belief if there are two persons named 'David Green' then he can have the belief if there is only one person named 'David Green'.

Notice, if there is only one famous physicist named 'David Green' then Jones has the same *identifying* description attached to both his uses of the name 'David Green', yet he still thinks that there are two persons named 'David Green'. Sosa's claim that Peter needs to have distinct senses for the name does not seem to be correct. As in the case of Jones, Peter may have the same sense and yet still believe that there are two persons named 'Paderewski'.

Second, in this version of the puzzle we did not use the disquotation principle though we could have (as Sosa notes). Still, *we* described Peter's beliefs (not unreasonably, given their sources) as (ii) and (iii) and we may very well have a single sense attached to the name. Of course, Sosa may have some principle that implies that an unambiguous (ii) and (iii) cannot describe Peter's beliefs and so if we have a single sense for the name we need to add something else in our description of Peter's beliefs, such as a parenthetical remark indicating some difference in Peter's belief state. This does not reject Kripke's puzzle but rather attempts to solve it. Sosa believes that we cannot generate the puzzle unless we assume a Millian perspective in the guise of H or some other similar principle. Yet, in the 'David Green' example above we explicitly assumed a non-Millian view of names and the puzzle still arose.

Still another way to avoid Kripke's conclusion is to deny the claim that if someone has contradictory beliefs then that person is not rational. But a simple denial of this principle cannot fully avoid the puzzle. In our discussion of Kripke's puzzle we focused on the positive belief claims, for example, that Pierre believes that London is pretty or that Peter believes that Paderewski had no musical talent. But this is not required. As Kripke points out in his paper, we could have considered Peter's or Pierre's lack of belief:

> Suppose Pierre's neighbours think that since they rarely venture outside their own ugly section, they have no right to any opinion as to the pulchritude of the whole city. Suppose Pierre shares their attitude. Then, judging by his failure to respond affirmatively to "London is pretty," we may judge, from Pierre's behavior as an *English* speaker, that he lacks the belief that London is pretty; never mind whether he disbelieves it, as before, or whether, as in the modified story, he insists that he has no firm opinion on the matter.
>
> Now (using the *strengthened* disquotation principle), we can derive a contradiction, not merely in Pierre's judgements, but in our own. (*PB*: 123)

The strengthened disquotation principle is a biconditional version of DP with the added requirement that the speaker not be reticent in the sense of being unwilling to express one's beliefs for any reason. Using that principle and Pierre's failure to affirm "London is pretty" we can derive the following claim:

(9)   It is not the case that Pierre believes that London is pretty.

Of course (9) contradicts

(5)   Pierre believes that London is pretty,

which we obtained from Pierre's French utterance, DP and TP. The result is that the contradiction lies not with Pierre but with us, for we are affirming (9) and (5).

Given that the result comes from the strengthened DP, some philosophers who accept some version of DP reject the strengthened DP. One cannot directly infer (9) from DP alone. Notice the difference between (6) (Pierre believes that London is not pretty) and (9). Strictly speaking, (6) and (5) only suggest a conflict with respect to Pierre's beliefs but (5) and (9) indicate a conflict in *our* beliefs. To avoid contradicting ourselves, we must be very careful in reporting Pierre's beliefs in the modified story. It is wrong to suppose that (6) is true, yet only presenting (5) as a description of Pierre's beliefs is, at best, misleading. Perhaps in a case like this, as well as the unmodified case of Pierre, we may need to abandon our ordinary practices of belief ascription for a somewhat more sophisticated account. What we should say is that when Pierre *thinks of* or *conceives of* London in one way – the way associated with his learning the word '*Londres*' – (5) is indeed true, but when he *thinks of* or *conceives of* London in a different way – the way associated with his present surroundings – (6) is true (or Pierre does not believe that London is pretty in that way). Ordinary practices are often just rough guides to the truth: good enough for many purposes, but susceptible to revision when the circumstances demand it. So even if Pierre has contradictory beliefs in this sense, it does not make him irrational. While this is an approach to a solution to the puzzle, more details are needed.

Chapter 4

Identity statements

Identity is perhaps the simplest of relations and yet it is at the centre of many philosophical controversies. For example, are mental states identical to physical states? The mind–brain identity theory holds that the mind is identical to the brain, at least in the sense that all mental states are identical to brain states. This theory depends, in part, on a certain view about the nature of identity; namely, that some identity statements express contingent truths or what are sometimes called *contingent identities*. Independent of the resolution of the mind–body problem, this view of identity has had wide support, in part because of the tradition that the distinction between contingent truths and necessary truths is equivalent to the distinction between analytic truths and synthetic truths (see pp. 3–6.). So, if a certain claim (such as brain state B is identical to mental state M) is not analytic, it must be contingent. This is acceptable to many philosophers because many identity statements can only be discovered empirically. Prior to investigation, it was not known that the morning star is, in fact, the evening star; knowledge that the morning star is the evening star was acquired though observation and experience. This is called a posteriori knowledge, to be contrasted with a priori knowledge, which knowledge is obtained from reason and logic alone. The claim that B is identical to M even if it is true is one that must be discovered through empirical means and hence it is not an example of a priori knowledge. Thus, it must be contingent. Contingent truths, it was held, are truths that we can only come to know empirically, via observation. They are a posteriori truths. Necessary truths, if there are any, are known by reason alone: they are a priori truths. We can thus tie together the epistemic, the linguistic and logical, with the metaphysical truths. Necessary truths are logical, analytic, a priori truths and contingent truths are empirical, synthetic, a posteriori truths.

I

The above description of the relationships between linguistic facts, epistemic facts and metaphysical facts presents problems, however. These problems come to the fore when considering identity statements. In his paper "Identity and Necessity", Kripke presents a known puzzle for those who wish to hold that some identity statements can be contingent truths. The problem can be seen by considering the following argument presented in the formal language of quantified modal logic (*IN:* 136):

(1) $(x)(y)[(x = y) \supset (Fx \supset Fy)]$

(2) $(x) \Box(x = x)$

(3) $(x)(y)((x = y) \supset [\Box(x = x) \supset \Box(x = y)]$

∴(4) $(x)(y)((x = y) \supset \Box(x = y))$

According to Kripke, (1) says: "Where [*F*] is any property at all including a property involving modal operators, and if *x* and *y* are the same object and *x* had a certain property *F*, then *y* has to have the same property *F*" (*IN:* 137). Line (2) says that everything is necessarily self-identical. Line (3) is supposed to follow from (1), where '$\Box(x =)$' is understood as an instance of '*F*'. Here the idea is that '$\Box(x =)$' expresses the property of being necessarily identical to *x*. Then (4) follows from (2) and (3). As Kripke acknowledges, this argument in favour of necessary identity is fairly well known. Marcus presented a rather different argument for the same conclusion in her paper "The Identity of Individuals in a Strict Functional Calculus of First Order" (1947). The version that Kripke discusses seems to have originated with Quine (1966a).

Kripke notes that the conclusion of the argument says nothing about the status of identity statements. It says that if entity *x* is identical to entity *y,* then it is necessary that *x* is identical to *y*. But if (4) is correct, then it seems to follow that identity statements are necessary and hence the puzzle. After all, there are "clear" examples of contingent identity statements; for example, Hesperus is the evening star, and the inventor of bifocals is the first Postmaster General of the US. Hence, it appears that we have the beginning of a paradox.

One can take different routes to avoid this paradox or puzzle. One is to argue that (4) and the argument that supports (4) have some problem. Kripke rejects this approach, claiming that anyone who accepts (2) should accept (4), although other philosophers have disagreed (we shall consider some of those positions below). Kripke takes an alternative approach. He argues for two theses concerning so-called contingent identity statements: (i) some ordinary identity statements turn out not to be simple identity statements of the form $\lceil \alpha = \beta \rceil$, and when one considers their logical form they cast no doubt on (4), and hence they present no paradox or puzzle; and (ii) the other ordinary identity statements that are of the form $\lceil \alpha = \beta \rceil$ are in fact necessarily true even though they have been thought to be contingent.

One standard example of a contingent identity is the statement

(5)   The inventor of bifocals is the first Postmaster General of the United States.

Although Benjamin Franklin was both the inventor of bifocals and the first Postmaster General, these are contingent facts about Franklin. So, although (5) is a true identity statement, it is a contingent one. This seems to conflict with (4), which appears to state that all identity statements are necessary. The answer, according to Kripke, is to be found in Russell's account of the scope of a description. Kripke says that we can avoid the problem:

> if we substitute descriptions for the universal quantifiers in (4) because the only consequence we will draw, for example, in the bifocals case, is that there is a man who both happened to have invented bifocals and happened to have been the first Postmaster General of the United States, and is necessarily self-identical. (*IN*: 139)

The idea is this: let '*Bx*' stand for '*x* is an inventor of bifocals' and '*Gx*' for '*x* is a first Postmaster General of the United States'. The logical form of the sentence "necessarily the inventor of bifocals is the first Postmaster General" will be

(6) $(\exists !x)(\exists !y) (Bx \ \& \ Gy \ \& \ x = y \ \& \ \Box(x = y))$

where '$\exists !x$' is read as 'there is a unique x such that'. The necessity in (6) covers only the simple identity claim and not the descriptive claim. Thus, the contingency of (5) is not a result of any "contingent identity", but rather the result of the fact it is contingent that who-ever satisfies 'Bx' also satisfies 'Gx'. The identity aspect of (5) is neces-sary, as indicated in (6).

On Kripke's view, true contingent identity statements (as in (5)) are not "contingent identities". What is contingent about these state-ments is not the claim of identity, but rather attributions of contin-gent properties to the object(s) involved in the identity claim. The situation is different, however, when we consider identity statements involving ordinary proper names.

Kripke claims that the following principle, along with (1), is also true:

(7) $(a = b \ \& \ Fa) \supset Fb$,

"whenever 'a' and 'b' stand in place of names and 'F' stands in place of a predicate expressing a genuine property of the object" (*IN*: 140). Given (7), an argument similar to the one given for (4) above can be presented to show that the following is true:

(8) $a = b \supset \Box a = b$.

But this creates problems for the claim that true identity statements between names are contingent. Quine addressed this in a famous debate with Marcus:

> Her [Marcus's] paradigm of assigning proper names is tagging. We tag the planet Venus some fine evening with the proper name 'Hesperus'. We may tag the same planet again someday before sun rise with the proper name 'Phosphorus'. When, at last, we discover that we have tagged the same planet twice, our discovery is empirical, and not because the proper names were descriptions. (1966b: 178–80)

We can understand Quine's complaint in the following way. We can infer

(9)   (Hesperus = Phosphorus) $\supset \Box$ (Hesperus = Phosphorus)

from (8) where 'Hesperus' and 'Phosphorus' are simple proper names. But given that we have named the same planet twice, it will follow from (9) that it is necessary that Hesperus is Phosphorus. Yet, our discovery of the truth of the simple identity claim is empirical. It is not analytic, and it is knowable only a posteriori. Hence it is a contin-gent and not a necessary truth. But in this case, unlike the case of (5),

we cannot point to any scope distinction to avoid the contingent identity (this is the point about names being simple tags).

There is more than one way to respond to this apparent conflict
between (4) and the contingency of Hesperus's being Phosphorus.
Russell rejected the idea that ordinary names could be simple tags
(logically proper names) and that they had to be understood as
disguised descriptions. In other words, we can avoid the puzzle if we
adopt descriptivism. As we have seen, Kripke rejects this view. An
alternative is to dispute Quine's claim that 'Hesperus is Phosphorus'
is not analytic. Marcus suggests such a view in her comments in the
debate: "Presumably, if a single object had more than one tag, there
would be a way of finding out such as having recourse to a dictionary
or some analogous inquiry, which would resolve the question as to
whether the two tags denote the same thing" (1962: 142). Some other
philosophers, for example, Scott Soames, hold that the statement in
question is knowable a priori. (Soames's view is discussed below in
Ch. 4. IV.)

Kripke's response to the puzzle is, itself, surprising. He claims
that while the identity sentence is indeed empirical, it is also necessary. He says:

> I thus agree with Quine, that "Hesperus is Phosphorus" is (or
> can be) an empirical discovery; with Marcus, that it is neces-
> sary. Both Quine and Marcus, according to the present stand-
> point, err in identifying the epistemological and the metaphysi-
> cal issues.   (*IN*: 154, n.13)

This is one of the positions for which Kripke is famous. Kripke suggested a revolutionary way of thinking about these matters. He
makes a distinction between the epistemological status of some
statement and its metaphysical status. Many philosophical confu-
sions or puzzles can be resolved if we are careful to distinguish these
two notions. This can be seen clearly, according to Kripke, in the case
of identity statements. Kripke claims that some true identity statements are both necessary and empirical: empirical in the sense that
one comes to know the truth of such statements through empirical
investigation and not a priori reasoning alone. They are necessary a
posteriori truths. Before we turn to Kripke's defence of this position,
we need to return to the question of whether (8) is true or not.

In "Identity and Necessity" Kripke suggests that we can infer (8)
from (7) using an argument similar to the argument that allowed us
to infer (4) from (1). Presumably the argument would go as follows:

(7) $((a = b) \ \& \ Fa) \supset Fb$

(7.2) $\Box(a = a)$

(7.3) $(a = b) \supset \Box((a = a) \supset \Box(a = b))$

(8) $(a = b) \supset \Box(a = b)$

where '*a*' and '*b*' are proper names. As in the case of the inference from (1) to (3), one might question the inference from (7) to (7.3) or perhaps the truth of (7). When Kripke presented (7) he indicated that there needs to be a restriction on the interpretation of '*F*'. '*F*' needs to stand in place of a predicate expressing a genuine property of the object in question, and without this restriction (7) is clearly false. Shorty may have been so called because of his size but John was not even though John is Shorty. With the restriction, however, arises the question of whether 'is necessarily identical to *a*' is an acceptable predicate. That is, is it a predicate that expresses a genuine property of the object(s) in question?

In *Naming and Necessity* Kripke considers the position that identity sentences in English involving proper names are to be understood as expressing relations between the names and not the objects named. He says:

> Suppose identity *were* a relation in English between names. I shall introduce an artificial relation called 'schmidentity' (not a word of English) which I now stipulate to hold only between an object and itself. Now then the question whether Cicero is schmidentical with Tully can arise, and if it does arise the same problems will hold for this statement as were thought in the case of the original identity statement to give the belief that this was a relation between names.   (*NN*: 108)

Kripke concludes that since the same problems arise with the introduced relation that arose with the original relation, it is most likely that the English 'is identical to' stands for the relation that obtains among objects. This, of course, is only half the problem. Even if one grants that the predicate 'is identical to *a*' expresses a genuine property of objects, it does not directly follow that the predicate 'is necessarily identical to *a*' also expresses a genuine property of objects.

Some philosophers have argued that 'is necessarily identical to *a*' expresses a genuine property of objects provided that the open sentence '$\Box(x = a)$' admits of substitution on *x* for codesignative names without loss of truth. Roughly speaking, what this means is that the predicate in question is a genuine property of objects only if the sentential context in question is not opaque. A sentential context is not opaque if it allows substitution of codesignative names without loss of truth. It is not clear that Kripke accepts this view, but Kripke argues that one *can* substitute codesignative names in contexts governed by the necessity operator. This is one of Kripke's points when he argues that ordinary proper names are rigid designators (see Chapter 2). In the current discussion of identity, Kripke claims that if proper names are rigid designators, then identity sentences containing names will be necessarily true:

> If names are rigid designators, then there can be no question about the identities being necessary, because '*a*' and '*b*' will be rigid designators of a certain man or thing *x*. Then even in every possible world, *a* and *b* will both refer to this same object *x*, and to no other, and so there will be no situation in which the object which we are also now calling '*x*' would not have been identical with itself. (*IN*: 154)

The idea here seems fairly clear. Consider the sentences

(10) Hesperus is Phosphorus,

(11) The morning star is Phosphorus,

and

(12) Phosphorus is Mars.

Sentences (10) and (11) express truths and (12) expresses a falsehood. Sentence (12) expresses the falsehood that Mars is identical to Venus, (11) that the morning star is identical to Venus and (10) that Venus is Venus. Or at least that is what they appear to express. The truth of (11) depends on the fact that Venus has the property of being the unique morning star. This is not a necessary property of Venus. Had the world been different in certain ways, Mars would have been the morning star and hence the truth that is expressed by (11) would have been false in such a counterfactual circumstance. In different counterfactual circumstances, different objects have the property of being the morning star and because the designation of the English expression 'the morning star' depends on which item has the property, we may safely conclude that the expression is not a rigid designator. Since the truth that (11) expresses would have been false, that truth is not a necessary truth. Notice that if 'the morning star' *were* a rigid designator then it would designate the same item in all counter-factual circumstances, including the one where Mars has the property of being the morning star. And hence we could not use the reasoning that we just did to show that (11) is not a necessary truth.

We need to be a bit careful here. What are we supposing when we consider a circumstance where 'the morning star' is a rigid designator? This is a tricky supposition since, in general, we have been using quotation marks to name interpreted items in a given language and not simply the marks that are so interpreted.

Quotation can be used in many ways and often the context of use makes it clear how it is to be understood. Kripke clearly relies on context in *Naming and Necessity* to help us understand a particular use of quotation. In certain situations, he uses quotation to name an interpreted expression in English, as when he says the name 'Hesperus' is a rigid designator. Clearly only with a given interpretation can a given expression be said to be rigid, because no intrinsic relation binds an expression to what it means or to what it refers. Other times, such as when he considers introducing the name 'Hesperus' to designate something other than Venus, he is using quotation to name an uninterpreted expression; otherwise the supposition would be nonsense. This point is relevant to our current supposition. It could plausibly be argued that it is an essential feature of the English phrase 'the morning star' that it designates what it designates via satisfaction conditions *à la* Russell (assuming that Russell's view is correct). This is treating our quotation as naming an interpreted phrase, as we have been doing. To suppose that 'the morning star' is a rigid designator is to apply an interpretation to the phrase that is not its actual interpretation. So, like Kripke, we shall sometimes use quotation to name the uninterpreted symbol(s). The context should make it clear what is being asserted. In the present case the purpose for considering the possibility that 'the morning star' is a rigid designator is to note that we could not avoid the claim of necessity for (11) the way we did if we were considering an expression that is a rigid designator.

So if the expressions in a given sentence designate rigidly, then the truth or falsehood expressed by such a sentence will depend on the same items in various counterfactual circumstances. Consider (12) and the counterfactual circumstance where Mars has the property of being the morning star. If 'Phosphorus ' were not rigid (again such a supposition needs to be considered in light of the remarks above) and, say, designates the item that has the property of being the morning star, then while (12) is false, it would have been true in the described counterfactual circumstances (assuming, of course, that 'Mars' is rigid). Yet, given that both 'Mars' and 'Phosphorus' are rigid, (12) is bound to be false in any counterfactual circumstance. In no counterfactual circumstance are distinct entities identical.

If names are rigid then one can substitute names in necessary identity sentences without loss of truth. So, for example, if (10) is true then one can replace one occurrence of 'Hesperus' with 'Phosphorus' in the true sentence

(11)   Necessarily Hesperus is Hesperus

yielding

(12)   Necessarily Hesperus is Phosphorus

without loss of truth. Given this, the reason offered above for concern over the property expressed by the open sentence '$\Box(x = a)$' evaporates. The property of necessarily being identical to Hesperus is a perfectly acceptable property and hence concerns over the acceptability of modalized identity properties should disappear. As indicated, if names were not rigid designators, then there might be a problem with holding that such predicates express genuine properties.

Of course, it is important to see that it is the relationship between rigidity and modality that yields the result, and not simply the rigidity of names alone. After all, even given that names are rigid, certain predicates cannot be said to express genuine properties as in the example discussed above: being so called because of one's size.

There is one caveat to all of this. Although Kripke holds that (12) is true, he explicitly says that it is true in a "weak" sense of necessity. That is, he does not hold that Venus is a necessarily existing object. One might hold that if (12) is true Venus must exist necessarily since its truth seems to require that the identity sentence is true for all possibilities or all possible worlds. Yet, surely there is a possible world w such that had w been actual, there would have been no Venus at all. What shall we say about the identity sentence with respect to that circumstance? Some philosophers would say that it is false while others would say that it lacks a truth-value since the items presupposed by the sentence fail to exist (in the imagined circumstance). In either case, the sentence does not seem to be true. Kripke avoids what he describes as delicate issues of existence by defining a *weak* sense of necessity. A statement is weakly necessarily true if the statement is true in every possibility where entities designated (in the statement) exist. We can avoid this weak sense of necessity if we conditionalize the statements in question. Thus, we can replace the weak necessity of (12) with *strong* necessity in the following sentence:

(13)   Necessarily if Hesperus and Phosphorus exist, then Hesperus is Phosphorus.

II

If Kripke is correct and identity statements between names are necessary when true, then the puzzle of identity reappears. As we noted, Kripke agrees with Quine that (10) is an empirical truth and not one that is known a priori. Why does Kripke hold that (10) is an empirical truth given his strong conviction that it is a necessary truth? Indeed, how is it even possible that an empirical truth be necessary? Kripke says:

> The evidence I have before I know that Hesperus is Phosphorus is that I see a certain star or a certain heavenly body in the evening and call it 'Hesperus,' and in the morning and call it 'Phosphorus.' I know these things. There certainly is a possible world in which a man should have seen a certain star at a certain position in the evening and called it 'Hesperus' and a certain star in the morning and called it 'Phosphorus'; and should have concluded – should have found out by empirical investigation – that he names two different stars, or two different heavenly bodies. ... So in that sense we can say that it might have turned out either way. Not that it might have turned out either way as to Hesperus's being Phosphorus. Though for all we knew in advance, Hesperus wasn't Phosphorus, that couldn't have turned out any other way, in a sense. But being in a situation where we have exactly the same evidence, qualitatively speaking, it could have turned out that Hesperus was not Phosphorus; that is, in a counterfactual world in which 'Hesperus' and 'Phosphorus' were not used in the way that we used them, as names of this planet, but as names of some other objects, one could have had qualitatively identical evidence and concluded that 'Hesperus' and 'Phosphorus' named different objects. ... So two things are true: first, that we do not know *a priori* that Hesperus is Phosphorus, and are in no position to find out the answer except empirically, Second, this is so because we could have evidence qualitatively indistinguishable from the

evidence we have and determine the reference of the names by the positions of the two planets in the sky, without the planets being the same. (*NN*: 103–4)

This passage is one of the more famous passages from *Naming and Necessity*. It is also a passage that has produced a wide variety of responses from its readers.

Kripke's basic view is relatively clear, although stating that view simply is another matter. Kripke imagines that he sees a certain object in the sky in the evening and dubs that object 'Hesperus' and in the morning he sees an object and dubs it 'Phosphorus'. For all he knows, he has named distinct objects and hence without some investigation he cannot know that Hesperus is Phosphorus. In fact (we are supposing), he has dubbed the same object twice, but from his perspective he cannot know that without some further evidence. One might thereby conclude that Hesperus might not have been Phosphorus since he *could have* dubbed distinct objects. But the sense in which Hesperus might not have been Phosphorus is an epistemic sense of 'might', not a metaphysical one. It is the sense of *for all Kripke knows* (at the time of the dubbing) the statement that Hesperus is Phosphorus is false. But given that Hesperus *is* Phosphorus, the identity is necessary. It is the identification of the epistemic status of the statement with its metaphysical status that leads to the puzzle about identity. Once we have distinguished the epistemic from the metaphysical, we can see that a statement that is not known to be true a priori may nonetheless turn out to be necessary.

Another example that might even be better than the identity claim that Hesperus is Phosphorus is the non-identity statement that Venus is not Mars. Again we can imagine someone pointing to an object in the sky and dubbing it 'Venus' and at some other time pointing to a object in the sky and dubbing it 'Mars'. For all we know at the time of the dubbings we have named the same object twice (as in the Hesperus case). Indeed, there is a possible situation that is qualitatively similar to our actual situation where we did name the same object twice. Yet in the actual situation we named distinct objects and hence the statement Venus is not Mars is true, but its truth is not one we can know by a priori reasoning alone. Still, it is necessarily true. Distinct objects are necessarily distinct just as identical objects are necessarily identical. Two objects cannot be one object (although there might have existed one object in place of the two objects).

So Kripke sees the puzzle about identity statements as a puzzle based upon a failure to carefully distinguish the metaphysical status of a statement from its epistemic status. It does not follow, according to Kripke, from the fact that something is not knowable a priori that it is contingent, nor does it follow from the fact that something is contingent that it is not knowable a priori. Kripke argues that there is a very sharp distinction between the epistemological status of a statement and its metaphysical status and the blurring of this distinction can lead to many contemporary puzzles in philosophy.

The examples of those statements that are necessary and not knowable a priori are not restricted to simple identity statements, such as (10), about objects. There are other examples of identity statements that are necessary a posteriori truths. Theoretical identifications also provide examples according to Kripke. A theoretical identification is a statement where one identifies an ordinary kind of thing with a scientific kind of thing. For example, we identity water with H_2O, heat with the motion of molecules and, according to the identity version of materialism, pain with certain physical states of the body. While issues involved in an account of such theoretical identifications are not completely detached from identity statements concerning objects, they are sufficiently different that we shall postpone any discussion of them until Chapter 5, where they are considered in detail. Kripke also provided arguments for the other half of his claim concerning the distinction between epistemological matters and metaphysical matters, namely that there are contingent a priori truths. Again, Kripke's examples of contingent a priori truths are best described as theoretical definitions, although one could formulate an example of a contingent a priori statement based on the examples that Kripke provides that does not involve any theoretical implications. The issues involved in a discussion of contingent a priori truths are different, so we shall also put off the presentation and discussion of them until Chapter 5.

Kripke's claim that true identity statements expressed by sentences containing distinct proper names are necessary, as well as his claim that such statements are necessary a posteriori truths, have produced considerable debate within the philosophical community, both in favour of his views and against them. We turn now to some of the responses.

III

A number of philosophers question the inference from (1) to (4) that Kripke defends. Here is the argument again:

(1) $(x)(y)[(x = y) \supset (Fx \supset Fy)]$

(2) $(x) \square (x = x)$

(3) $(x)(y)((x = y) \supset [\square(x = x) \supset \square(x = y)]$

∴(4) $(x)(y)((x = y) \supset \square(x = y))$

One of the more interesting discussions of this inference is Richard Cartwright's in his article "Indiscernibility Principles" (1979). According to Cartwright, (1) (in Kripke's intended interpretation of it) is what Cartwright calls an *indiscernibility principle*, and (3) is also an example of an indiscernibility principle. Indeed, any principle of the form

(ID) $(\alpha)(\alpha')(\alpha = \alpha' \supset (\varphi \supset \varphi'))$

where α and α' are distinct variables and φ and φ' are open sentences that are alike, except that φ' has one or more free occurrences of α' where φ has free occurrences of α, is an indiscernibility principle. One example of an indiscernibility principle that Cartwright offers is:

(14) $(x)(y)(x = y \supset (\text{astro}(x = \text{Phosphorus}) \supset \text{astro}(y = \text{Phosphorus}))$

where 'astro' abbreviates the operator 'it is a truth of astronomy that'.

It is not a truth of astronomy that Phosphorus is Phosphorus even though it is a truth of astronomy that Hesperus is Phosphorus. Hence it appears that (14) is false. What can we conclude from this with respect to (1)? Either (1) is false or the following "comprehension principle" is false:

(15) $(\exists z)(x)(z$ is a property of $x \equiv \text{astro}(x = \text{Phosphorus}))$.

In other words 'astro(x = Phosphorus)' does not express a genuine property of objects. Line (1) is taken to be true in so far as 'F' expresses a genuine property of objects. This condition is made explicit by Cartwright in providing comprehension principles for indiscernibility principles.

We return now to the argument from (1) to (4). Cartwright notes that from (2) and (3), (4) follows. He also notes that Kripke includes (1) as part of an argument for necessary identity. This suggests that Kripke uses (1) to justify (3). But according to Cartwright, (1) by itself cannot do the job. What is needed is a comprehension principle along the following lines:

(16) $(x)(\exists z)(y)(z$ is a property of $y \equiv \square (x = y))$.

Again, this says that '$\Box(x = y)$' expresses a genuine property of objects. Cartwright takes Kripke's comment "Where [*F*] is any property at all including a property involving modal operators, and if *x* and *y* are the same object and *x* had a certain property *F*, then *y* has to have the same property *F*" (*IN*: 137) to be Kripke's acceptance of (16).

Cartwright thinks, as do many others, that the '$\Box$' introduces an opaque context in much the same way as does 'astro'. If we understand ⌈astro φ⌉ to be true if and only if φ is a truth of astronomy, then we cannot accept (14). In effect 'astro(*x* = Phosphorus)' fails to express a property of objects because 'astro' introduces an opaque context. We know that 'astro' introduces an opaque context because we cannot substitute 'Phosphorus' for 'Hesperus' in:

(17)   astro(Hesperus = Phosphorus)

without a loss of truth. Cartwright makes a similar point with respect to '$\Box$':

> ['$\Box$'] is sometimes so used that ⌈$\Box$φ⌉ counts as true if and only if φ itself counts as necessary. If that is all there is to go on, we have no option but to count the '$\Box$'-construction opaque and hence [(3)] unintelligible. But [(3), (2) and (4)] are witnesses to a contemplated transparent '$\Box$'-construction. ... The problem remains of settling, somehow, which sequences of objects satisfy ⌈$\Box$φ⌉ where φ is an open sentence.   (1979: 213)

But why does Cartwright think that '$\Box$' produces an opaque context in the same way that 'astro' does?

First, one might think that '$\Box$' produces an opaque context because of Quine's argument concerning the number of planets. As discussed in Chapter 1, Quine was suspicious of quantified modal logic and he offered an argument to the effect that the modal operators produced opaque contexts. The argument that Quine offered went something like this:

(i)   9 = the number of planets

(ii) $\Box(9 > 7)$

(iii) $\Box$(the number of planets > 7)

(iv)   not: $\Box$ (the number of planets > 7)

However, this argument can be avoided with the use of Russell's scope distinctions (see the discussion on pp. 29–30, 89–90).

Secondly, one might think that it is intuitive that Hesperus might not have been Phosphorus and hence, like 'astro', '□' produces an opaque context. Kripke would respond by claiming that one's intuition that Hesperus might not have been Phosphorus is best understood as an intuition about an epistemic possibility, not a metaphysical one. This is why Kripke claims that (10) is an empirical truth (more on this case below).

Thirdly, one might argue for opacity from the fact that different statements that have the same truth-value cannot be replaced inside the scope of '□' without fear of a change in truth-value. For example, we cannot replace the statement that $1 + 1 = 2$ in the sentence 'it is necessary that $1 + 1 = 2$' with the statement that snow is white without loss of truth, even though both statements are true. Thus, the necessity operator creates a non-extensional context and substitution within such a context may be restricted.

It is true that '□' produces a non-extensional context. Yet Cartwright seems to ignore Kripke's point about names being rigid designators. The fact that names are rigid designators does not mean that one can safely replace codesignative names in any context whatsoever. Kripke's remarks about the empirical nature of (10) make this clear. But one can replace them in *modal* contexts. Hence, in an important sense '□' is very different from 'astro' and we have no reason to reject (16). Cartwright's final concern over which sequence of objects satisfies $\lceil \Box \varphi \rceil$ when φ is an open sentence seems to me to be based on Quinean misgivings over how we refer to the objects in the sequence that satisfies the modal claim. Those misgivings seem to be based on treating necessity as analyticity. Consider the open sentence '$\Box(x > 7)$'. It does not matter if we refer to the object that satisfies the open sentence using '9' or 'the number of planets' since we are simply designating the *object* that satisfies the open sentence; we are not replacing 'x' with our means of designating that object. In one sense, this worry of Cartwright's does not matter, because the arguments that suggest that something is wrong with either (16) or (4) all seem to fail. There really is no reason to doubt (4).

As Kripke notes, (4) is a statement about the identity of objects and not a claim about the necessity of identity statements. Hence an acceptance of (4) does not entail that one accept:

(8) $(a = b) \supset \Box(a = b)$

where (8) is understood to be the form of certain English sentences and not just a formula of a formal modal language. The following sentence is an example of (8):

101

(18) If Hesperus is Phosphorus, then necessarily Hesperus is Phosphorus.

Kripke actually offers a more general claim than (8). When we presented (8) above as the conclusion of an argument we restricted '*a*' and '*b*' to proper names. Kripke claims that (8) is true if '*a*' and '*b*' are rigid designators, whether those designators be proper names, rigid descriptions, indexicals or demonstratives. Since those who object to Kripke's claim that (8) is true for rigid designators usually focus on proper names, it does no real harm to restrict our attention to names. From Kripke's perspective, however, it is the rigidity of the terms that guarantees that (8) is true.

Whereas the truth of (4) is accepted by many and rejected by few, the truth of (8) is considerably more controversial. Some reject the notion of rigid designation. The rejections come in various forms. One sort of rejection is that the notion of rigid designation presupposes a metaphysics of possible worlds and that metaphysics is unacceptable. In my view this sort of objection misses the point. As we noted in Chapter 1, Kripke's talk of possible worlds is just another way of talking about modality and it is not intended to imply commitment to any unusual metaphysical entities. Moreover, the notion of a rigid designator can be defined in terms of modal contexts without reference to possible worlds.

Others have objected that the notion of a rigid designator assumes a notion of transworld identity and that notion is suspect. Kripke explicitly comments on such a view:

> Those who have argued that to make sense of the notion of rigid designator, we must antecedently make sense of 'criteria of transworld identity' have precisely reversed the cart and the horse; it is *because* we can refer (rigidly) to Nixon, and stipulate that we are speaking of what might have happened to *him* (under certain circumstances), that 'transworld identifications' are unproblematic in such cases. (*NN*: 49)

Kripke's point here is that we describe counterfactual possibilities using the names of the objects that we are considering in the possibility in question. If we consider the possibility of Nixon's losing the election in 1968, we are considering a possibility where *Nixon* loses. We do not have to search, as it were, among all the possibilities looking for one where it is Nixon who loses as opposed to someone else. We stipulate that the possibility we want to consider is one where Nixon loses.

Some may see Kripke's claim that names are rigid designators as trivial given his view that we stipulate who is involved in the various counterfactual possibilities. But to some extent such comments are based on a misunderstanding of Kripke's view. Kripke is not stipulating that ordinary names are rigid designators; rather he is pointing out how we use names in describing various counterfactual possibilities. And in fact we use names as rigid designators when describing these possibilities.

This objection is related to another objection that has been offered to Kripke's notion of a rigid designator. If α is a rigid designator for x, then α designates x at every world (where x exists). But, it is objected, we cannot understand the claim that α designates x at every world to mean that it is true in each world w that α designates x. So how are we to understand it? (See Rosenberg 1994.)

The reason we cannot take 'α designates x at every world' to mean 'in each world w, α designates x in w' is because the expression α can be used in different ways in different worlds. Kripke is clear that when we talk about the reference of an expression relative to worlds, it must be understood that we are considering the expression as we use it to describe these other possibilities, not how it might be used by people in the described situation. This should not cause confusion over the meaning of 'rigid designator'. If α is a rigid designator for x, then when we describe various possibilities and use α in those descriptions, α designates x. I suspect that Rosenberg would not be satisfied, yet I fail to see the difficulty here. Part of the problem is that Rosenberg mixes the question of whether proper names are rigid designators with what it means to be a rigid designator. Even if ordinary proper names are not rigid designators as Kripke claims, what it would take for something to be a rigid designator is clear: "a term d is a rigid designator of an object x if and only if d designates x at every possible world where x exists and does not designate anything other than x at any possible world" (see pp. 36–7). Of course, this definition does not provide an account of designation in general, but that is not the purpose. Suppose that all designation occurs via some satisfaction conditions or via some relation not yet discovered. Still, we can make sense of the notion of a rigid designator even if no such expressions occurred in natural language.

Again, Rosenberg may not be satisfied, because he doubts the expression–object relation in the first place. He thinks that the apparent relation 'term d refers to object x' is to be understood in terms of 'speakers S_1 and S_2 use d *confluently*', by which he means that their uses converge under certain conditions, the details of which need not concern us. Yet, even if Rosenberg is correct and there is no relation of designation between expressions in natural languages and objects, such a relation could be introduced. We certainly do introduce it into our interpretations of formal languages when we *assign* objects from domains to the variables in our formal language. So imagine that there is a language *L* like English, except that its singular terms do designate objects. Is this so hard to do? I think not. Further, imagine that there are name-like expressions in *L* that are rigid designators. We know how these expressions function in *L* and so we understand the notion of a rigid designator. Consequently, to the extent that Rosenberg's objection to (8) is based on the idea that rigid designation is unworkable due to obscurity, his objection seems to fail. One could take much of what Rosenberg says to be part of an argument to the effect that ordinary proper names are not rigid designators, the idea being that to the extent that we can understand the notion of a rigid designator, it does not apply to ordinary proper names. Yet we have evidence that names are rigid designators. When describing various counterfactual situations in which Nixon did this or that, the name 'Nixon' in the descriptions of the counterfactual situations designates Nixon in the counterfactual situations. This seems to be true for other names as well, which suggests that names are rigid designators.

Not all philosophers who object to Kripke's conclusion that true identity statements between rigid designators are necessary question the notion of a rigid designator. David Bostock (1977) and Michael Wreen (1998) are examples of two philosophers who think that the problem with Kripke's argument from rigid designators to necessary identity statements is not with his definition of a rigid designator. Bostock says the following of Kripke's argument:

> For surely when Kripke claims (speaking loosely) that '*a* = *b*' is a necessary truth we are able to understand him as intending to rule out the possibility of *a* existing while *b* does not (and *vice versa*). But this does not follow simply from the stated definition of a rigid designator. That definition does not by itself rule out the possibility that '*a*' designates while '*b*' does not.
>
> (1977: 313)

Clearly something has gone wrong here. Kripke explicitly states that when he loosely says that '*a* = *b*' is a necessary truth he means *weak necessity*. Given this, and given that if *a* is a rigid designator for *x* and *b* is a rigid designator for *x*, it follows that there is no possibility where a designates and b does not, for any possibility in which x exists, a and b will (since they are rigid designators) designate x. So it is hard to see why Bostock holds that this conclusion does not follow.

In any case, his main objection seems to arise from the function of names in certain counterfactual conditionals:

(19) If Everest and Gaurisanker had turned out to be different mountains, there would have been no border dispute between India and Tibet.

Here we are to imagine the following "facts": the mountain when seen from India was named 'Everest' and it was called 'Gaurisanker' when seen from Tibet. Each country claimed that the mountain belonged to it, which led to a border dispute. In the imagined circumstances, not only does Bostock take (19) to be true, but he also assumes that the antecedent of the conditional in (19) is *prima facie* possible. But if the antecedent of (19) is *prima facie* possible, then there is *prima facie* a possibility that Everest and Gaurisanker are distinct entities and hence it is not necessarily true that Everest = Gaurisanker, even though it is true.

Suppose Bostock is correct and the antecedent is possible (a tricky supposition). Let us also assume that 'Everest' and 'Gaurisanker' are rigid designators. Because 'Everest' is a rigid designator and it designates an object m, it follows that in each described possibility it designates m. The same is true for 'Gaurisanker'. So consider the counterfactual possibility Bostock describes. Since 'Everest' is a rigid designator, it designates m with respect to that possibility, as does 'Gaurisanker'. Thus we have described a possibility where m is not m, or, in other words, where $m \neq m$. This, of course, is not at all possible so at least one of our assumptions must be mistaken. Yet, Bostock seems to think that we can keep both of them:

> Our original example with 'Everest' and 'Gaurisanker' ... is a case where in specifying the situation I refer (twice) to one mountain, and in the situation specified there are two. There seems to me nothing amiss with this suggestion, and if I am right then it seems quite clear that there is no inference from rigidity of designation (as defined by our counterfactual criterion) to what can coherently be supposed to happen in counterfactual situations. And with this Kripke's main argument for the necessity of identity statements collapses.   (1977: 319)

It is difficult to see what has gone wrong here. If 'Everest' and 'Gaurisanker' are rigid designators, then the situation Bostock describes is not possible. It would have been better, however, if Bostock had argued against the claim that names are rigid designators. On the face of it, it may seem that we have the choice of accepting the scenario as possible and rejecting the claim that names are rigid designators, or accepting the claim that names are rigid designators and rejecting the scenario as possible. What we cannot do is accept both. We have many cases that seem to confirm Kripke's claim that names are rigid designators and Kripke has an account of the plausibility of the antecedent that does not require us to reject necessary identity (see the discussion of Hesperus/Phosphorus above), therefore this argument does not seem very convincing.

Wreen's objection is subtler. He offers the following argument:

(21) 'Hesperus' designates Hesperus.

(22) 'Phosphorus' designates Phosphorus.

(23) 'Hesperus' and 'Phosphorus' designate the same object.

(24) Hesperus is Phosphorus.

(25) (21) is contingent.

(26) (22) is contingent.

(27) (23) is contingent.

(28) (23) is logically equivalent to (24).

(29) (24) is contingent.

If (29) is true then it is contingent and not necessary that Hesperus is Phosphorus and Kripke is mistaken in holding that identity statements between coextensive names are necessary.

One concern with this argument is (28). Certainly Kripke argues that (23) entails (24). That is, if the two names name the same thing, then the identity statement is true. Here we are assuming, as we have been all along, that all the sentences in question are in the same language: English. This is true for the metalanguage claims (21)–(23) and the object language (24). What about the claim that (24) entails (23)? Wreen argues for that entailment by asking us to restrict those worlds under consideration to be worlds where Venus, 'Hesperus' and 'Phosphorus' all exist, then remarks:

> given the existence assumption just mentioned – and, remember, it's our term 'Hesperus' (with its meaning (if any) and its referent (if any)) and our term 'Phosphorus' (with its meaning

(if any) and its referent (if any)) which figure in [(23) (as Kripke insists; *NN*: 77)] – [(24)] entails [(23)] as well.   (1998: 322)

This presents a potential problem. It is not clear that *our* term 'Hesperus' exists in other possible worlds. That is, it may be that the origin of a word is essential to that word, but this is a controversial issue. If we restrict the worlds under consideration to those where the terms 'Hesperus' and 'Phosphorus' have the designations they have in the actual world, then it may not matter. Such a restriction, however, leads one to question the truth of (25) and (26).

Wreen argues for the truth of (25) and (26) on the grounds that what a term designates is partially a function of the causal relations between the term and the objects in the world and causal connections are contingent (a principle he labels CC). Kripke holds that the reference of a given use of a name is determined by the historical connections between that use and the introduction of that name. Yet if we allow our names to exist in other possible worlds (as seems reasonable), the particular historical connections between a name and its bearer need not be the same. That is, for a term to be a *name* (as opposed to a description or an abbreviation) there must be a causal–historical connection from its use to its introduction. (There are some subtle issues about the introduction of a name that were discussed in Chapter 2. There may be a time when a term is not fully introduced and yet it is used, as in the Madagascar example. We shall ignore these issues in the present context.) Hence if 'Hesperus' is used as a name on a given occasion in some possible world, there will be some causal connection from its use to its introduction as a name of Venus in that world. But the causal connections need not be the same, so, in that sense, the causal connections are contingent. But it is not contingent that there are such connections. It cannot be that the term 'Hesperus' in some world w designates what it does depending on who is President of the US and it also be true that it is our name 'Hesperus'. Still, it seems plausible that the introduction of 'Hesperus' might have occurred on a different night than it actually occurred and it be our name 'Hesperus'. So while the particular causal history of the term 'Hesperus' is contingent, for the name to be our name it must have some causal history that ends in the introduction of 'Hesperus' as a name for Venus.

What then about (25)? It depends in part on our understanding of (21), which can be read in two possible ways. On one reading the quotation marks are used to name an interpreted expression in our language and on the other they are used to name a particular symbol.

As we have noted above, quotation is used in both ways and usually the context indicates the interpretation. Because symbols by themselves do not designate anything – they need to be assigned a meaning or reference – one would naturally read (21) as saying that an interpreted expression in English designates a certain object. The question of whether or not such designation is contingent depends on whether that expression *so interpreted* could designate something other than what it does designate. If Kripke is correct that names are rigid designators then (21) is not contingent. Hence, (25) is false and the argument fails.

Wreen considers something like this type of response to his argument when he considers what he calls the *referent theory* of name-types. On the referent theory, name-types are identified as inscriptions plus an object. Quotation is understood to be used to name name-types. Wreen says that Kripke does not hold the referent theory of name-types since Kripke says that he does not think that it is necessary that Socrates is called 'Socrates'. But again we need to be careful in how quotation is being used. In this case it seems clear that quotation is used to name the sign design and not the interpreted expression. As we have noted before, Kripke uses quotation in both ways, relying on the context of use to make his meaning clear. Kripke is not obscure on this issue. No doubt Kripke could have distinguished various uses of quotation as well as linguistic items and introduced some artificial devices to track the various items being mentioned, used and discussed. But even if Kripke's exact views concerning quotation and use and mention are not entirely clear, his meaning at the various places seems clear enough. Sometimes he mentions symbols and sometimes he mentions interpreted expressions. So I do not think it is absolutely clear that Kripke would reject interpreting (21) as involving a mention of an interpreted expression.

If one interprets (21) as I have suggested, then Wreen thinks this requires holding that the causal connections between names are necessary. But again we need to distinguish particular causal connections from the fact that there are causal connections. It is not going to be necessary that a particular causal chain be associated with a particular use of a name for it to be our name. It is necessary, of course, that there be some such chain associated with a use of the name. It is no different for other terms in our language. The symbol 'vixen' is not the English expression if it means something other than being a female fox. The history of how that expression came to be used to mean what it does might have been slightly different and yet the expression could still be considered the English expression (this point is not one universally agreed upon). If we understand (21) as not involving the mention of an interpreted expression but rather the mention of a symbol that happens to have an interpretation in English, is (21) true? As mentioned above, symbols do not by themselves have any function at all. This includes the function of referring or designating, and hence, strictly speaking, on this interpretation (21) is false. But one can understand (21) as:

(21*) 'Hesperus' (as used by us) designates Hesperus.

It is, of course, true that we use the symbol 'Hesperus' to designate Venus. It is also true that we did not have to do that. It might have happened that no one ever dubbed Venus with the symbol 'Hesperus' and as a result we never used that symbol to designate Venus. So (21*) is contingent. We can interpret (22) and (23) along the lines of (21*) producing the result that (25)–(27) are true. But the problem with Wreen's argument comes when we consider (28). Line (23) is no longer equivalent to (24), even in Wreen's limited sense of equivalence (i.e. we only consider those worlds in which the symbols exist and Venus exists). While it is true that we use the symbol 'Hesperus' to designate Venus, we also use that symbol to designate various ships, my dog and so on. When we understand (21) as (21*), the strong connection between (23) and (24) is broken; they are materially equivalent, but only because they are both factually true. There is no logical connection because there are possibilities where (24) is true but (23) is not. The only way the limited logical connection between (23) and (24) made sense was if (21) was (and (22) and (23) were) understood to mention interpreted expressions whose interpretations fixed the designations of the names in question to the object mentioned in (24). Without that strong connection, there is no reason to accept (28).

Any plausibility that Wreen's argument has is a result of reading (21) in one way to get the truth of (25) and then reading it another way to get the truth of (28). When read the same way throughout, either (25) is false or (28) is false. This is true, even though Wreen himself offers two interpretations of (21) that are similar to the two uses of quotation just discussed.

Before we turn to consider the other side of Kripke's claim, namely that (10) (Hesperus is Phosphorus) is an a posteriori truth, please note that in the above discussions of the commentaries of Rosenberg, Bostock and Wreen, I have made extensive use of quotation marks.

Usually, but not always, what is quoted is an interpreted expression in English; other times I am quoting what might be called a symbol or sign design. Sometimes, to be as clear as possible, I indicate how to interpret the quotation by prefacing it with comments such as 'our name' or 'the symbol' and so forth. Like Kripke, I believe that the context of the quotation indicates what is meant.

IV

Kripke's claim that statements such as 'Hesperus is Phosphorus' are both necessarily true and known only a posteriori has produced a wide range of responses. In 1976, I offered an argument against Kripke's view that there are necessary a posteriori truths of the sort he suggested (Fitch 1976). Here is a revised version of that argument:

(1)   The terms 'Hesperus' and 'Phosphorus' are rigid designators.

(2)   The objects of knowledge are propositions.

(3)   If a and b are coextensive rigid names then $\lceil a = b \rceil$ expresses the same proposition as does $\lceil a = a \rceil$.

(4)   We know a priori that Hesperus is Hesperus.

Hence

(5)   We know a priori that Hesperus is Phosphorus.

If what we know when we know something is a proposition or the truth of a proposition, then it does not really matter how we express that proposition. If we know it a priori when expressed by a certain sentence, then we know it a priori when expressed by another sentence because it is the proposition and not the sentence that is known a priori. One might question (4) on the grounds that Hesperus is a contingent object, but as noted above we could replace (4) with 'If Hesperus exists then Hesperus is Hesperus', and avoid the existence question.

This argument is similar in spirit to an argument offered by Soames (2002) to the effect that (5) is true. (Nathan Salmon presents a similar argument (1986: 133–42).) Soames argues that there is an important distinction between the following two claims (Soames's numbering in Soames 2002):

(4a)   Hesperus = Phosphorus

(4b) 'Hesperus = Phosphorus' expresses a truth in our language.

Kripke's argument for the falsity of (5) (the long quote at the beginning of Ch. 4.II), according to Soames, only shows that (4b) is not known a priori and not that (4a) is not a priori. Soames says:

> Proposition (4b) is knowable only a posteriori. But that has no obvious bearing on the question of whether (4a) is a priori. The agents of Kripke's imagined world do not know the proposition they use the sentence *Hesperus = Phosphorus* to express, for the simple reason that the proposition they use the sentence to express is false in their world. But this does not show that the different proposition we use the sentence to express isn't known by us; nor does it show that it isn't known by us independent of empirical investigation. (2002: 8)

In presenting (4b), Soames is clearly using quotation to name symbols and not to name certain English names. Hence, (4b) is understood to mean that we use or interpret the symbolic string 'Hesperus is Phosphorus' in such a way that it expresses a truth. On the other hand the speakers in Kripke's imagined world use that same string in such a way that it expresses a falsehood. According to Soames, Kripke's imagined world only proves that (4b) is not knowable a priori; it does not show that (4a) is not a priori.

In the preface to *Naming and Necessity*, Kripke makes the following claim,which is relevant to both my argument and Soames's argument:

> My view that the English sentence 'Hesperus is Phosphorus' could sometimes be used to raise an empirical issue while the sentence 'Hesperus is Hesperus' could not shows that I do not treat the *sentences* as completely interchangeable. Further, it indicates that the mode of fixing the reference is relevant to our epistemic attitude toward the sentences expressed. How this relates to the question of what 'propositions' are expressed by these sentences, whether these 'propositions' are objects of knowledge and belief, and in general, how to treat names in epistemic contexts are vexing questions. I have no 'official doctrine' concerning them, and in fact I am unsure that the apparatus of 'propositions' does not break down in this area.
> (*NN*: 20–21)

Clearly, Kripke rejects or at least questions premise (2) of my argument and Soames's assumption that propositions are the objects of our knowledge. But if Kripke was not assuming any doctrine of propositions then how *are* we to understand his claims concerning necessary a posteriori truths? What does he have in mind by the term 'truths'?

Kripke may not have had anything like a theory or even a picture of the nature of truths in mind when he presented his arguments. Still, it is interesting that Kripke says that it is the *English sentence* that raises the empirical issue and not simply the symbols. So one might argue that what we know when we know something is that a certain statement is true or false. The statement that Hesperus is Hesperus is not the same as the statement that Hesperus is Phosphorus even if it is the same state of affairs or fact that makes the statements true, namely Venus's being Venus. Since the statements are different, it may turn out that the truth of one of them is knowable a priori while the truth of the other is only knowable a posteriori. We have then what might be the beginning of a view that is consistent with what Kripke says and yet yields the required consequences.

If we take this approach, then for something to be both necessarily true and knowable only a posteriori, the statement must have both properties. Is the statement that Hesperus is Phosphorus a necessary truth? This depends in part on how we are using the expression 'statement'. I take the term 'statement' to mean a completed interpreted sentence: something like Kripke's phrase 'English sentence' but completed with respect to any necessary contextual elements (it is a disambiguated 'eternal sentence', to use a phrase from Quine (1960)). So is the statement a necessary truth? If we ignore the existence issue, then the answer seems to be yes. That is, (4b) expresses a necessary truth if we understand the quotation marks to name an interpreted sentence and not just a name of the symbols involved. This does not seem to be the way that Soames interpreted (4b), but there is no reason why we cannot do so. Even if we interpret (4b) as I am suggesting and hence it turns out to be a necessary truth, it will remain only knowable a posteriori given the way the reference of the names are fixed. This can account for Kripke's comment that the mode of fixing the reference is relevant to our epistemic situation.

Perhaps Salmon, Soames, myself and others have fixed our attention on the wrong item. We naturally took it that it is the proposition that Hesperus is Phosphorus that Kripke intended to be both necessary and only known a posteriori. Maybe the proposition we should have considered instead is the proposition that the statement that Hesperus is Phosphorus is true. This proposition, which differs from the proposition that the statement that Hesperus is Hesperus is true, appears to be both necessary and knowable only a posteriori. Or if one is willing to accept the idea that statements themselves may be the objects of knowledge and belief, one can hold the even simpler view that it is the statement that Hesperus is Phosphorus that is the necessary a posteriori truth. (See Fitch (2004) for a more detailed account of this position.)

Chapter 5

Definitions and theoretical identifications

One of Kripke's principal themes in *Naming and Necessity* and elsewhere is the distinction between the metaphysical status of a statement and its epistemic status. In Chapter 4 we considered the status of identity statements involving ordinary proper names and Kripke's arguments that such claims are examples of necessary a posteriori truths. In this chapter we continue Kripke's theme of the importance of separating the epistemic status of a statement from its metaphysical status by first considering the claim that there are contingent a priori truths; then we consider Kripke's views on theoretical identifications. Kripke argues for a version of what is now called *scientific realism*. We conclude with his argument against materialism.

I

Kripke provides us with a number of examples of contingent a priori statements based on a single idea. One example comes from Wittgenstein. Wittgenstein remarks that the bar in Paris that (at that time) was the standard for the length of one metre cannot itself be a metre long. It is not completely clear why Wittgenstein thought the standard for something cannot have the property that it is the standard for. In any case, Kripke makes the following remarks about this example (where 'S' is the standard metre bar):

> We could make the definition more precise by stipulating that one meter is to be the length of stick S at a fixed time t_0. Is it then a necessary truth that stick S is one meter long at time t_0? Someone who thinks that everything one knows *a priori* is

> necessary might think: "This is the *definition* of a meter. By
> definition stick S is one meter long at t_0. That's a necessary
> truth." But there seems to me to be no reason so to conclude,
> even for a man who uses the stated definition of 'one meter.' For
> he's using this definition not to *give the meaning* of what he
> called the 'meter,' but to *fix the reference*.   (*NN*: 55)

Here Kripke distinguishes between giving the meaning of an expression
and fixing the reference of that expression. Both are forms of definition,
but different kinds of definition, and they have different features. One
gives the meaning of an expression α in a definition when one provides
an alternative expression or phrase β such that α and β are synonymous.
'A vixen is a female fox' is an example of such a definition. When, on the
other hand, one fixes the reference of an expression α in a definition one
provides an expression or phrase β that determines which item is to be
referred to by α. If, for example, I were to institute a system of temperature, I might fix the reference of '100°' as the temperature at which
water boils at sea level (this is one of Kripke's examples). In so doing I
have provided a definition of '100°' by fixing its reference.

There are, however, important differences in providing these different kinds of definitions. When one provides the meaning of an expres-
sion α by β, then it will be necessary that α is β. It is necessary that
vixens are female foxes. But when one gives a definition by fixing the
reference, the connection in the definition need not be a necessary one,
as in the example of 'one metre'. The expression 'one metre' designates
a certain length and it is the length that stick S has at t_0. Still, the
length of S is not a necessary feature of S. At different temperatures
and relative speeds the length of S varies. So S *might* have been longer
or shorter than one metre at t_0. Thus, it is not necessary that S is one
metre long at t_0. Kripke continues his discussion of S as follows:

> What then, is the *epistemological* status of the statement 'Stick
> S is one meter long at t_0', for someone who has fixed the metric
> system by reference to stick S? It would seem that he knows it *a
> priori*. For if he used stick S to fix the reference of the term 'one
> meter', then as a result of this kind of 'definition' (which is not an
> abbreviative or synonymous definition), he knows automati-
> cally, without further investigation, that S is one meter long.
>   (*NN*: 56)

Thus according to Kripke we have an example of a statement that is
both contingent and known a priori. This is a rather surprising result
and many philosophers have taken exception to it. We consider their

views shortly. We should perhaps note here that Kripke's main point with this example is to distinguish between two kinds of definitions to help in his discussion of descriptivism and not to provide an account of contingent a priori truths. Although this does not mean that Kripke does not view the example as providing a case of a contingent a priori truth, Kripke qualifies his claim in a footnote:

> But, merely by fixing a system of measurement, has he [the fixer] thereby *learned* some (contingent) *information* about the world, some new *fact* that he did not know before? It seems plausible that in some sense he did not, even though it is undeniably a contingent fact that *S* is one meter long. So there may be a case for reformulating the thesis that everything *a priori* is necessary so as to save it from this type of counterexample.
>
> (*NN*: 63, n.26)

Kripke does not, however, offer a different formulation of the claim that all a priori truths are necessary and holds that on the standard formulations his example is a counter-example.

The "one metre" example is not the only example that Kripke offers for the view that there are contingent a priori truths. In a footnote he offers the following example:

> Neptune was hypothesized as the planet which caused such and such discrepancies in the orbits of certain other planets. If Leverrier indeed gave the name 'Neptune' to the planet before it was ever seen, then he fixed the reference of 'Neptune' by means of the description just mentioned.   (*NN*: 79, n.33)

The statement that Neptune is the planet that causes such and such discrepancies in the orbits of other heavenly bodies is, according to Kripke, an example of a contingent a priori truth. It is contingent because those discrepancies might have been caused by something other than Neptune, but given that Neptune did cause the discrepancies, those who fixed the reference of the name 'Neptune' knew without further investigation that Neptune is the cause of the discrepancies. Thus, we have an example of a contingent a priori truth.

To understand the implications of Kripke's claim, we again need to be clear about what entity has the property of being knowable a priori and again Kripke does not provide a clear account. As we noted in Chapter 4, in the 1980 preface to the book version of *Naming and Necessity*, Kripke explicitly questions whether propositions are the objects of knowledge of any kind, including a priori knowledge.

Hence, any discussion of this matter will involve a certain level of speculation regarding Kripke's view, as Kripke himself does not offer an official position on many of the relevant issues. In particular, Kripke does not provide an account of the nature of the truths that have both the metaphysical and epistemic properties we are considering. We shall follow Kripke and hold that it is statements that have the properties in question (Kripke says "The terms 'necessary' and '*a priori*', then, as applied to statements, are not obvious synonyms" (*NN*: 38)) and leave the nature of statements somewhat open (see pp. 112–13).

Kripke's argument for the existence of contingent a priori truths is simple enough. Suppose Jones defines the expression 'one metre' by fixing its referent via the description 'the length of stick S at time t_0'. It follows that Jones knows, without further enquiry, that the statement that S is one metre long at t_0 is true. But the statement that S is one metre long at t_0 is not a necessary truth since S might have been longer than in fact it is. Hence, there is a possible circumstance in which the statement is false. Thus, for Jones, the statement that S is one metre long at t_0 is something that he knows to be true without empirical enquiry and it is something that is only contingently true.

II

Let us begin our discussion of Kripke's contingent a priori truths by avoiding one issue that often arises in such discussions, namely the existence of the objects to which the statements in question purport to refer. Can one have a priori knowledge of the existence of an object whose existence is only contingent? This depends, in part, on how narrowly or widely one uses the term 'a priori'. Some use the expression to mean something like knowledge that one acquires without any *external* empirical evidence. So knowledge of one's own headaches (as well as one's existence) would count as a priori knowledge since that knowledge is acquired without any *external* empirical evidence. Others use the expression to rule out any empirical evidence whatsoever, including the observations of one's own internal states. Kripke uses the phrase "independently of any experience" but that cannot be taken literally. Obviously one must have some experience to have knowledge at all. It is reasonable to understand Kripke to mean something like the following: a priori truths for S are those statements that are known (or knowable) to be true by S and that the warrant for the knowledge of them for S is not based on any empirical evidence (i.e. evidence from observation and experience). Given this account of a priori truth, one cannot know a priori that x exists if x is a contingently existing object. Since the truth of the statement that S is one metre long at t_0 depends, it would seem, on the existence of S, it cannot be exactly that statement that is known a priori by Jones. The a priori truth must instead be the statement that:

(1)   If S exists, then S is one metre long at t_0.

Now a number of philosophers, including me, have questioned these examples as truly being examples of contingent a priori truths. Moreover, as we noted above, Kripke himself wonders whether these examples can demonstrate that there are contingent truths that are knowable a priori.

To understand the difficulties, consider the distinction that Donnellan (1977) makes between the following two claims:

(A)   Provided the φ exists, "t is the φ" expresses a contingent truth

and

(B)   Provided the φ exists, t is the φ.

Donnellan argues that while instances of the form (B) are indeed contingent, one can only know them a posteriori. The inclination to think that one could know instances of (B) a priori seems based on the fact that instances of (A) are knowable a priori. Jones, in our example above, defines the term 'one metre' by reference to the stick S and as a result of that kind of definition Jones is assured that the sentence 'If S exists, then S is one metre long at t_0' expresses a truth. But Donnellan argues that knowing that a given sentence expresses a truth is not the same thing as knowing the truth expressed by the sentence. So, (B) does not follow from (A) and it is (B), not (A), that is claimed to be known a priori by Jones. But unless Jones inspects S, Jones cannot know the length of S. Simply by fixing the referent of the term 'one metre', Jones does not thereby learn S's length. (Compare Donnellan's point to Soames's argument, pp. 110–11.)

What can we conclude about Jones's epistemic situation with respect to the statement that S is one metre long at t_0? Donnellan makes an interesting remark about this:

> I am not sure whether in the circumstances what sentences of form (A) express are both contingent and *a priori*. But if they are, they are harmless varieties of the contingent *a priori*,

> examples of which we produce without recourse to stipulations
> introducing rigid designators. ... Suppose I stipulate that
> 'Widgit' shall mean by definition "green cow," then I know the
> truth of what the following expresses:
>
> (C) Provided there are any green cows, "Widgits are green
>   cows" expresses a truth.
>
> But the same considerations would argue for this being *a priori*
> knowledge of a contingent truth. If this proves that there can be
> *a priori* knowledge of the contingent, then it seems to me that
> the contingent *a priori* is not very scary and not very interest-
> ing.   (1977: 23)

The considerations that Donnellan uses to argue for (C)'s being a
contingent truth concern the contingency of the stipulations that lead
to (C). But this seems to be the wrong place to locate contingency for
such cases. Clearly, what a given string of symbols expresses in a given
language is a matter of convention and hence to that extent the claim
that any given string of symbols expresses a truth is contingent. Once
we have interpreted these symbols in the language, however, the question of whether that interpreted sentence expresses a truth may not be
contingent. In particular, (C) does not appear to be contingent. The
statement that a vixen is a female fox is not contingent, or in other
words, it is not contingent that the interpreted sentence "A vixen is a
female fox" expresses a truth. Some sentences express truths solely in
virtue of their "meaning" or semantic properties; others express truths
because of the way the world happens to be, together with their semantic properties. Given the meaning of (C) established by Donnellan's
stipulations, not only does (C) express a necessary truth, but it is
necessary that it (so interpreted) expresses a truth.

The situation seems very different for (1). The statement made by
an utterance of (1) is not a necessary truth. Not only does (1) not
express a necessary truth, but it is not necessary that it expresses a
truth at all. Again, what we mean by saying that (1) does not express
a necessary truth is that the proposition that an utterance of (1)
expresses (in standard contexts) is not necessary. The proposition
expressed is that if S exists, then S is a metre long at t_0, and as we
have noted, the length of S varies from world to world. But it is also
not necessary that (1) expresses a truth at all. It is true that our
world happens to be one where (1) does express a truth. But if we
uttered (1) in a context that involves a world where S exists, but is
less than a metre in length, (1) would still mean what it means in our

world; that is, it would make the same statement and express the proposition that it expresses in our world, but that statement would be false. This is not the case for (C). In every world, the statement that an utterance of (C) would make and the proposition that would thereby be expressed (again keeping the meaning fixed across contexts) would be true.

This difference between (1) and (C) suggests that Kripke's example is not trivial in the way Donnellan suggests. (1) is contingent not simply because meaning is conventional, and hence it is a contingent fact that a given term in a language means what it does. Once meaning is fixed, however, there remains the question of whether it is necessary that the sentence so interpreted is true (or that it expresses a true proposition).

Donnellan is right when he remarks that Kripke's examples of contingent a priori truths are not "scary". Any term α that is introduced by fixing its referent by the description 'the φ' will provide those that introduce it with contingent a priori statements of the form ⌈if α exists, then α is the φ⌉. To be somewhat more cautious, we can add the condition that the sentences must express a proposition for the statement to be a contingent a priori truth.

I add the above condition for those who hold that if one attempts to fix the referent of a term that one is introducing by a description that is not satisfied by anything, then even given the explicit existence condition of the antecedent, sentences containing that term do not express propositions and hence cannot be true or false. For example, suppose I say let 'Spaceman' be the first person on Mars in the 1990s. Since no one actually set foot on Mars in the 1990s, some might claim that the sentence 'If Spaceman exists, then Spaceman was the first person on Mars in the 1990s' fails to express any proposition and hence cannot be true.

Kripke's examples demonstrate that when we introduce terms via a fixing definition of the sort described, we (the fixers) are in a position to know certain statements are true without empirical enquiry, even though it is not necessary that those statements are true and they do not express necessary truths. As Kripke himself notes, one does not thereby learn some new (non-linguistic) information about the world. One does not come to learn the length of S by fixing the referent of 'one metre'. Similarly, if one is lost and one utters the sentence 'I am here, now', one is assured of having said something true without knowing one's location. These examples of contingent a priori truths should not seem "scary".

III

Kripke argues that we should carefully distinguish the metaphysical status of a claim from its epistemological status. As a result of this distinction, he argues that identity statements between codesignative proper names provide examples of necessary a posteriori truths. Kripke identifies at least two other classes of statements that are semantically similar to identity statements involving proper names. One class Kripke calls *theoretical identifications* and the other class are general statements concerning natural kind terms. Theoretical identifications are statements in which one identifies a natural kind with a scientific kind. Examples of this class are 'Water is H_2O' and 'Gold is the element with atomic number 79'. Kripke's examples of general statements involving natural kinds are 'light is a stream of photons' and 'lightning is an electrical discharge', as well as more ordinary statements such as 'cats are animals'.

Kripke does not explicitly distinguish between the various statements concerned with natural kinds, even though different statements involving kinds have different logical forms. What Kripke notices is the similarity between the way natural kind terms function and the way that proper names function. Consider, for example, Kripke's comments concerning the statement 'cats are animals':

> Cats are in fact animals! Then is this truth a necessary truth or a contingent one? It seems to me that it is necessary. Consider the counterfactual situation in which in place of these creatures – these animals – we have in fact little demons which when they approached us brought bad luck indeed. Should we describe this as a situation in which cats were demons? It seems to me that these demons would not be cats. They would be demons in a cat-like form. We could have discovered that the actual cats that we *have* are demons ... Although we could say cats *might turn out* to be demons, of a certain species, given that cats are in fact animals, any cat-like being which is not an animal, in the actual world or in a counterfactual one, is not a cat. (*NN*: 125–6)

Kripke's argument for the necessity of the statement that cats are animals is strikingly similar to his Hesperus/Phosphorus argument (see Ch. 4.II.) The sense in which cats might have turned out to be demons is the same as the sense in which it might have turned out that Hesperus is not Phosphorus. The circumstances surrounding our introduction for such terms is such that, for all we knew at the time of the introduction, we were naming different heavenly bodies or demons in the case of 'cat'. Hence, we were in no position to know a priori that cats are animals. This required some empirical investigation. In addition, the introduction of the term 'cat' is, according to Kripke, similar in certain respects to the introduction of a proper name: "The original concept of cat is: *that kind of thing*, where the kind can be identified by paradigmatic instances. It is not something picked out by any qualitative dictionary definition" (*NN*: 122). The term 'cat' is introduced to designate a certain kind of creature and not as synonymous for some description. Hence, the meaning of natural kind terms like proper names is not to be found in some version of descriptivism. The statement that cats are animals is an example of a necessary a posteriori truth. It is a necessary truth since in all possible worlds cats are animals. Yet the fact that cats are animals was something that we could only know after empirical investigation into cats. Kripke's position with respect to general terms like 'cat' is one that is shared by Hilary Putnam (1962, 1973), although each arrived at their conclusions independently. Kripke's and Putnam's view that the underlying properties that science discovers with respect to a given natural kind are essential to that kind is often called *scientific essentialism*. (Putnam, however, has come to question this metaphysical thesis (1990).)

The statement that water is H_2O is another example that Kripke offers of a necessary a posteriori truth:

> It certainly represents a discovery that water is H_2O. We identified water originally by its characteristic feel, appearance and perhaps taste, (though the taste may usually be due to the impurities). If there were a substance, even actually, which had a completely different atomic structure from that of water, but resembled water in these respects, would we say that some water wasn't H_2O? I think not. We would say instead that just as there is a fool's gold there could be a fool's water; a substance which, though having the properties by which we originally identified water, would not in fact be water.   (*NN*: 128)

Again, Kripke argues as follows. Consider various counterfactual situations in which we come across something that has many of the properties that we used when we fixed the meaning of the term 'water' but lacks the underlying physical structure of water. Would we say that such stuff is water? Kripke claims not. We would call it 'fool's water' or something similar.

Kripke considers a wide range of cases involving general terms. In addition to the examples of water and cats, he discusses gold, heat, light, lightning, tigers and pain. Kripke concludes his discussion of these examples by indicating that he takes general kind terms to be similar to ordinary proper names:

> my argument implicitly concludes that certain general terms, those for natural kinds, have a greater kinship with proper names than is generally realized. This conclusion holds for certain for various species names, whether they are count nouns, such as 'cat,' 'tiger,' 'chunk of gold,' or mass terms such as 'gold,' 'water,' 'iron pyrites.' It also applies to certain terms for natural phenomena, such as 'heat,' 'light,' 'sound,' 'lightning,' and, presumably, suitably elaborated, to corresponding adjectives – 'hot,' 'loud,' 'red.' (*NN*: 134)

Kripke is not explicit concerning the nature of this kinship between general kind terms and proper names. At one point (*NN*: 140), he says that theoretical identities involve rigid designators and this suggests that the kinship between natural kind terms and proper names includes the fact that both sorts of expressions are rigid designators. This may be the case when these general terms are being used as abstract nouns in such identity sentences as 'water is H_2O' (assuming, for the moment, that these are identity sentences), but it is difficult to see how the notion of 'rigid designator' applies to such expressions generally. Consider the sentence 'Fluffy is a cat'. It is difficult to see how the expression 'cat' in this sentence is a rigid designator. What does it rigidly designate? It does not rigidly designate the set of cats since the extension of the predicate varies from world to world. Perhaps it is the intension of the predicate, which is often associated with the corresponding property (in this case *being a cat*). The problem with this approach is that the intension of every predicate is fixed across worlds and hence every predicate would be rigid. Soames suggests that one might try to define the notion of a rigid predicate in terms of an associated singular term that is rigid, but he concludes that such an approach is hopeless (see Soames 2002: 259–62).

Except perhaps in special cases such as 'water is H_2O', the kinship between proper names and natural kind terms for which Kripke argues is not one of rigid designation. In what, then, does this kinship consist? The answer, I believe, lies in Kripke's rejection of descriptivism for natural kind terms and all that is implied by such a rejection. Recall that the doctrine of descriptivism as it applies to proper names is the view that associated with each name is a description that is the meaning of the name and the description determines the referent of the name. Descriptivism as it applies to natural kind terms is the view that associated with each natural kind term is a description that is the meaning of the term and the description determines the extension of the term. Consider, for example, what descriptivism would say about the meaning of 'cat'. Presumably such a view would hold that the meaning of 'cat' is (or is similar to) 'a small soft-furred domesticated animal kept as a pet or for killing mice'. The meaning of 'cat' determines the extension of cat in every counterfactual circumstance in much the same way that the meaning of a name determines the referent of that name in each counterfactual circumstance, and, as in the case of names, there are corresponding epistemic and metaphysical truths that result from accepting descriptivism for natural kind terms. Hence, on such a view, it is analytic, necessary and a priori that cats are soft-furred domesticated animals that are kept as pets or for killing mice. According to Kripke, the problems that arose for descriptivism for names also arise for descriptivism for natural kind terms. We do not know a priori that cats are animals and it is not necessary that they are domesticated pets.

The similarity between natural kind terms and proper names lies in the rejection of descriptivism as providing the meaning of a natural kind term and replacing it with a form of the causal–historical view. In his discussion of the natural kind term 'gold', Kripke remarks:

> More important, the species-name may be passed from link to link, exactly as in the case of proper names, so that many who have seen little or no gold can still use the term. Their reference is determined by a causal (historical) chain, not by use of any items. (*NN*: 139)

The same is true for 'cat', ' water' and other natural kind terms. There is, of course, an important difference between proper names and natural kind terms. Proper names designate particulars and are introduced via some attempted dubbing (intentional or not) of that particular. What corresponds to the dubbing of a particular in the case of a natural kind term?

Kripke holds that natural kind terms are introduced to refer to natural kinds and it is the kind itself that determines the extension of the term. Hence, as we noticed above, the term 'cat' refers to the kind *cat*. Ideally, this is done by pointing to a number of cats and saying that we shall introduce the term 'cat' as a name for that kind of creature of which all these are samples. In the case of a substance term such as 'gold', we have a collection of samples and decide to name the substance of which all these are samples: 'gold'. Of course things do not always work out the way one expects. Kripke notes:

> If, on the other hand, the supposition that there is one uniform substance or kind in the initial sample proves more radically in error, reactions can vary: sometimes we may declare that there are two kinds of gold, sometimes we may drop the term 'gold'. (These possibilities are not supposed to be exhaustive.)
>
> (*NN*: 136)

In practice, all sorts of factors enter into the process that results in a term being a natural kind term. For example, it may just turn out that the sample we picked was not a typical sample of those items that had the surface features that we used to pick out the sample. We might suppose that the items we picked are the only items in the world that share their internal structure, but there are many items that have a common internal structure that happen to share their surface properties with the items of our sample. At first it seems reasonable to think that we would refer to all the items that share the surface features with the same general term (say β). Once we discovered the facts about the sample (and the other similar items), however, it seems likely that we reserve our term 'β' for the large majority of the items and no longer use 'β' to refer to the items in the original sample. There will also be examples of empty general terms and reference shifts as in the case of proper names.

Kripke's main point in most of his discussions concerning what he calls natural kind terms is that such general terms actually function more like proper names than do general predicate expressions. Most predicate expressions are descriptive. So, for example, 'bachelor' simply means 'an unmarried adult human male' and the extension of the term is determined by that meaning. The extension of a natural kind term, according to Kripke, is a certain kind that does not necessarily have the features that we commonly use or once used to pick out the members of that kind. So although we may use the feature of being a shiny yellow metal to pick out examples of gold and to that extent 'gold' has a "common" meaning of being the stuff that is a shiny yellow metal (or something similar), what determines whether something *is* gold is the structure of gold (i.e. being an element with atomic number 79).

IV

One of Kripke's more controversial claims concerning natural kind terms is his claim that 'water is H_2O' is an identity statement between rigid designators and as such it is a necessary a posteriori truth. One standard objection to Kripke's example is the complaint that one or both of the terms flanking the identity is not a rigid designator. Helen Steward's comments (Steward 1990) offer a typical version of this kind of objection. Steward imagines that we discover that there are two types of protons: the ordinary proton and the rare proton-B. In addition, when we have a large concentration of H_2O molecules whose atoms all have protons-B we have an opaque pink solid. She then asks:

> What would happen to the claim that, necessarily, water is H_2O in such a case as this? Would we continue to insist that all the range of substances, from the pink and opaque to the clear and colorless, which are chemically composed of H_2O are in fact different kinds of water? Surely not; surely we would use different names for the widely varying kinds of substance produced by the substitution of protons-B for ordinary protons.
>
> (Steward 1990: 390)

Steward concludes that 'H_2O' is not a rigid designator because it *can* designate both water and the opaque pink solid made up of proton-B atoms.

One response to Steward is to claim that our term 'H_2O' does not designate compounds primarily composed of proton-B atoms and hence it does not designate the pink solid substance. Steward anticipates this response:

> It simply ignores the fact that there is descriptive complexity in a term like 'H_2O', that it is a shorthand for a chemical structure and not just an arbitrary name, so that while that chemical structure (two atoms of hydrogen to one atom of oxygen, arranged in the particular way characteristic of the water molecule) remains intact, the term must continue to apply.
>
> (1990: 391, n.7)

The expression 'H_2O' is a chemical formula and as such it carries with it a certain amount of information. Hence, a kind of descriptive complexity is associated with any such formula. But it does not follow from this that any combination of two hydrogen atoms with one oxygen atom is designated by 'H_2O'. For example, we do not use 'H_2O' to designate heavy water (which is designated by 'D_2O'), which contains two atoms of hydrogen to one atom of oxygen, even though a certain amount of D_2O is in all of our samples of (pure) water. So what reason do we have to suppose along with Steward that *our* expression 'H_2O' designates compounds composed of two hydrogen proton-B atoms and one oxygen proton-B atom in any world? Given the way we introduce chemical formulas, if we discovered protons-B, we would distinguish between compounds containing such protons from those that do not. But even if we would not so distinguish them, given that there are no protons-B, our chemical formulas do not designate any compounds containing them, since *our* chemical formulas designate *our* chemical kinds. Putting the point in a slightly different way, *our* chemical symbol O designates ordinary oxygen atoms, not oxygen proton-B atoms.

A different kind of objection is presented by Mark Johnston (1997). He argues that such statements as 'water is H_2O' should be viewed as claims of constitution and not identity. The claim that

(W)   Water is H_2O

should be understood to mean that water is constituted by H_2O, according to Johnston.

Johnston's argument that the statement that water is H_2O should not be viewed as an identity statement is relatively straightforward. Assume that it is an identity statement. That is, assume:

(1)   Water = H_2O.

Next Johnston asserts:

(2)   If water = H_2O then water vapour = H_2O and snow = H_2O.

From (1) and (2) we can derive

(3)   Water vapour = H_2O and snow = H_2O.

Clearly (3) is false (because it implies that water vapour = snow), so either (1) or (2) must be false. But Johnston argues that any reason you have for rejecting (2) is a reason to reject (1). Hence (1) is false.

One reason for thinking that (2) is true is that if the kind water is the kind H_2O then certainly the kind water vapour (or snow) is also the kind H_2O, for what else could the kind water vapour be if not the kind H_2O? However, this reasoning assumes that water vapour is itself a kind as opposed to a state of the kind water. One might think this because the term 'water' has two ordinary uses. One use of the term designates the substance *kind* water. This is the use that we have been assuming Kripke intended in his statements concerning water. There is another ordinary use in which the term 'water' is used to designate a particular state of the kind water, namely the liquid state. We use terms like 'ice', 'snow', 'steam', 'water' and so on to refer to particular states of a given kind of substance; namely, the substance water. Given that we use the same expression to refer both to the substance and to a state of the substance, it is easy to see that (W) is ambiguous. It can be interpreted to mean 'liquid water is identical to the substance H_2O' (where 'liquid water' is understood to mean 'the substance water in a liquid state') or to mean 'the substance water is identical to the substance H_2O'. It is reasonable to assume that it is the latter claim that Kripke intended.

For these reasons, (1) is to be understood as an identity claim between a natural kind substance and a scientific kind substance. How then are we to understand (2)? The most straightforward reading of (2) is the following:

(2*)   If the substance water is identical to the substance H_2O, then water vapour is identical to the substance H_2O and snow is identical to the substance H_2O.

Yet clearly (2*) is false. Water vapour is not identical to the substance H_2O for the expression 'water vapour' designates the state of a substance and not the substance itself. Hence the argument fails.

Johnston considers this response to his argument or at least one similar to it. Johnston claims that we can replace the false (2) with the following true claim and still produce unacceptable results (his numbering):

(7)   Water vapour = H_2O in a vaporous condition and snow = H_2O in powdery condition.

We get the unacceptable results when we add the following premise:

(9) H_2O = H_2O in a vaporous condition.

Clearly Johnston is correct that from (1), (9) and (7) we get the unacceptable result that snow is identical to water vapour. It also seems obvious that anyone who rejects (2) will reject (9) (as Johnston acknowledges). But before we reject (9), we should consider exactly what statement (9) makes. What (9) seems to claim is that the substance H_2O is identical with – what? How do we understand the phrase 'H_2O in a vaporous condition'? Does it also designate a sub-stance? If so, what substance? Since Johnston takes (7) as obviously true, perhaps it designates the substance water vapour. But there is no such substance. Johnston claims the expression 'water vapour' designates what he calls a 'manifest kind' which he defines as 'a kind whose instances we identify and re-identify on the basis of their manifest properties' (1997: 565). So we should understand the phrase 'H_2O in a vaporous condition' to designate a manifest kind. But now, according to Johnston, we run into a problem.

Consider a certain quantity of water vapour. Certainly that is noth-ing but a quantity of molecules of H_2O. But the quantity of molecules of H_2O might have been powdery (and hence it might have been snow), but the water vapour could not be snow, so the quantity of water vapour cannot be the quantity of H_2O molecules. So, Johnston con-cludes that water cannot be H_2O. Instead, it is constituted by H_2O.

The key to this argument is Johnston's claim that the quantity of water vapour could not have been snow. Why would anyone think this? Johnston offers the following example concerning fog:

> I do not mean to ask whether the fog could solidify into a block of ice or liquefy into a puddle of water. I know that it could. I mean to ask whether the fog could *be* either of these things. It seems to me that the fog could not be either of these things. For when the fog solidifies or liquefies, that is the end of the fog. A vapor like the fog is essentially a vapor … To summarize: the instances of H_2O in a vaporous condition, that is the water vapors, are essentially instances of that kind.   (1997: 568)

What plausibility there is in Johnston's claim that a quantity of water vapour is essentially vaporous comes from Johnston's further claim that water vapours are kinds of entities. Yet one should ques-tion whether or not such expressions as 'snow' and 'water vapour' really designate *kinds* if 'kind' is used in its ontologically significant sense. Traditionally, membership in a kind is an essential feature of the entity in question. Hence water is essentially water, gold is essen-tially gold, and if water vapours are kinds then there are essentially water vapours. A yellow car, on the other hand, is not essentially yel-low and hence the phrase 'yellow car' does not designate a kind. Of course, in one ordinary use of the term 'kind', a yellow car is a kind of thing. In this sense of the term 'kind', being a certain kind of thing carries with it no metaphysical importance. In particular, there are no essentialist connections with kinds of this sort.

I suggest that water vapours are no more a metaphysical kind than yellow cars. That is, just as yellow cars are not essentially yellow, water vapour is not essentially vaporous. Of course, for the term 'yellow car' to apply correctly to some item, that item needs to be yellow and in order to apply correctly the expression 'water vapour' to an item that item needs to be vaporous. But the item that is a yellow car is not necessarily yellow, nor is the item that is a water vapour necessarily vaporous. So I do not find Johnston's argument convincing.

Kripke's view of natural kind terms and his theoretical identifications involve a number of issues. I refer the reader to Salmon (1982), Soames (2002), Fitch (2001) and others listed in the bibliography for further discussion on these topics.

V

One of Kripke's more famous arguments is his argument against the mind–body identity theory: the theory that the mental is identical to the physical. There are a number of different versions of this theory. According to one version, every particular mental event or state is identical to some particular physical state. This view is often called the *token identity theory* in contrast to the *type identity theory*. According to the type theory, every mental event type is identical to a physical event type. There are other versions as well. Kripke offers arguments against both the type theory and the token theory. His argument against the token theory is the following:

> Let 'A' name a particular pain sensation, and let 'B' name the corresponding brain state, or the brain state some identity theorist wishes to identify with A. *Prima facie*, it would seem that it is at least logically possible that B should have existed (Jones's brain could have been in exactly that state at the time in question) without Jones feeling any pain at all, and thus without the presence of A. Once again, the identity theorist cannot admit the possibility cheerfully and proceed from there; consistency, and the principle of the necessity of identities using rigid designators, disallows any such course. If A and B were identical, the identity would have to be necessary. The difficulty can hardly be evaded by arguing that although B could not exist without A, *being a pain* is merely a contingent property of A, and that therefore the presence of B without pain does

not imply the presence of B without A. Can any case of essence be more obvious than the fact that being a pain is a necessary property of each pain? The identity theorist who wishes to adopt the strategy in question must even argue that being a sensation is a contingent property of A, for *prima facie* it would seem logically possible that B could exist without any sensation with which it might plausibly be identified. Consider a particular pain, or other sensation, that you once had. Do you find it at all plausible that *that very sensation* could have existed without being a sensation, the way a certain inventor (Franklin) could have existed without being an inventor? (*NN*: 146)

We can recast Kripke's argument as follows:

(1)   Let '*A*' name a particular pain and '*B*' its corresponding brain state.

(2)   If $A = B$, then necessarily $A = B$.

(3)   It is possible that B exist and A not exist.

(4)   It is possible that $A \neq B$.

(5)   Therefore $A \neq B$.

The conclusion, (5), contradicts the token identity thesis. The key premise is (3). Kripke argues that (3) is true on the grounds that it is possible for someone to be in a particular brain state (B) and yet not feel pain; as he puts it, Jones's brain could have been in state B without Jones feeling any pain at all.

A natural response to the suggestion that it is *possible* that Jones be in state B without feeling pain is that the identity between the pain state and the brain state is only contingent and based on the laws of nature. But such a response cannot be correct, because (2) is true. Kripke has argued that true identities are necessary (see Chapter 4).

Still, some argue that the necessity of identity is beside the point. Premise (3) is false, not because identity might be contingent, but rather because Jones's being in state B without being in pain does not mean that state B can exist without state A existing. It just means that state A can exist without Jones being in pain. Kripke rejects this move when he says "Can any case of essence be more obvious than the fact that *being a pain* is a necessary property of each pain?" (*NN*: 146) Still, it is not obvious to everyone. Consider Fred Feldman's remarks on the issue:

For any serious materialist should recognize that his view entails that painfulness is never part of the essence of a pain-event. Pain-events are experienced as they are only as a result of contingent laws of nature ... These very brain-events, had the laws of nature been different, would of course still have been self-identical, but would not have been identical to anything that would, under those circumstances, have been a pain-event. Thus, such events are not essentially painful. (1974: 675)

What is contingent, according to Feldman, is not the identity between events, but rather the mental–physical status of the events themselves. According to Feldman, having a certain mental property is a contingent property of the physical state.

The other side of the coin needs to be considered as well. In addition to claiming that *being a pain* is an essential feature of A, Kripke also claims that *being a brain state* is an essential feature of B. Kripke says, "The configuration of brain cells whose presence at a given time constitutes the presence of B at that time is essential to B, and in its absence B would not exist" (*NN*: 147). But A could have existed without that very configuration of brain cells, and thus we could replace (3) in the above argument with

(3*) It is possible that A exist without B existing,

and achieve the same result. But a token materialist could reject the claim that A could exist without that brain state. Perhaps a different and qualitively similar pain could have existed, but not A. It is also unclear whether *being a brain state* is an essential feature of B; B is, after all, simply a certain physical state. Does it have to be a state of a *brain*? This depends to some extent on exactly what 'B' designates. What is reasonably clear is that token identity theorists can avoid Kripke's argument, but they do so by giving up what Kripke takes to be plausible essentialist claims.

Kripke's argument against the type identity thesis is similar to his argument against the token identity thesis. The type identity thesis differs from the token thesis in that kinds of mental states are identified with kinds of physical states as opposed to particular mental and physical states. So the type identity thesis is an example of the general class of theoretical identifications that includes identifying water with H_2O, gold with the element with atomic number 79 and so on. Kripke's example of the type theory is the identification of the mental kind pain with the physical state of the stimulation of C-fibres. Although Kripke uses the phrase 'C-fibre stimulation' as the name of the scientific kind correlated with pain, it does not really matter if pain is discovered to be a more complicated physical state than simply C-fibre stimulation. We can use the phrase 'C-fibre stimulation' to designate whatever physical state science determines correlates to pain states. The argument against the type identity thesis parallels the above argument:

(1') If pain = C-fibre stimulation, then necessarily pain = C-fibre stimulation.

(2') It is possible that C-fibre stimulation occur without pain occurring and that pain occur without C-fibre stimulation occurring.

(3') Therefore, pain ≠ C-fibre stimulation.

A defender of the identity thesis could claim that (2') is not, in fact, true. It *seems* as though C-fibre stimulation could occur without pain occurring but that "possibility" is merely epistemic in much the same way as it seemed that one could have a drop of water without thereby having a drop of H_2O.

Kripke argues that the identity theorist cannot resort to the strategy that he himself employed to explain the apparent contingency of such theoretical identifications as 'water is H_2O' or 'gold is the element with atomic number 79'. As we explained in Ch. 5.III, Kripke argued that such scientific identifications with our ordinary kind terms are necessary, but empirical and hence knowable only a posteriori. It would be natural for an identity theorist to claim that the identity between a mental state and a brain state is a theoretical identification like the identity between water and H_2O. But according to Kripke, there is a difference between the water–H_2O identification and the pain–C-fibre stimulation identification. It is not a priori that water is H_2O because we could be in a situation that is qualitatively identical to our actual situation and yet the stuff in question not be water. Something other than water might have the superficial properties of water, that is, the properties that we use to individuate water. Turning to the pain–C-fibre stimulation case, we can ask whether we could be in a situation that is qualitatively identical to our actual situation and the state in question not be a state of pain. Could it be a state that simply resembles the pain but not be a pain in the way that something could resemble water and not be water? Kripke denies that this is possible. How can a state be qualitatively identical to a state of pain and not be a pain? We know that x is qualitatively identical to y provided the *qualities* of x and y are the same, including the qualities of sensation. So the only states that can be qualitively identical to a state of pain are states that are themselves pains. Thus, pain is different from water in that nothing can be qualitatively identical to a pain except another pain, while some stuff can be qualitatively identical to water without being water.

Kripke tries to make the point with an imaginative example. If God were creating the world, what would God have to do to make it the case that heat is the motion of molecules? All he needs to do, Kripke claims, is create the heat. Kripke continues:

> How then does it appear to us that the identity of molecular motion with heat is a substantive scientific fact, that the mere creation of molecular motion still leaves God with the additional task of making molecular motion into heat? This feeling is indeed illusory, but what *is* a substantive task for the Deity is the task of making molecular motion felt as heat. To do this He must create some sentient beings to insure that the molecular motion produces the sensation S in them. Only after he has done this will there be beings who can learn that the sentence 'Heat is the motion of molecules' expresses an *a posteriori* truth in precisely the same way that we do.
>
> What about the case of the stimulation of C-fibers? To create this phenomenon, it would seem that God need only create beings with C-fibers capable of the appropriate type of physical stimulation; whether the beings are conscious or not is irrelevant here. It would seem, though, that to make the C-fiber stimulation correspond to pain, or be felt as pain, God must do something in addition to the mere creation of the C-fiber stimulation; He must let the creatures feel the C-fiber stimulation as pain, and not as a tickle, or as warmth, or as nothing, as apparently would also have been within His powers ... The same cannot be said for pain; if the phenomenon exists at all, no further work should be required to make it into pain.   (*NN*: 153–4)

The point Kripke is making is clear enough. The relationship between C-fibre stimulation and pain is contingent. There could be a possible world where C-fibre stimulation is felt as a tickle. But there could be no possible world where pain is not felt as pain. Any world where a given state *M* is not felt as a pain is a world where *M* is not a pain. Whether Kripke is correct about this remains to be seen. The debate concerning the relationship between mental states and physical states is far from over. I refer the reader to the bibliography for additional reading on this topic.

Chapter 6
Truth

In the 1970s, Kripke turned his attention to the problem of semantic paradoxes. It is not surprising that Kripke was interested in this issue, given his interest in puzzles and formal logic. The problem, in a nutshell, is how is it possible to have a truth predicate apply to sentences that themselves contain a truth predicate? This is an ancient problem and it is often called the problem of the liar. According to the ancient version of the liar paradox, Epimenides, a Cretan, is supposed to have asserted the sentence 'All Cretans are liars'. Given certain empirical assumptions, this sentence yields the result that it is true if and only if it is false. A more direct version of the problem can be seen with the following sentence:

(1)   This sentence is false.

(1) is true if and only if it is false. It would be a mistake to think that the problem that is expressed by "liar sentences" such as (1) is only a problem for a very special class of sentences, namely those that involve self-reference, as (1) does. In fact, there are many ways that such paradoxical results can obtain. For example, consider the pair of sentences

(2)   Sentence (3) is false.

(3)   Sentence (2) is true.

Sentence (2) does not involve self-reference (at least not directly), yet (2) is true if and only if (2) is false. The paradox of the preface is another example. Suppose that someone writes in the preface to her book that there is at least one false sentence in the book. If, as a matter of fact, all the other sentences in the book are true then that sentence is true if and only if it is false.

Liar sentences in the language give rise to an obvious problem. How is it possible to assert that something is true or false without (possibly) involving oneself in a contradiction or paradox? Almost any sentence that we utter concerning what is true or false may lead to a paradox given the right set of empirical facts about the world. In essence, the problem is providing an account of the truth of sentences without thereby becoming involved in the paradoxes. In his paper "Outline of a Theory of Truth", Kripke presented a formal way of avoiding these paradoxes that avoided the philosophical problems of the then "orthodox" view. Kripke is cautious with respect to the claims he makes for his own view of the problem, but before we discuss Kripke's contribution to this important area of philosophy, we shall first briefly present the orthodox view.

I

The orthodox view is essentially the view of Alfred Tarski (1944, 1956). Tarski argued that any language that accepts the classical laws of logic and is *semantically closed* is inconsistent. By "semantically closed" he meant a language that contains its own truth predicate, that is, a language (such as English) that contains a truth predicate such as 'is true' that applies to the very sentences of that language. While there is some question about exactly what Tarski meant by saying that a language is inconsistent, we may avoid these issues and focus on Tarski's proposal for avoiding this inconsistency. Tarski's solution to the problem of the semantic paradoxes was to offer an account of truth that did not depend on a semantically closed language. Tarski argued that to provide an account of truth for a given language, say L_0, one needed to present that account in a different language: the metalanguage for L_0.

The idea is this. We start with a first-order language L_0 (see PL, Ch. 1.II) that has the usual connectives and operations together with a set of primitive predicates. To talk about the truth (and falsity) of the sentences of L_0, we need a metalanguage L_1 that contains a truth predicate (relation of satisfaction, etc.) that applies to sentences of L_0 but not to sentences of L_1. The same will be true for the sentences of L_1 and hence we shall need a language L_2 to talk about the truths of L_1. A sentence such as (1) will not be well formed since the truth predicate of (say) L_1 only applies to sentences of L_0 and not to sentences of L_1, assuming that (1) is a sentence of L_1. The result is an infinite hierarchy of languages, each one (except the first level) containing a truth predicate for the language at the level below.

Tarski's hierarchy avoids the paradoxes, but at a cost. As Kripke and others mention, it does not appear that English has a hierarchy of truth predicates but rather just the simple predicate 'is true'. It appears that Tarski thought that natural languages were hopeless and we should present a language that is not semantically closed for scientific purposes. Still, some would defend Tarski's account for natural languages. Those who do might claim that our ordinary predicate, 'true', is actually ambiguous between the various truth predicates and the one expressed depends on the context of use. If, for example, one is talking about sentences that do not contain truth predicates, then 'true' means something like 'true of sentences not involving the semantic notion of truth'. If, on the other hand, one is talking about sentences that involve the notion of truth, then one is using 'true' to mean something like 'true of sentences that are a level below this one'.

Kripke pointed out, however, that many of our most ordinary sentences talk about truth without implying any given level of discussion. Kripke asks us to consider the following sentence uttered by John Dean:

(4)   All of Nixon's utterances about Watergate are false.

It is difficult to tell what level of truth we are dealing with, yet it seems as though we can perfectly well understand (4). The situation is even worse if, among the things that Nixon utters about Watergate, is:

(5)   Everything Dean says about Watergate is false.

Dean wishes to include (5) in his assertion and Nixon wishes to include (4) in his. On Tarski's view, this is not possible because this would imply that at least one of the truth predicates is "saying" something about sentences of its own level. Yet, as Kripke argues, we can intuitively assign truth-values to (4) and (5) even if both are viewed as saying something about the other. This seems to be a serious problem of Tarski's view when considered as an account of truth in a natural language. Kripke also claims that there are some mathematical difficulties with extending Tarski's hierarchy to transfinite levels, yet clearly Tarski's hierarchy is intended to include transfinite levels.

So, Kripke offers an alternative formal account of truth based on the idea that sentences such as (1) do not have a truth-value. The reason that they lack a truth-value is that when we try to determine the truth-value of such sentences there does not appear to be any foundation or ground on which to base a truth-value. The problem is not confined to just those sentences that lead to paradox. Consider the following sentence:

(6)   (6) is true.

Sentence (6) is not paradoxical in the sense that (1) is (that is, it is not the case that (6) is true if and only if (6) is false). Still, (6) is problematic. What makes it the case that (6) is true (or false)?

Kripke defines a sentence as *grounded* if the sentence asserts that some (all, most, etc.) sentences of a given kind or class have a certain truth-value and some of these sentences also assert that some other sentences are true and so on, and if this process terminates in sentences that do not mention the concept of truth so that the original sentence's truth can be determined (*OTT*: 694). As the examples of (4) and (5) indicate, whether a given sentence is grounded can depend on certain empirical facts. Sentence (6), however, is clearly ungrounded. What shall we say about these ungrounded sentences? Kripke's idea is that such sentences should lack a truth-value and that there are truth-value gaps in our language. What Kripke did is present a formal framework within which a definition of truth can be presented and the language will contain its own truth predicate.

Kripke describes the intuitive idea behind his formal structure as follows. Suppose we are explaining to someone the use of the word 'true'. He describes how we would explain when to apply that predicate to a given sentence and when to refrain from applying it:

> We may say that we are entitled to assert (or deny) of any sentence that it is true precisely under the circumstances when we can assert (or deny) the sentence itself. Our interlocutor then can understand what it means, say, to attribute truth to ['snow is white'] but he will still be puzzled about attributions of truth to sentences containing the word true. Since he did not understand these initially, it will be equally nonexplanatory, initially, to explain to him that to call such a sentence "true" ("false") is tantamount to asserting (denying) the sentence itself.
>
> (*OTT*: 701)

After our learner applies the predicate to various sentences that do not themselves contain the notion of truth, he will be able to apply 'true' to certain sentences that do contain the predicate. For example, consider the sentence:

(7)   Jim just said something true.

If what Jim just said is "Snow is white" then since our subject is willing to apply the predicate 'true' to 'snow is white', he will, after a moment's reflection, be willing to assert

(8)   (7) is true.

Kripke argues that all grounded sentences will eventually receive a truth-value in such a process, but some sentences will never receive a truth-value. Sentence (6) is an example. At no time during the process will the learner assign 'true' to it. But also the learner will not be able to assert that (6) is not true. This is because the rules state that the learner can deny the truth of a sentence only if he can deny the sentence itself. This results in truth-value gaps. Some sentences, the ungrounded ones, never receive a truth-value. So not every sentence is either true or false; some simply lack any truth-value at all.

   We can present Kripke's idea in a slightly more formal way that may help in understanding Kripke's rich formal structure. The *extension* of a predicate F is the class of items to which F applies and the *anti-extension* is the class of items to which F does not apply. A predicate is *completely defined* if every item is either in the extension or in the anti-extension and is only partially defined if some items are members of neither the extension nor the anti-extension of the predicate. When some of the predicates of a given language are only partially defined, then our definitions of the logical connectives (e.g. negation and disjunction) need to be changed from their classical definitions. Definitions must be changed because if a is neither in the extension nor in the anti-extension of the predicate F, then the sentence 'Fa' is undefined. What shall we say about '$\sim Fa$' and '$Fa \lor Gb$' (where 'Gb' is defined)? One has a number of choices, including S. C. Kleene's strong three-valued logic (1952). On this account, if p is undefined then the negation of p is undefined and a disjunction is true if one disjunct is true; false if both disjuncts are false, and undefined otherwise. A quantified sentence '$\exists x \varphi x$' is true if 'φx' is true for some assignment to x, false if 'φx' is false for all assignments to x, and undefined otherwise. Kripke chose Kleene's strong three-valued logic because although sentences such as (6) are ungrounded, they are not meaningless, so Kripke takes it that the sentence '(6) or $2 + 2 = 4$' is true. We can use this three-valued logic to construct a language that will contain its own truth predicate, but will avoid the paradoxes by containing truth-value gaps. The construction proceeds, intuitively, along the lines of the informal account presented above.

We begin with a classical first-order language L that contains a denumerable list of fully defined predicates (including relational predicates) over a given domain D. We shall assume that L is rich enough to contain sentences about the sentences of L (via some coding scheme *à la* Gödel). We then extend L to $\mathfrak{L}$ by adding a monadic predicate 'T'. So $\mathfrak{L}$ is a language just like L except that $\mathfrak{L}$ contains the uninterpreted predicate 'T'. That is, the syntax and semantics of L is exactly the syntax and semantics of $\mathfrak{L}$ except that $\mathfrak{L}$ contains the predicate 'T'. Because this predicate is not part of the syntax of L, it has no interpretation in the semantics of L and hence it is uninterpreted in $\mathfrak{L}$. By 'uninterpreted', all that is meant is that it has no assignment in the semantics.

Let us now add an interpretation for $\mathfrak{L}$ so that all the predicates of $\mathfrak{L}$ are interpreted. Let $\mathfrak{L}(S_1, S_2)$ be the interpretation of $\mathfrak{L}$ such that all predicates and terms of $\mathfrak{L}$ that are also part of L are interpreted as before (as they were interpreted in the semantics of L). Secondly, S_1 is the extension of T and S_2 is the anti-extension of T. This may result in the fact that T is only partially defined. Let S_1' be the set of true sentences of $\mathfrak{L}(S_1, S_2)$ (in D) and let S_2' be the set of either those items in D not sentences of $\mathfrak{L}(S_1, S_2)$ or those sentences of $\mathfrak{L}(S_1, S_2)$ that are false.

We can then define a hierarchy of interpretations or languages. Let $\mathfrak{L}_0$ be $\mathfrak{L}(\varnothing, \varnothing)$ (where $\varnothing$ is the null set). This is where 'T' is completely undefined having no members in the extension or anti-extension. This corresponds to the learner's first step in using 'true'. Then for any integer α, if $\mathfrak{L}_\alpha = \mathfrak{L}(S_1, S_2)$, then $\mathfrak{L}_{\alpha+1} = \mathfrak{L}(S_1', S_2')$.

Given the definitions, intuitively $\mathfrak{L}_{\alpha+1}$ extends the interpretation of T in $\mathfrak{L}_\alpha$. As we move up the hierarchy, the extension and anti-extension of T increase by adding new members while retaining the previous members. Once a sentence is added to the extension of T in the hierarchy, it remains in the extension at all higher levels. No sentence ever changes its status from true or false to undefined as we move up the hierarchy, although many sentences change from undefined to true or false.

Clearly, the process just described can go on infinitely. Still, as Kripke showed, it is possible to define transfinite limits. For any finite ordinal α, let (S_1^α, S_2^α) be the interpretation of T in $\mathfrak{L}_\alpha$. Define the transfinite limit $\mathfrak{L}_\omega$ to be (S_1^ω, S_2^ω) where S_1^ω is the union of all S_1^α for finite α and S_2^ω is the union of all S_2^α for finite α. For each higher limit ordinal λ, $\mathfrak{L}_\lambda$ can be defined in a similar way.

At some point in the hierarchy we reach a point where the extension and anti-extension of T does not increase in the sense that no new sentences are added from one level to the next. This is a point where $(S_1^\alpha, S_2^\alpha) = (S_1^{\alpha+1}, S_2^{\alpha+1})$. Kripke calls this a *minimal fixed point* (in what follows I shall, following Kripke, refer to both the language and the pair as a fixed point). This result is called Kripke's fixed point theorem. Kripke was the first to show that there was a minimal fixed point. As Kripke notes in his paper, however, Robert Martin and Peter Woodruff (1975) had independently proved the existence of maximal fixed points (in a different framework that is not as general in its application as Kripke's framework).

All fixed points contain their own truth predicates. The differences between the various fixed points concern the way we interpret T. In Kripke's minimal fixed point, the language was constructed from a language where T was completely undefined. Moreover, at each level only those sentences that were determined to be true (false) by the rules (which were limited) would be included in the interpretation of T. Some sentences (such as the formal version of (6)) never received a truth-value and hence would not be included in the extension or anti-extension of T at the minimal fixed point: $\mathcal{L}_\sigma$. Still, we could consistently extend $\mathcal{L}_\sigma$ by adding (the code of the formal version of) (6) to the extension of T. The result would be a language $\mathcal{L}_\sigma'$ that is not constructed by the rules that we used to construct $\mathcal{L}_\sigma$ since those rules left (6) without a truth-value. Still, $\mathcal{L}_\sigma'$ is a fixed point. Alternatively, we could have put (6) in the extension (anti-extension) of T at the very beginning of the hierarchy and proceeded as we did before. The result would be a fixed point where (6) has a truth-value. A maximal fixed point is one such that no proper extension of it is a consistent fixed point. As Kripke notes, maximal fixed points assign truth-values to as many sentences as possible. A sentence such as (6) would have a truth-value in every maximal fixed point even though (6) is ungrounded. Still, the smallest fixed point is, as Kripke notes, the most natural model for the ordinary notion of truth. This is because fixed points, other than the smallest fixed point, involve some arbitrary decision with respect to assignments of truth-value to various sentences. For example, (6) can be assigned either true or false (but not both) . Hence, there is a maximal fixed point where (6) is true and one where (6) is false. Why should one of these maximal fixed points be thought to model the ordinary notion of truth rather than the other?

Kripke points out that some fixed points other than the smallest fixed point have special interest as models of truth. An example of one such point is what Kripke calls the largest *intrinsic* fixed point. An *intrinsic* fixed point is a fixed point that assigns no sentence a truth-value that conflicts with the truth-value of that sentence in any other fixed point. Maximal fixed points are not intrinsic because they will assign some sentence (such as (6)) a truth-value that differs from its assignment at another maximal fixed point. A sentence has an *intrinsic truth-value* if it has a truth-value at some intrinsic fixed point. It can be shown that there is a largest intrinsic fixed point. Such a point has as many non-arbitrary truth assignments to sentences as consistently possible and hence it is a candidate for the model of our ordinary notion of truth.

Although Kripke's theory is presented using Kleene's strong three-value logic, Kripke shows that his results are not dependent on this theory. Alternative schemes for dealing with truth-value gaps can be substituted and the same results achieved provided that the rules for extending the interpretation of the truth predicate up the hierarchy do not allow a sentence to change its truth-value once one has been assigned.

Kripke's solution to the paradoxes is rather different from Tarski's, even though both make use of a hierarchy of languages. In Kripke's hierarchy, unlike Tarski's, the various levels of language leading up to the fixed point are really not that important to the overall goal. They are not intended to model anything related to our natural language; they are simply better and better approximations of the minimal fixed point. It is only when we consider a fixed point that we have a possible model of truth. On Tarski's account, however, each level of language models a level of natural language (to the extent that Tarski's account applies to natural languages at all). Hence, on such an account a natural language such as English is not really a single language at all. Instead it is an infinite hierarchy of languages, each of which contains a truth predicate for the language at the level below (except, of course, the first-order language, which does not contain a truth predicate at all). On Kripke's account, a natural language is a single language that contains it own truth predicate together with truth-value gaps. Moreover, Kripke's hierarchy involves a single truth predicate (if it really makes sense to identify predicates that have distinct interpretations) increasing in its interpretation. Tarski's heirarchy, on the other hand, involves an infinite number of distinct predicates (these are the subscripted predicates).

Kripke is cautious about the conclusions one can draw from his formal account. He explicitly says "I do not regard any proposal, including the one to be advanced here, as definitive in the sense that it gives *the* interpretation of the ordinary use of 'true', or *the* solution to the semantic paradoxes" (*OTT*: 699). For some alternatives to Kripke's account (some based on Kripke's results) the reader should review Burge (1979a), Gupta (1982), Herzberger (1982) and McGee (1991). Still, Kripke's view has substantially advanced our understanding both of the concept of truth for formal languages and the concept of truth for natural languages. One of the important points in Kripke's theory is the idea that truth (falsity) is basically a property of grounded sentences and the paradoxes arise because we attempt to apply the truth predicate to ungrounded sentences. As noted above, not every instance of applying truth to an ungrounded sentence leads to paradox, but many such applications seem completely arbitrary even when no paradox results from such an application of the truth predicate. Also, Kripke's account of groundedness helps explain why the empirical facts can play a role in whether a given sentence leads to paradox. There is nothing intrinsic in the fact that sentence (2) leads to paradox. If sentence (3) had been 'Snow is white', sentence (2) would not be paradoxical. This is because (2) would then have been grounded and hence an application of the truth predicate would not cause problems. As it is, (2) is ungrounded and this provides a partial account of why it lacks any clear truth-value.

II

Although Kripke's account of truth has expanded our understanding of truth predicates for formal and natural languages, it does not provide a complete account of truth; nor does it provide a complete account of the semantic paradoxes. Some have criticized Kripke's view on the grounds that it does not solve what has been called the *strengthened liar paradox*. The strengthened liar paradox is a version of the liar paradox presented above (see sentence (1)) that is designed to apply to theories, like Kripke's, that reject bivalence.

On Kripke's view, there are truth-value gaps: some sentences (such as (6) above) are neither assigned true nor are they assigned false in the smallest fixed point. Yet this fact seems to lead to another paradox. Consider the following sentence:

(9)   (9) is not true.

Sentence (9) appears to be an ungrounded sentence and hence is not in the extension of the truth predicate; nor is it in the anti-extension at the smallest fixed point. Since (9) is not in the extension of the truth predicate it seems to follow that it is not the case that (9) is true or (9) is not true. But if (9) is *not* true then what (9) says is true (namely that it is not true) and hence it is true. And if it *is* true then what it says is the case and hence it is not true. So, (9) is true if and only if it is not true; in other words, it is paradoxical. It appears to involve the very sort of paradox that Kripke's theory was designed to avoid. Moreover, (9) is paradoxical even though we have given up the assumption that every sentence is true or false.

Whether Kripke's view is susceptible to the strengthened liar paradox seems to depend on the interpretation of Kripke's truth-value gaps. According to Kripke, certain sentences, such as (6), lack a truth-value because they fail to express propositions:

> Under the influence of Strawson, we can regard a sentence as an attempt to make a statement, express a proposition, or the like. The meaningfulness or well-formedness of the sentence lies in the fact that there are specifiable circumstances under which it has determinate truth conditions (expresses a proposition), not that it always does express a proposition. A sentence such as (1) [Most (i.e. a majority) of Nixon's assertions about Watergate are false] is always *meaningful*, but under various circumstances it may not "make a statement" or "express a proposition." *(OTT*: 699)

Yet, as Soames (1999) has pointed out, it is odd to think that when he utters the sentence "Most of Nixon's assertions about Watergate are false" Jones fails to express a proposition simply because one of Nixon's assertions is that everything Jones says about Watergate is true (and that Nixon's other assertions about Watergate are evenly balanced). Strawson's idea that certain sentences fail to express propositions was based on the failure of reference for singular terms in the indicated sentence. For example, consider the sentence 'This ball is red' when no object is being demonstrated. In such a case, it is reasonable to hold that the sentence does not express a proposition. Yet nothing like this is going on in the liar paradox sentences or in examples like Kripke's (1). Soames (1999: 195) also argues that Kripke's choice of strong Kleene truth-tables is at odds with the idea that the truth-value gaps are a result of the fact that certain sentences fail to express propositions. According to strong Kleene, an undefined sentence (such as (6)) disjoined with a true sentence is true (e.g. '(6) or 2 + 2 = 4' is true), yet if (6) really fails to express a proposition, such disjunctions should also fail to express propositions and hence fail to have a truth-value.

The fact that many sentences that lead to paradox seem to express propositions, the fact that Kripke uses strong Kleene, the fact that Kripke rejects the idea that 'undefined' represents a third truth-value (see *OTT*: 700, n.18), and other items, leads Soames to a different interpretation of Kripke's truth-value gaps than Kripke explicitly claims.

According to Soames (who credits Salmon with suggesting the initial idea of this interpretation of Kripke), the truth-value gaps in Kripke's system do not arise because some sentences fail to express propositions, but rather because some predicates may be only partially defined. The idea is this. Suppose we define the predicate F as follows: *x has F* just in case *x* has G and H and *x does not have F* just in case *x* has E and I. At the time of our definition we may think that everything either has G and H or has E and I (but not both). We later discover something *y* that has G and E. (Perhaps our early attempts at defining 'is an animal' is an example.) Since *y* does not have E and I we cannot correctly say that *y* does not have F, nor can we correctly say that *y* has F (since *y* does not have G and H). It turns out that the extension and anti-extension of our predicate F is not exhaustive; there are some things that are members of neither the extension nor the anti-extension.

In such a case we need to consider what we can say about the claim:

(10)   *y* has F.

Is it true or not? If we assign truth to a sentence based on the idea that we can affirm that sentence, then we cannot assign truth to (10). Can we then perhaps assign it as not true? Not if we understand the claim that '*y* has F' is not true just in case *y* does not have F. As we pointed out above, *y* is not a member of the anti-extension of F and hence we cannot correctly assert that *y* does not have F. Thus, (10) is truly undefined and we can say neither that it is true nor that it is not true. If Kripke's truth predicate is like F, then (9) does not lead to a paradox. For (9) will be undefined with respect to that predicate and hence we can say neither that it is true nor that it is not true. So, if Kripke's gaps arise as a result of the fact that the truth predicates are only partially defined as is the case for F, he can avoid the strengthened liar paradox.

Still, it is clear that there is something that we wish to say about liar sentences that we are unable to say in the fixed point language. McGee describes the problem as follows:

> The fundamental thesis motivating Kripke's theory, that the liar sentence λ is neither true nor false, can be represented by a sentence of $\mathcal{L}^+$, namely
>
> $$\sim(Tr(\lceil\lambda\rceil) \vee Tr(\lceil\sim\lambda\rceil)).$$
>
> But this fundamental thesis of Kripke's theory is itself, according to Kripke's theory, semantically defective and so untrue.
>
> (1991: 90)

Kripke knew that he could not truly express many of his basic insights in the language he constructed:

> there are assertions we can make about the object language which we cannot make in the object language. For example, Liar sentences are *not true* in the object language, in the sense that the inductive process never makes them true; but we are precluded from saying this in the object language by our interpretation of negation and the truth predicate. If we think of the minimal fixed point, say, under Kleene valuation, as giving a model of natural language, that a Liar sentence is not true must be thought of as associated with some later stage in the development of natural language, one in which speakers reflect on the generation process leading to the minimal fixed point. It is not itself a part of the process. The necessity to ascend to a metalanguage may be one of the weaknesses of the present theory. The ghost of the Tarski hierarchy is still with us.
>
> (*OTT*: 714)

Thus, Kripke's response to an objection such as McGee's is to remark that there are some insights that can only be expressed in the metalanguage and not in the object language. This is, of course, to weaken somewhat the results that Kripke obtained. But Kripke never thought that he was presenting a "universal language" and he provides us with some deep insights into the nature of truth as it occurs in a natural language.

Chapter 7

Wittgenstein and meaning

One of the features of Kripke's philosophical preoccupations that can be seen in much of his work is his interest in puzzles and paradoxes. We find him commenting on the paradox of identity, the puzzle of belief, the paradox of the liar, the surprise exam paradox (unpublished) and so on. So it is perhaps not too surprising that in 1982 Kripke published in book form his commentary on Wittgenstein's famous private language argument. *Wittgenstein on Rules and Private Language: An Elementary Exposition* presents a skeptical paradox and a "skeptical solution" based on Kripke's reading of Wittgenstein's *Philosophical Investigations*. Like all of Kripke's work, it has produced a wide range of responses. It is, however, different in certain respects from his other work.

First of all, Kripke explicitly states that the arguments and positions that he presents in this book are not to be taken as his views. He says "It deserves emphasis that I do not in this piece of writing attempt to speak for myself, or, except in occasional and minor asides, to say anything about my own views on the substantive issues" (*WRPL*: ix). Because Kripke explicitly denies offering his own views in this essay, it would be natural to assume that his goal is to provide a correct historical account of Wittgenstein's views. It is not clear, however, that Kripke is claiming to provide us with a piece of Wittgensteinian scholarship:

> In the following, I am largely trying to present Wittgenstein's argument, or more accurately, that set of problems and arguments which I personally have gotten out of reading Wittgenstein ... So the present paper should be thought of as expounding neither 'Wittgenstein's argument nor Kripke's':

rather Wittgenstein's argument as it struck Kripke, as it presented a problem for him. (*WRPL*: 5)

Thus, the primary goal is not historical exegesis but, as Kripke says
in the preface, "The primary purpose of this work is the presentation
of a problem and an argument, not its critical evaluation" (*WRPL*: ix).

I

The problem that Kripke presents is one that he finds in §201 of the
Philosophical Investigations, in which Wittgenstein says: "this was
our paradox: no course of action could be determined by a rule,
because every course of action can be made out to accord with the
rule". This is puzzling, if true, because what we mean by our sentences and words is clearly rule related. That I mean x by α is related
to the rules that govern my use of the term α. If those rules do not
determine a specific meaning for the term α, then it may turn out
that there is no fact that I mean x by α and hence no fact that I mean
anything at all by α. The conclusion that is drawn from the skeptical
argument is that there are no facts about meaning. This is, of course,
a radical conclusion because, if true, then it appears that we are
unable to state it. Kripke presents the argument that leads to such a
radical result by first considering what one means on a particular
occasion when using the term 'plus'.

We all, at some time in our lives, have had to produce the sum of
two (or more) numbers. We do this, we suppose, by grasping the
mathematical function of addition (a rule concerning numbers) and
applying that function to the arguments or numbers that we are
given. Of course, we have not done all possible additions so let us
suppose that '68 + 57' is one problem that I have not done. Suppose I
encounter a bizarre skeptic who asks me "What is 68 plus 57?" I do a
quick calculation and answer '125'. But the skeptic says that given
my *past use* of the term 'plus' the correct answer should be 5. Of
course, I disagree with her, but how am I to prove to the skeptic that
the correct answer is '125' and not '5'?

As I slowly start to go over my work in reaching my conclusion that
the answer is '125', the skeptic stops me and says that she does not
doubt that '125' is the sum of 68 and 57; the problem she has is with
my current choice of that particular function to answer her question.
Why pick addition as the function to use in answer to the question
"What is 68 plus 57?"

Naturally, I answer by saying that 'plus' means addition, but the skeptic is not convinced. The skeptic points out that there is another function called 'quaddition' that is like addition in that it gives the same answer that addition gives for all pairs of numbers that I have considered in the past, and yields the answer '5' to all other pairs. I respond by saying that while the skeptic may have meant quaddition by 'plus', I mean and have always meant addition. But the skeptic asks me what is it about my past usage, mental states or whatever that determines that I meant addition by 'plus' and not quaddition? Kripke describes the situation as follows:

> The basic point is this. Ordinarily, I suppose that, in computing '68 + 57' as I do, I do not simply make an unjustified leap in the dark. I follow directions I previously gave myself that uniquely determine that in this new instance I should say '125'. What are these directions? By hypothesis, I never explicitly told myself that I should say '125' in this very instance. Nor can I say that I should simply 'do the same thing I always did,' if this means 'compute according to the rule exhibited by my previous examples.' That rule could just as well have been the rule for quaddition (the quus function) as for addition. (*WRPL*: 11)

Kripke considers a range of possible answers that one might give to the skeptic, but finds that each answer is lacking in some essential aspect.

First, we cannot simply point to my past calculations. No collection of finite calculations can, by itself, show that it was addition and not quaddition that I applied in the various cases (since the results of all actual cases are the same for both functions). One might argue that it is what I *would* do or say in various cases that distinguishes my using addition from quaddition. The idea is this: even though I had not yet (we have been assuming) encountered the particular problem '68 + 57', I was disposed to answer '125' (as I in fact did) if asked. Hence, what determines that I meant addition by 'plus' in the past is that I would have given the sum of any two numbers n and m if I had been asked "What is n plus m?"

Kripke raises three objections to this dispositional view. First, my dispositions, like my actual calculations, are finite. There are numbers that are so large that I am not disposed to give their sum. As Kripke says, "When given such sums, I may shrug my shoulders for lack of comprehension; I may even, if the numbers involved are large enough, die of old age before the questioner completes his question" (*WRPL*: 27).

Saul Kripke

The second objection to this answer to the skeptic is that I am disposed (sometimes) to make a mistake when adding large numbers. Yet, if I am disposed to make a mistake when adding *n* and *m*, then the function distinguished by my dispositions will not turn out, after all, to be addition. Hence, my dispositions do not assure me that I mean addition by 'plus'. That is, my dispositions together with my actual answers in the past do not determine that the function I was using in the past is addition. Finally, there is the problem of correctness. Kripke describes the problem thus:

> The dispositionalist gives a *descriptive* account of this relation: if '+' meant addition then I will answer '125'. But this is not the proper account of the relation, which is *normative*, not descriptive. The point is *not* that, if I meant addition by '+', I *will* answer '125', but that, if I intend to accord with my past meaning of '+', I *should* answer '125'. (*WRPL*: 37)

But how can a dispositional account of meaning include the normative aspect of meaning? A dispositional account offers what we are disposed to do under certain circumstances, not what we *ought* to do. Yet, the fact that I am disposed to answer '125' to the question 'What is 68 plus 57?' does not imply that '125' is the *correct* answer. It is the correct answer only if addition is the function I mean by 'plus'. But we are trying to use my dispositions to establish this very fact: that it is addition I meant by 'plus'.

Kripke makes it clear that the puzzle about meaning that he is presenting is not essentially an epistemological problem. That is, the puzzle is not how we can *know* that we mean addition by 'plus' and not quaddition, but rather whether there is any *fact* of the matter. The skeptic says that even given all the facts about one's past usage and one's mental states, including one's intentions, no determinate fact results that I meant addition instead of quaddition. We may assume that we have complete knowledge of all the relevant facts. Still, the skeptic argues that these facts will not result in the view that the correct answer for me to the question 'What is 68 plus 57?' is '125'.

Why not simply say that it is a brute fact that I mean and have always meant addition by 'plus'? Perhaps the skeptic is right in thinking that the fact that I have meant addition by 'plus' is not to be explained in terms of or reduced to other facts about me. Still, there is a primitive fact that I have meant addition by 'plus'. One way to understand this response to the skeptic is to view meaning addition (by 'plus') as on a par with (say) being in pain. There is an inner state that I am in when I am in pain and while this state cannot be explained or reduced to other states, I know it when I am in that state. Similarly, there is a state of meaning addition (by 'plus') that cannot be reduced or explained in terms of other states and I know it when I am in that state. But the skeptic (through Kripke) argues that such a state cannot do the job it is intended to do:

> Well, suppose I do in fact feel a certain headache with a very special quality whenever I think of the '+' sign. How on earth would this headache help me figure out whether I ought to answer '125' or '5' when asked about '68 + 57'? If I think the headache indicates that I ought to say '125', would there be anything about it to refute a sceptic's contention that, on the contrary, it indicates that I should say '5'?   (*WRPL*: 41–2)

The idea here is that even if there is a special mental state associated with my use of the term 'plus', there is no way to determine that the special state is associated with addition as opposed to quaddition because these functions agree on all my past usages of 'plus'.

Kripke concludes his discussion of the skeptical problem with the following consideration:

> Perhaps we may try to recoup, by arguing that meaning addition by 'plus' is a state even more *sui generis* than we have argued. Perhaps it is simply a primitive state, not to be assimilated to sensations or headaches or any 'qualitative' states, nor to be assimilated to dispositions, but a state of a unique kind of its own.
>
> Such a move may in a sense be irrefutable, and taken in an appropriate way Wittgenstein may even accept it. But it seems desperate: it leaves the nature of this postulated primitive state – the primitive state of 'meaning addition by "plus"' – completely mysterious.   (*WRPL*: 51)

The suggestion is that we can refute the skeptic only by positing a primitive state that is, in Kripke's phrase, "completely mysterious". Yet somehow it is a state that we know we are in whenever we are in it, even though it is not a qualitative state. How is this even possible?

If there is no fact of the matter that I meant addition by 'plus', then it seems to follow that it is not the case that I meant addition as opposed to quaddition (or an infinite number of other functions). However, there is no fact of the matter that I meant quaddition (or any function whatsoever). So it seems to follow that there is no fact of the matter that I meant anything at all by 'plus'. But the same argument presented for the conclusion that there is no fact of the matter that I meant anything at all by 'plus' can be applied to any term I use. Hence, it appears that there is no fact of the matter that I meant anything at all by any term. This conclusion applies to any current use of any term, and hence we can draw the radical conclusion that we do not mean anything by any of our words or sentences.

Kripke claims that in addition to presenting a skeptical argument, Wittgenstein presents a *skeptical solution*. A skeptical solution to a skeptical argument is to be distinguished from a *straight* solution. A skeptical solution is one that *accepts* the skeptical argument in question, but claims that the conclusions that can be drawn from that argument are not what the skeptic thinks they are. Kripke offers Hume's problems on induction as a historical example of a skeptical problem and solution that one can compare with the problem and solution offered by Wittgenstein. Kripke often compares Hume's skepticism to Wittgenstein's in *Wittgenstein on Rules and Private Language*, but a detailed comparison of the two philosophers will take us too far afield. A rather simple example can illustrate the idea that Kripke has in mind. Suppose a skeptic argues that one cannot be certain that there is an external world. A skeptical solution would admit that we are not *certain* that there is an external world, but certainty is not required for us to have knowledge of an external world. This is a skeptical solution because the solution grants the skeptic the conclusion of the skeptical argument; namely, that we are not certain that there is an external world. But it is a solution because it denies the main goal of the skeptic; namely, to get us to doubt that we have knowledge of the external world. A straight solution, on the other hand, denies that the skeptical argument is sound. One of the premises in the argument is false or the inference that is used in the argument is invalid, and thus it rejects the skeptical conclusion that we are not certain that there is an external world.

So how does this distinction apply in the present case? The skeptical argument concludes that there is no fact of the matter that I meant addition (as opposed to quaddition) by 'plus'. Thus a skeptical solution to the skeptical argument is one that accepts this conclusion, but denies the general goal of the skeptic that I do not mean anything by any term. This is, in effect, what Kripke claims Wittgenstein does. It may seem impossible to accept the conclusion that there is no fact of the matter that I meant addition by 'plus' while at the same time rejecting the idea that I do not mean anything by my use of language:

> Wittgenstein holds, with the skeptic, that there is no fact as to whether I mean plus or quus. But if this is to be conceded to the skeptic, is this not the end of the matter? What *can* be said on behalf of our ordinary attributions of meaningful language to ourselves and to others? Has not the incredible and self-defeating conclusion, that all language is meaningless, already been drawn?   (*WRPL*: 70–71)

The answer to this problem can be found, according to Kripke, by considering what Wittgenstein meant by a "fact about meaning". There is some room to wiggle between the *facts* of meaning and whether we mean anything by our use of language, but we must be careful not to confuse some general notion of *fact* with the notion of *meaning fact* that is at issue here. In some general sense, if we do ordinarily mean addition by 'plus', then it is a fact that we do so. Thus in this sense, the claim that there are no meaning facts conflicts with the claim that I ordinarily mean addition by 'plus'. But, according to Kripke, this is not what Wittgenstein's solution claims:

> We do not wish to doubt or deny that when people speak of themselves and others as meaning something by their words, as following rules, they do so with perfect right. We do not even wish to deny the propriety of an ordinary use of the phrase 'the fact that Jones meant addition by such-and-such a symbol', and indeed such expressions do have perfectly ordinary uses. We merely wish to deny the existence of the 'superlative fact' that philosophers misleadingly attach to such ordinary forms of words, not the propriety of the forms of words themselves.
>
>   (*WRPL*: 69)

It is the philosopher's superlative fact that the skeptical argument is designed to call into question. Thus, it is claimed that the skeptical argument shows that there are no "philosophical superlative" meaning facts. But what exactly are these superlative facts that it is claimed the skeptical argument is attacking?

The answer comes in Wittgenstein's own early account of meaning. This view is characterized by Kripke as follows:

> To each sentence there corresponds a (possible) fact. If such a fact, obtains, the sentence is true; if not, false. For atomic

> sentences, the relation between a sentence and the fact it alleges is one of a simple correspondence or isomorphism. The sentence contains names, corresponding to objects. An atomic sentence is itself a fact, putting the names in a certain relation; and it says that (there is a corresponding fact that) the corresponding objects are in the same relation. Other sentences are (finite or infinite) truth-functions of these ... a declarative sentence gets its meaning by virtue of its *truth conditions*, by virtue of its correspondence to facts that must obtain if it is true.   (*WRPL*: 71–2)

The superlative facts that are called into question are the supposed interpretation rules in the form of truth-conditions that are supposed to provide the meaning of our expressions. It is these *meaning rules* that the skeptical argument calls into question. The skeptical argument then is designed to show that the meaning of an expression like 'plus' cannot be determined by some rule of interpretation based on the truth-conditions of sentences. Any "meaning" can be found to accord with such a rule (addition or quaddition for example) and hence there can be no such meaning facts.

It is natural to ask: "If there are no such meaning facts, how can there be any meaning at all?" This is where the skeptical solution enters. According to Kripke, Wittgenstein accepts the conclusion that there can be no such meaning facts of the sort described by his earlier self (hence there is a certain irony in Kripke questioning what we meant in the past in the skeptical argument). Nonetheless, we still can mean what we ordinarily mean:

> Wittgenstein replaces the question, "What must be the case for this sentence to be true?" by two others: first, "Under what conditions may this form of words be appropriately asserted (or denied)?"; second, given an answer to the first question, "What is the role, and the utility, in our lives of our practice of asserting (or denying) the form of words under these conditions?" ... [for the case of declarative sentences] we can say that Wittgenstein proposes a picture of language based, not on *truth conditions*, but on *assertability conditions* or *justification conditions*: under what circumstance are we allowed to make a given assertion?   (*WRPL*: 73–4)

The meaning of a sentence is not to be associated with some truth-condition associated with the sentence for, strictly speaking, sentences are not true or false in *that sense*. Rather meaning (in the ordinary sense of meaning) is to be found in our acceptance and rejection of certain statements in certain circumstances. Hence, one who says '5' in response to our question "What is 57 plus 68?" has said something that is unacceptable or incorrect, while one who says '125' has said something correct. That is, we agree (or most of us do at any rate) that '125' is the right thing to say in the circumstance in question (i.e. the circumstance of the question "What is 57 plus 68?") and '5' is the incorrect thing to say.

Kripke has the following to say about these assertability conditions that replace the standard truth-conditions:

> we must consider how we actually use: (i) the categorical assertion that an individual is following a given rule (that he means addition by 'plus'); (ii) the conditional assertion that "if an individual follows such-and-such a rule, he must do so-and-so on a given occasion" (e.g., "if he means addition by '+', his answer to '68+57' should be '125'") ... When the community accepts a particular conditional (ii), it accepts its contraposed form: the failure of an individual to come up with the particular responses the community regards as right leads the community to suppose that he is not following the rule. On the other hand, if an individual passes enough tests, the community (endorsing assertions of the form (i)) accepts him as a rule follower, thus enabling him to engage in certain types of interactions with them that depend on their reliance on his responses. Note that this solution explains how the assertions in (i) and (ii) are introduced into language; it does not give conditions for these statements to be true ... The success of the practices [above] depends on the brute empirical fact that we agree with each other in our responses. (*WRPL*: 108–9)

We are individually inclined to respond in certain ways in certain circumstances. It turns out as a matter of course that many of us are inclined to respond in the same way in similar circumstances. Those who do not agree with the majority are "corrected" and hence learn to respond with the rest of us. So if the majority agrees that '125' is the "correct" response – that is, they say it is the correct response – then it is the correct response. Note this is not to say that it is true that 68 plus 57 is 125 if everyone says that it is true. As Kripke points out, this would be a kind of community version of the dispositional view discussed above and would suffer from similar objections. Simply because everyone thinks that it is true, it does not follow that it is true (in the sense of representing or designating a fact). Remember, Kripke holds that Wittgenstein accepts the conclusion that there is no fact of the matter that someone meant addition by 'plus'. All we can say is that the person meant what we meant and we meant addition by 'plus' because the person agrees with our *use* of the word. What determines that we meant addition by 'plus'? We use the words 'addition' and 'plus' in such and such ways, and that is all there is to it. That is what it means (or at any rate the most it can mean) to say that we mean addition by 'plus'. If you look for some other form of meaning (so Kripke's Wittgenstein claims) you will land yourself in the radical position of concluding that you cannot mean anything by what you say, because you will have to face the skeptical argument.

II

We can roughly separate two distinct lines of commentary on Kripke's presentation of Wittgenstein. One concerns the accuracy of Kripke's account of Wittgenstein; the other concerns the force of the skeptical argument and/or the correctness of the skeptical solution, regardless of whether Wittgenstein actually held the positions that Kripke attributes to him. To discuss the accuracy of Kripke's interpretation would take us beyond our main purpose in describing Kripke's philosophy and his contributions to a detailed discussion of Wittgenstein's philosophy. For various reasons there is considerable disagreement about how to interpret Wittgenstein and there is disagreement over whether Kripke's interpretation is accurate. Kripke's presentation of Wittgenstein has, in any case, re-energized those interested in the interpretation of Wittgenstein.

What about the skeptical argument and the skeptical solution? Kripke has presented a puzzle, regardless of whether that puzzle was exactly the one Wittgenstein had in mind. And he offers us a solution to that puzzle to consider, again whether Wittgenstein would have endorsed that solution or not.

Kripke's skeptical argument may seem clear, but there have been a large number of different responses to it. One of the most common responses to the skeptical argument is to propose a straight solution to the argument. There is, however, some disagreement over the exact nature of that solution. Some argue that the skeptical arguments against the dispositional view fail (see, for example, Ginet

(1992), and Martin & Heil (1998)) and hence the solution to the skeptical argument is the dispositional view. Others, Colin McGinn (1984), for example, argue that there are facts that determine meaning that the skeptic has not considered; still others that meaning facts are basic or primitive and are not determined by other facts (see Feldman (1985), Soames (1998a,b) and D. Lewis (1999)).

Given the detailed objections that Kripke offers, it is hard to see how a dispositional account can avoid the objections. For example, one of the objections raised by the skeptic is that when we consider someone's actual dispositions to use 'plus' we find that people are disposed to make mistakes and, hence, Jones may be disposed to answer "126" when asked "What is 57 plus 68?" It seems to follow on the dispositional account that Jones does not mean addition by 'plus'. In response to this objection, Martin and Heil (1998) argue that the fact that x has a disposition to do A in c does not imply that x does A in c because other factors may interfere. So the fact that Jones is disposed to respond by saying "126" instead of "125" (in answer to our question) does not mean that Jones does not mean addition by 'plus':

> Don, for instance, in acquiring the plus rule, has acquired a disposition of a particular sort. (We leave aside, for the moment, the character of this disposition.) But his having acquired, and continuing to possess, the disposition does not mean that Don will manifest it on every occasion in which its manifestation is called for. Don's overall dispositional state could be such that, on particular occasions, the manifestation of the disposition constituting his possession of the plus rule is blocked or inhibited. (Martin & Heil 1998: 291)

In one sense what Martin and Heil say is correct, but what they say has a certain presupposition; namely, that Don's disposition is the disposition that constitutes the plus rule. If we do not describe Don's dispositions in semantical terms but in purely behavioural or physical terms, what determines that a particular disposition of Don's is the disposition that constitutes meaning addition by 'plus'? It is true that having dispositions to do something does not entail that you do it in every circumstance that it is called for. But the problem of error that Kripke identifies for the dispositional account cannot be avoided simply by pointing this out. The problem is connecting particular dispositions to particular rules. Or to put the point another way, what is it about this particular disposition that makes having it constitute meaning addition by 'plus'? Couldn't another person have that very same disposition and not mean addition by 'plus'? Certainly it seems possible for two agents to be disposed to act in exactly the same way and yet mean different things by a given term if their patterns of error and correctness just happen to fit. So it seems possible that they do have the same disposition.

One might argue that two agents are not acting in the same way or cannot have the *same* disposition if they mean different things by a given term, even if it appears that they are acting in the same way. This may be correct but it is based on the idea that the reason why the agents are not acting alike is due to the fact that one of them means (say) φ by the term in question and the other means something different. Hence, the distinction in action–disposition is based on a distinction in meaning and not the other way around. This is no help for the dispositional view since that view was to provide an account of meaning in terms of dispositions.

McGinn claims that Kripke's skeptical argument fails in its conclusion because "we can point to other sorts of facts which will do what those Kripke considers admittedly fail to do" (1984: 141). What sort of facts does he have in mind? He suggests that we can account for the fact that Jones meant addition by his use of 'plus' by considering Jones's *capacities*:

> In Kripke's favourite example, the suggestion would be that it is the concept of *addition* that I exercise when I do computations involving '+', and not the concept of *quaddition*, because the capacity that gets brought to bear is the capacity *to add* and not *to quadd*, where the former capacity is conceived as a capacity to recognize what is the *sum* of pairs of numbers ... to mean addition by '+' is to associate with '+' the capacity to add, i.e. to exercise *that* capacity in response to questions involving '+' ...
> (1984: 169–70)

McGinn's idea seems to be this: what determines that Jones meant addition by 'plus' is that when he used 'plus' (or responded to questions containing 'plus') he brought a certain capacity to bear and when he exercises that capacity it follows that he means addition.

We need to be a bit careful in considering McGinn's response to the skeptical argument. Suppose I were to offer the following "solution" to the skeptical argument: what determines that Jones meant addition by 'plus' is that he *is disposed* to add when he uses 'plus'. Naturally, Kripke's skeptic might reply by asking, "What determines that Jones's *disposition* is a disposition to add as opposed to quadd?" And suppose we answer that it is simply a brute fact about Jones that he is disposed to add. It cannot be reduced or explained in terms of other facts. Jones *just is* disposed to add in such cases. Of course, having such a disposition, as noted above, does not mean that one does not make mistakes or that one always acts according to the disposition. Is this a solution to the skeptical argument?

Well, the skeptic questions whether there is any fact of the matter that Jones meant addition by 'plus' given that all Jones's past uses of the term 'plus' are consistent with Jones's meaning quaddition by 'plus'. It does not seem like much of an answer to the skeptic to simply claim that Jones was disposed to add rather than quadd when he used 'plus' or to claim that when using 'plus' Jones brought the capacity to add to bear rather than the capacity to quadd. The reason why it does not seem like much of an answer is that, in effect, the skeptic questions whether one can distinguish Jones's dispositions or capacities in this case. Or to put it another way, what fact determines that Jones was disposed to *add* as opposed to *quadd* or brought the capacity to add to bear as oppose to quadd when using 'plus' in the past? Admittedly, this is not exactly the same question as what fact determines that Jones meant addition (as opposed to quaddition) when using 'plus' in the past, but they are very close. This form of answer appears to be a version of the view that meaning facts really are just brute facts and are not themselves determined by other facts.

McGinn is aware that someone might respond to his suggestion to use *capacities* as indicated above: "I think it is clear that this protest is misplaced: it can be prompted only by an unargued reductionism about the notion of *capacity* – a reluctance to accept that capacities might be factual just as they stand" (1984: 174). In a footnote to that passage, McGinn adds the following: "Capacities are, of course, distinguished (individuated) by what they are capacities *to do*; so there is no particular difficulty in saying what a difference of capacity consists in" (*ibid.*: 174, n.47). But everything that McGinn says with respect to capacities can just as well apply to dispositions. Dispositions are also individuated by what they are dispositions to do and they may be basic as well. In this respect anyway there is not much difference between dispositions and capacities. But even if we grant McGinn that capacities are, in some sense, basic – that is, the notion of a capacity to do something is not to be reduced or explained in terms of other facts (such as counterfactual conditionals) – there remains the question of which capacity Jones brings to bear when using the expression 'plus'. We may assume that Jones has the capacity to add and the capacity to quadd. But what determines which capacity Jones brought to bear in the past when using 'plus'? It is not as though we can determine which capacity Jones used in the past by looking at the answers he gave since they are consistent with his exercising either capacity. Nor is it the case that the capacity to add has a certain felt quality distinct from the capacity to quadd. So what is it about Jones that determines that it is the capacity to add and not to quadd that he brought to bear in the past? The answer that McGinn offers, as far as I can tell, is that it is just a brute fact about Jones that he brings the capacity to add to bear when using 'plus' and not the capacity to quadd. One might as well say that it is just a brute fact that Jones meant addition when using 'plus' in the past. It is not a fact that is determined by other facts about Jones (a point that McGinn also mentions).

A number of philosophers have responded to the skeptical argument by claiming that the skeptic rules out certain facts about meaning when asking what fact determines that Jones meant addition by 'plus'. Indeed, Soames (1998a,b) argues that the skeptical argument is based on an equivocation on this very point. Soames presents the skeptical argument as follows:

P1. If in the past it was a fact that I meant addition by '+', then either:

(i) this fact was determined by non-intentional facts of the following sorts: ...

or

(ii) the fact that I meant addition by '+' was a primitive fact; that is, a fact not determined by non-intentional facts.

P2. It is not the case that non-intentional facts of type (i) determined that I meant addition by '+'.

P3. It is not the case that the fact that I meant addition by '+' was a primitive fact.

C1. Therefore, in the past there was no fact that I meant addition by '+'. (1998a: 314)

The ellipsis is to be filled in by the various accounts offered, such as the dispositional account. The problem with the argument, according to Soames, is that there is an equivocation in the argument with respect to the use of the term 'determines'. It is because there are two senses of that term in play in the argument that the argument seems plausible. One sense of the term is the sense of 'deducible'. To say that fact X determines Y is to say that one can deduce Y from X. In the case at hand, to say that the fact that I meant addition by 'plus' is determined by non-intentional (non-meaning) facts is to say that we can deduce the fact that I meant addition by 'plus' from the non-intentional facts about me. Soames agrees with the skeptic that we cannot provide a deduction from the non-intentional facts to facts about meaning, and hence P2 is true in this sense of 'determines'. But the fact that we cannot provide such a deduction should not lead us to believe that I did not mean addition by 'plus'.

The other sense of 'determines' is the sense of 'entails' or 'is a necessary consequence of'. In this sense, to say that I meant addition by 'plus' is determined by the non-intentional facts is to say that those facts entail that I meant addition by 'plus'. Hence, on this view there is no possible world where the facts about me in the past are as the actual facts about me and I not mean addition by 'plus'. Soames thinks that this is clearly true. He says:

> Is there a possible world in which someone conforms to all those facts – precisely the facts that characterize me in the actual world – and yet that person does not mean anything by '+'?
>
> I think not. Given my conviction that in the past I did mean addition by '+', and given also my conviction that if there are intentional facts, then they don't float free of everything else, I am confident that there is no such world. Although I cannot identify the smallest set of nonintentional facts about me in the actual world on which meaning facts supervene, I am confident that they do supervene.   (1998b: 229)

Soames comments that the skeptic will not be happy with this response since the skeptic does not assume that I did mean addition by my use of 'plus' in the past. The skeptic wants us to prove that we meant addition by 'plus'. In effect, a demonstration is required. But this we have already granted we cannot do. Still, the sense in which it is true that meaning facts are *not* primitive facts is only the sense in which such facts supervene on non-meaning facts and not the sense in which I can demonstrate (in the sense of providing a proof) that I meant addition by 'plus'. Hence, the sense in which P3 (above) is true is the sense in which P2 is false and vice versa. This is because, according to Soames, there are two notions of determination at work in the argument.

There is a lot to be said for Soames's response to the skeptical argument and I certainly agree with him that it seems obvious that meaning facts do supervene on non-meaning facts even though we cannot demonstrate this. But I am not certain that Soames's response constitutes a complete response to the problem that Kripke's skeptic raises. If one is going to claim, as Soames does, that the meaning facts supervene on the non-meaning facts, then even if one cannot provide a demonstration of how the supervenience goes, it does seem that one ought to provide a rough account of how it works. After all, the skeptic doubts that any such account can be provided and it is not clear that simply insisting that some account must work really avoids the problem. That is, suppose we use 'determines' to mean 'entails' in the above argument throughout. In such a case Soames grants P3 is true, but denies that P2 is true. This is the case even though Soames himself grants that he cannot provide the set of non-intentional facts upon which the meaning facts supervene. One might wonder if such a set of facts actually exists.

Feldman (1985) offers a version of the view that meaning facts are brute facts by presenting what he calls *robust platonism*. According to robust platonism, one directly *grasps* properties and presumably functions as well. Hence, I directly grasp the function of addition when using 'plus' and thus the fact that I meant addition by 'plus' is determined by the fact that when I use 'plus' I grasp the function of addition. Kripke does consider platonism but his comments are brief. At one point he says that Wittgenstein found appeal to platonic objects unhelpful. He also remarks "Platonic objects may be self-interpreting, or rather, they may need no interpretation; but ultimately there must be some mental entity involved that raises the skeptical problem" (*WRPL*: 54). But Feldman wants to claim that the only mental "item" involved is the grasping itself. One simply grasps the property or function in question and *grasping* is a brute relation that cannot be defined or analysed in terms of other relations or properties. Many philosophers reject this sort of platonism and thus they look elsewhere for an answer to the skeptic's argument.

In "New Work for a Theory of Universals" (1999), David Lewis offers an interesting response to the skeptical puzzle. Lewis says the fact that everything known up to the time of the question "What is 68 + 57?" is consistent with either answer (i.e. 125 or 5) being correct – that is, it is consistent with one's adding or quadding up to that time – provides us with a good reason for holding that the correct answer is 125 and that what we have been doing all along is adding and we are to continue on in the same way:

> How ironic that we were worried to find nothing positive to settle the matter in favor of addition! For the lack of anything positive that points either way just *is* what it takes to favor addition. Quaddition, being less natural and eligible, needs something positive in its favor. Addition can win by default.
>
> (D. Lewis 1999: 54)

On Lewis's view, properties are more or less natural. The naturalness of a property is a matter of degree. When we consider addition and quaddition, we see that addition, while not perfectly natural, is more natural than quaddition and hence other things being equal it is the more natural property that applies. In order to intend to quadd one needs to be in a state that rules out addition, since quaddition is the less natural of the two to intend to follow.

Lewis's solution depends on the idea that properties come in varying degrees of naturalness, quaddition is less natural than addition, and what one intends to do, other things being equal, is to instantiate the most natural (relevant?) property. Each of these claims can, of course, be questioned. Certainly the claim that addition is more natural than quaddition seems to beg the question against the skeptic. What could be more natural, one might ask, than a function that always produces the value 5 for any pair of numbers greater than a certain number? Lewis's solution is an interesting one and certainly one that deserves to be considered.

III

Kripke claims that Wittgenstein offered an answer to the skeptical argument: what Kripke called the skeptical solution. The skeptical solution accepts that there are no *facts* about meaning even though we do mean things. Meaning something is not constituted by a correspondence to facts or truth-conditions but rather by conditions of assertability. These conditions require us to be members of a linguistic community. As we noted above, Kripke offers rough assertability conditions, which involve the agreement of members of the community. Hence, to say that my use of the term 'plus' has meaning is to say that my use is in agreement with its use in my linguistic community. Some philosophers have questioned the involvement of the community in the skeptical solution. McGinn, for example, questions the need for agreement between members of the community as part of the assertability conditions:

> My first objection to this is that the reference to my own responses is strictly *redundant* in this assertability condition: for the correct condition is simply that I observe that you give the sum of pairs of numbers sufficiently often. This condition is, of course, entirely individualistic in that it refers only to the person to whom the rule is ascribed and to his behavior – no mention here of me or my community. Moreover, unless Kripke's community condition somehow embeds this individualistic condition it cannot give the right results: it is only if your agreement of response with me is correlated with your giving the sum of pairs of numbers that it is right for me to use such agreement as a basis for ascribing the rule of addition to you.
>
> (1984: 185)

McGinn's idea seems to be that you mean addition by 'plus' if I observe you giving sums or adding numbers when using 'plus'. Hence, the assertability condition for meaning 'plus' is based on your giving sums and not on any agreement between your responses and the rest of the community. This appears to be an acceptable description of our assertability conditions for meaning addition by 'plus' provided we have agreed on what it means to give the *sum* of two (or more) numbers. Yet this agreement – that is, the agreement of what we mean by 'sum' – requires community involvement. McGinn realizes that some might misunderstand the condition he offers, and so adds the following comment in a footnote:

> This assertability condition should not be read in such a way as to presuppose that the speaker has the concept of addition: that is, we should not assume that the computational behaviour is intentional under a description in which the concept of addition figures; the condition is rather that the speaker gives what is *in fact* the sum of pairs of numbers sufficiently often.
>
> (1984: 185, n.65)

Yet we need to be careful. There are many functions available for us to designate and we assumed for the purposes of presenting the skeptical argument that we use 'addition' to designate a particular function, but when considering the skeptical solution we must not assume too much about facts about meaning. The skeptical solution only applies *if* we accept the skeptical argument. So in discussing the "correctness" of the skeptical solution we cannot assume any facts about meaning (including facts about our own use of terms). The person to whom we ascribe meaning does and says various things. If we agree to use 'sum' to designate a certain function – namely, the function that we agree gives the answer *x* to the question 'what is *n* plus *m*?' – then to say that the speaker gives what is in fact the sum of pairs of numbers is to say that the person gives what we accept is the right answer for the use of 'plus'. This is just the function that we use 'sum' to designate. But the community is not redundant here. If there is no community, then the speaker cannot give the sum of pairs of numbers for the expression 'sum' would not designate any function (so the argument goes). We can only describe the speaker as giving the sum because *we* have agreed that by sum we shall mean the function described above.

Paul Boghossian, who agrees with McGinn that the community is not needed in giving assertability conditions, makes the following comment:

> It would be absurd for me, under conditions where I had good reason to believe that I had become prone to making arithmetical mistakes – perhaps owing to intoxication or senility or whatever – to insist on agreement with me as a precondition for crediting Jones with mastery of the concept of addition.
>
> (1989: 522)

Boghossian is right that if I am unsure about my own application of a concept or word, it would make little sense to require agreement with me to assert that Jones means what the community means by 'plus' (what we are calling 'addition'). But this is really beside the point. In discussing the issue at all, it is agreed or conceded that we (i.e. Kripke, the skeptic Kripke imagines, McGinn, Boghossian, the reader and I) mean something by our use of words. Otherwise we cannot even state the problem. Hence, the question to be answered is what is the basis for this meaning that we agree on? So although it is agreed we mean something and that we mean addition by 'plus', it cannot be assumed that the meaning is independent of agreement by the community with our responses. If there were no such agreement with respect to a given term α, in what sense could we say that my use of the term α is correct? It is not obvious that the community should play no role in the assertability conditions that are to replace the standard truth-conditions.

Another apparent problem with the skeptical solution is that a view of meaning that denies that there are any facts about meaning seems incoherent. Soames is one of the philosophers who has argued that a non-factual solution leads to a kind of incoherence. Soames's argument is based on the idea that while meaning statements are non-factual (and hence neither true nor false) they can be correct or incorrect depending on whether or not they satisfy the assertability conditions. So consider a particular sentence such as:

(1)   'plus' means addition.

Since (1) is neither true nor false it does not, as Soames puts it, express a proposition. Still, as Kripke pointed out, (1) is assertable (according to our conditions of assertability) while

(2)   'plus' does not mean addition

is not, or it is not correct to assert it. Similarly we can say that

(3)   '"plus" means addition' expresses a proposition

is also neither true nor false and hence does not itself express a proposition. However it, like (1), is assertable while:

(4)   '"plus" means addition' does not expresses a proposition

is not assertable. The idea is that we use phrases like 'expresses a proposition' and 'x means φ' in our language, so certain utterances of such expressions are acceptable (we all agree so) while others are not. But this leads to a problem, according to Soames:

> So we have it that ~S, but it is incorrect or mistaken for one seriously to utter that very sentence. In addition, the proponent of the skeptical solution must say something of the form *s does not express a proposition* on the basis of [(1)'s not expressing a proposition] and something of the form *s does express a proposition* on the basis of [3]. According to the non-descriptive version of the skeptical solution, this may not be a case of asserting contradictory propositions. Presumably, though, it is still incoherent – like ordering someone both to close the door and not to close it.   (1998a: 326)

By "non-descriptive version of the skeptical solution", Soames means what we have been calling the non-factual view. The problem should be clear. The solution has the consequence that (1) does not express a proposition, yet it also tells us that (4) (which says that (1) does not express a proposition) is not correct or assertable. Hence the very consequences of the solution to the skeptical argument are themselves not correct on the basis of the solution.

The skeptical solution may not be incoherent in the way that Soames suggests. It is not incoherent to order someone to both close the door and not close the door if two doors or two different times are involved. It is only incoherent if one orders someone to both close the door and not close the door at the same time with respect to the same door. In Kripke's interpretation of Wittgenstein, the conditions of assertability involve the circumstances of utterance or, in other words, he takes the context in which one utters a given sentence into account. Someone who accepted the non-factual skeptical solution may be able to offer a defence to the objections of Soames and others by noting that the same utterances may or may not be acceptable depending on the circumstance. When we are in the "philosophy room" (3) is not assertable, since (1) does not express a fact (proposition). Outside the philosophy room, (3) may be acceptable, but only if our ordinary practice permits it. So while our ordinary practice finds such sentences as "It is a fact that I meant addition by 'plus'" acceptable, it would be a mistake to read into that acceptance any suggestion that there are meaning facts of the sort that Russell, G. E. Moore and the early Wittgenstein claimed. Or to put the point another way, in the philosophy room it is *not* acceptable to assert "It is a fact that I meant addition by 'plus'" but it is acceptable in common speech. Clearly, Soames, Kripke, Wittgenstein and I are in the philosophy room, and hence the claim that (3) is acceptable is not acceptable here. Whether this kind of defence can really save the non-factual skeptical solution to the skeptical problem remains to be seen.

Conclusion

Saul Kripke's philosophy has had a great influence on the direction of analytic philosophy in the latter part of the twentieth century. His published work on logic, modality, reference, truth and meaning is widely discussed today and the literature related to Kripke's ideas is vast (as a simple glance at the limited Bibliography in this book will attest). Among the views that Kripke has presented and developed is the view that the relation of reference between words and the world is not what had been thought for most of the twentieth century. The traditional view was that reference takes place via descriptions of some sort: the descriptivism discussed in Chapter 2. As we discussed in that chapter, Kripke argued that reference takes place via some sort of chain of reference dependent on uses of expressions. This view is what some philosophers, such as Gareth Evans (1973), have labelled the *causal theory of names*.

The phrase 'causal theory of names' is not Kripke's, although in at least one place in the lectures he does mention that reference is determined by a causal chain (*NN*: 139). In any case, although the phrase now has common currency in philosophy, it is best used with caution. The phrase suggests that there is a cause-and-effect relation that obtains between the name and its bearer. Unless reference itself is a causal relation, however, Kripke's suggested programme for a theory does not imply any particular causal relation between a name and its bearer. Hence, it is not an objection to Kripke's view of naming that we have names for objects to which we do not stand in any (obvious) causal relation, such as mathematical objects or logical objects (as some have claimed). To avoid misunderstandings concerning Kripke's view it would be best if we chose another label for Kripke's view.

Kripke's position is also associated with the phrases 'the new theory of reference' and 'the direct theory of reference'. There are, however, some disadvantages in referring to Kripke's position with either phrase. First, Kaplan (1989b) introduced the phrase 'the direct theory of reference' to refer to his view of designation. One way that Kaplan defines the view of direct reference is in terms of the constituents of propositions. It is not clear that Kripke would agree with Kaplan's account of the nature of propositions and hence it is unclear that Kripke really accepts some of the basic tenets of Kaplan's direct theory. There is no doubt that there are many similarities between the two positions and that is why Kaplan's, Kripke's and other philosophers' views are often categorized under the 'direct reference theory' label. Still, Kripke's views should not be confused with Kaplan's, despite the level of agreement between them.

Stephen Schwartz (1977) introduced the phrase the 'new theory of reference' to refer to the views of a number of philosophers, including Donnellan, Putnam and Kripke. Again, the views of Kripke are very similar in many respects to the views of Putnam, Donnellan, Marcus and others but, as in the case of Kaplan, they differ in important respects. Moreover, when various philosophers speak of the new theory of reference, often they are not completely clear as to what is included in the theory. For example, in describing the new theory, Schwartz mentions Donnellan's rejection of (part of) Russell's theory of definite descriptions in favour of one that allows one to designate an object using a definite description, even if the description fails to describe the object. Donnellan called this use of descriptions the *referential use* (see Chapter 3). Kripke explicitly rejects Donnellan's view of the referential use of descriptions, however, and some have used Donnellan's distinction between two uses of descriptions as a way of defending descriptivism (although Donnellan has not done so). Given that Kripke rejects this aspect of Donnellan's view, it may not be wise to refer to Kripke's position as the 'new theory of reference'. It will depend on what is included in the "new theory".

Another reason for being cautious in labelling Kripke's views is the controversy over the origins of the views that have been labelled the *new theory of reference*. (For details on this controversy see Humphreys & Fetzer (1998).) Some suggest that Kripke has received too much credit for the ideas that comprise the new theory of reference. Given that Schwartz introduced the phrase to describe the views of a number of philosophers, Kripke included, it is less than charitable to deny Kripke's role in the presentation and development of the ideas contained in this theory. This is not to say that Kripke was the only philosopher working on these issues in the 1960s and 1970s. Yet Kripke's presentation and development of the ideas contained in the new theory have been a major influence on contemporary philosophy.

Some of Kripke's views are startling. His claim that there are necessary a posteriori and contingent a priori truths has resulted in a re-evaluation of the relationship between metaphysics and epistemology. Yet, I must agree with Robert Stalnaker's recent assessment of Kripke's views on reference and essence:

> while Kripke defends these theses about the descriptive semantics of names, the way the reference relation is determined, and the capacities and dispositions of human beings and physical objects (and I think he makes a persuasive case for each of them), his most important accomplishment is in the way he posed and clarified the questions, and not in the particular answers that he gave to them. (1997: 536–7)

What Stalnaker says about Kripke's views on reference applies to all of Kripke's work. What is special about Kripke is the philosophical and logical framework that he develops to answer various questions or to solve some puzzle or paradox. As we noted in the introduction, Kripke cannot be said to be a system-building philosopher in the manner of Kant or Leibniz. Instead, Kripke is a philosopher who finds puzzles or paradoxes in our way of thinking and then tries to unravel the Gordian knot for us. In the process, we find the connections to all sorts of other problems and issues that have been unnoticed before. I suspect that we will be talking about Kripke's philosophy for a long time to come.

The published work of Saul Kripke

1959. "A Completeness Theorem in Modal Logic", *The Journal of Symbolic Logic* **24**(1) (March), 1–14.

1959. "Distinguished Constituents" (abstract), *The Journal of Symbolic Logic* **24**(4) (December), 323.

1959. "Semantical Analysis of Modal Logic" (abstract), *The Journal of Symbolic Logic* **24**(4) (December), 323–4.

1959. "The Problem of Entailment" (abstract), *The Journal of Symbolic Logic* **24**(4) (December), 324.

1962. "'Flexible' Predicates of Formal Number Theory", *Proceedings of the American Mathematical Society* **13**(4) (August), 647–50.

1962. "The Undecidability of Monadic Modal Quantification Theory", *Zeitschrift für mathematische Logik und Grundlagen der Mathematik* **8**, 113–16.

1963. "Semantical Considerations on Modal Logic", *Acta Philosophica Fennica* **16**, 83–94. Reprinted in *Reference and Modality: Oxford Readings in Philosophy*, L. Linsky (ed.), 63–72. Oxford: Oxford University Press (1971).

1963. "Semantical Analysis of Modal Logic I. Normal Propositional Calculi", *Zeitschrift für mathematische Logik und Grundlagen der Mathematik* **9**, 67–96.

1964. "Transfinite Recursions on Admissible Ordinals, I" (abstract), *The Journal of Symbolic Logic* **29**(3) (September), 161–2.

1964. "Transfinite Recursions on Admissible Ordinals, II" (abstract), *The Journal of Symbolic Logic* **29**(3) (September), 162.

1964. "Admissible Ordinals and the Analytic Hierarchy" (abstract), *The Journal of Symbolic Logic* **29**(3) (September), 162.

1963. "Semantical Analysis of Intuitionistic Logic I". In *Formal Systems and Recursive Functions (Proceedings of the Eighth Logic Colloquium at Oxford, July, 1963)*, J. N. Crossley & M. A. E. Dummett (eds), 92–129. Amsterdam: North Holland.

1965. "Semantical Analysis of Modal Logic II. Non-Normal Modal Prositional Calculi". In *The Theory of Models (Proceedings of the 1963 International Symposium at Berkeley)*, J. W. Addison, L. Henkin & A. Tarski (eds), 206–20. Amsterdam: North Holland.

1967. "An Extension of a Theorem of Gaifman–Hales–Solovay", *Fundamenta Mathematicae* **61**, 29–32.

1971. "Identity and Necessity". In *Identity and Individuation*, M. K. Munitz (ed.), 135–64. New York: New York University Press.

1972. "Naming and Necessity". In *Semantics of Natural Language*, 2nd edn, D. Davidson (ed.), 253–355; addenda, 763–69. Dordrecht: Reidel. This paper was later published as a book with a foreword.

1975. "Outline of a Theory of Truth", *The Journal of Philosophy* **72**(19) (November), 690–716.

1976. "A Theory of Truth I. Preliminary Report" (abstract), *The Journal of Symbolic Logic* **41**(2), 556.

1976. "A Theory of Truth II. Preliminary Report" (abstract), *The Journal of Symbolic Logic* **41**(2), 556–7.

Saul Kripke

1976. "Is There a Problem about Substitutional Quantification?" In *Truth and Meaning*, G. Evans & J. McDowell (eds), 325–419. Oxford: Oxford University Press.

1977. "Speaker's Reference and Semantic Reference", *Midwest Studies in Philosophy* **II**, 255–76.

1979. "A Puzzle About Belief". In *Meaning and Use*, A. Margalit (ed.), 239–83. Dordrecht: Reidel.

1980. *Naming and Necessity*. Oxford: Basil Blackwell.

1981. "Wittgenstein on Rules and Private Language: An Elementary Exposition". In *Perspectives on the Philosophy of Wittgenstein*, I. Block (ed.), 238–312. Oxford: Basil Blackwell. This paper was later expanded into a book.

1982. *Wittgenstein on Rules and Private Language*. Oxford: Basil Blackwell.

1982. "Non-standard Models of Peano Arithmetic", with Simon Kochen. In *Logic and Algorithmic: An International Sumposium held in Honor of Ernst Specker*, H. Lanchi (ed.), 277–95, Monographies de L'Enseignement Mathématique 30. Geneva: University of Geneva Press.

1985. "Review of Three Articles by Kit Fine", *Journal of Symbolic Logic* **50**, 1083–93.

1986. "A Problem in the Theory of Reference: The Linguistic Division of Labor and the Social Character of Naming". In *Philosophy and Culture (Proceedings of the XVIIth World Congress of Philosophy)*, Editions du Beffroi, Editions Montmorency (Montreal), 241–7.

1992. "Individual Concepts: Their Logic, Philosophy, and Some of Their Uses", *Proceedings and Addresses of The American Philosophical Association* **66**(2) (October), 70–73. Summary of invited paper given at American Philosophical Association Eastern Division Meeting, Washington, D.C., December 1992.

Bibliography

Ackermann, D. F. 1979. "Proper Names, Essences and Intuitive Beliefs", *Theory and Decision* **11**, 5–26.

Ackermann, D. F. 1983. "Wittgenstein, Rules and Origin-Privacy", *Journal of Indian Council of Philosophical Research* **1** (Autumn), 63–9.

Akiba, K. 2000a. "Identity is Simple", *American Philosophical Quarterly* **37**(4), 389–401.

Akiba, K. 2000b. "Vagueness as a Modality", *Philosophical Quarterly* **50**, 359–70.

Aldridge, V. C. 1987. "Kripke on Wittgenstein on Regulation", *Philosophy* **62**, 375–84.

Allen, B. 1989. "Gruesome Arithmetic: Kripke's Sceptic Replies", *Dialogue* **28**, 257–64.

Allwein, G. & M. J. Dunn 1993. "Kripke Models for Linear Logic", *Journal of Symbolic Logic* **58**(2), 514–45.

Almog, J. 1981. "Dthis and Dthat: Indexicality Goes Beyond That", *Philosophical Studies* **39**, 347–81.

Almog, J. 1984a. "Believe it or Not: It is a Puzzle. Rejoinder to Suppes", *Synthese* **58**, 51–61.

Almog, J. 1984b. "Semantic Anthropology", *Midwest Studies* **9**, 479–89.

Almog, J. 1986. "Naming Without Necessity", *Journal of Philosophy* **83**(4), 210.

Almog, J. 1996. "The What and the How II: Reals and Mights", *Noûs* **30**(4), 413–33.

Anderson, E. 1994. "Kant, Natural Kind Terms, and Scientific Essentialism", *History of Philosophy Quarterly* **11**, 355–73.

Anscombe, G. E. M. 1985a. "Critical Notice: *Wittgenstein on Rules and Private Language*", *Canadian Journal of Philosophy* **15**(1), 103–9.

Anscombe, G. E. M. 1985b. "Review of Saul Kripke's *Wittgenstein on Rules and Private Language*", *Ethics* **95**, 342–52.

Armstrong, B. 1984. "Wittgenstein on Private Languages: It Takes Two to Talk", *Philosophical Investigations* **7**, 46–62.

Ayer, A. J. 1985. *Wittgenstein*. New York: Random House.

Bach, K. 1994. *Thought and Reference*. Oxford: Clarendon Press. First published 1987.

Baker, G. P. 1985. *Wittgenstein: Rules, Grammar and Necessity*. Oxford: Basil Blackwell.

Baker, G. & P. Hacker 1984a. "On Misunderstanding Wittgenstein: Kripke's Private Language Argument", *Synthese* **58**(3), 407–50.

Baker, G. & P. Hacker 1984b. *Scepticism, Rules and Language*. Oxford: Basil Blackwell.

Baker, G. & P. Hacker 1990. "Malcolm on Language and Rules", *Philosophy* **65**, 167–79.

Baker, J. M. 1981. "Kripke and Necessary Identity", *Dialogue* **20**, 19–22.

Baker, L. 1982. "Underprivileged Access", *Noûs* **16**, 227–41.

Baldwin, T. 1978–79. "Kripke, Pseudo-Kripke, and Wallace", *Analysis* **38–9**, 173–81.

Bales, S. 1993. "On Wittgenstein and Kripke: Mastering Language in Wittgenstein's Philosophical Investigations". In *Pursuits of Reason: Essays in Honor of Stanley Cavell*, T. Cohen, P. Guyer & H. Putnam (eds). Lubbock, TX: Texas Tech University Press.

Ballie, J. 1990. "Identity, Survival and Sortal Concepts", *Philosophical Quarterly* **40**, 183–94.

Bar-On, D. 1992. "On the Possibility of a Solitary Language", *Noûs* **26**(1), 27–46.

Barnette, R. 1977. "Kripke's Pains", *Southern Journal of Philosophy* **15**, 3–14.

Saul Kripke

Bayne, S. 1988. "Kripke's Cartesian Argument", *Philosophia* 18(2), 265–8.
Bayne, S. 1988–89. "On the Appearance of Contingency: A Rejoinder To Blum", *Philosophia* 19(4), 457–60.
Bealer, G. 1982. *Quality and Concept*. Oxford: Clarendon Press.
Bealer, G. 1987. "The Philosophical Limits of Scientific Essentialism", *Philosophical Perspectives* 1, 289–365.
Bealer, G. 1996a. "A Priori Knowledge and the Scope of Philosophy", *Philosophical Studies* 81, 121–42.
Bealer, G. 1996b. "Mental Properties", *Journal of Philosophy* 91, 185–208.
Bealer, G. 1996c. "On the Possibility of Philosophical Knowledge", *Philosophical Perspectives* 10, 1–34.
Bealer, G. 2000. "A Theory of the A Priori", *Pacific Philosophical Quarterly* 81(1), 1–30.
Belshaw, C. 1998. "Gold", *Theoria* 13, 415–26.
Benfield, D. 1974–75. "The Apriori–Aposteriori Distinction", *Philosophy and Phenomenological Research* 35, 151–66.
Benfield, D. & E. Erwin 1975. "Identity, Schmidentity – It's Not All the Same", *Philosophical Studies* 27, 145–8.
Bennett, D. 1969. "Essential Properties", *Journal of Philosophy* 66, 487–99.
Bertolef, R. 1980–81. "Kripke's Speaker Reference", *Analysis* 40–41, 70–72.
Bird, A. 2001. "Necessarily, Salt Dissolves in Water", *Analysis* 61(4), 267–74.
Blackburn, S. 1984. "The Individual Stikes Back", *Synthese* 58, 281–302.
Bloor, D. 1997. *Wittgenstein, Rules and Institutions*. London: Routledge.
Blum, A. 1989. "Bayne on Kripke", *Philosophia* 19(4), 455–6.
Blumenfeld, J. 1975. "Kripke's Refutation of Materialism", *Australasian Journal of Philosophy* 53, 1–6.
Boer, S. 1985. "Substance and Kind: Reflections on the New Theory of Reference". In *Analytical Philosophy in Comparative Perspective*, B. K. Matilal & J. L. Shaw (eds), 103–50. Dordrecht: Reidel.
Boghossian, P. A. 1989. "The Rule-Following Considerations", *Mind* 98, 507–49.
Boghossian, P. A. 1993. "Sense, Reference, and Rule Following". In *Naturalism and Normativity*, E. Villanueva (ed.), 135–41. Atascadero, CA: Ridgeview.
Bolton, C. J. 1996. "Proper Names, Taxonomic Names and Necessity", *Philosophical Quarterly* 46(183), 145–57.
Bostock, D. 1977. "Kripke on Identity and Necessity", *Philosophical Quarterly* 27(109), 313–24.
Bostock, D. 1988. "Necessary Truth and A Priori Truth", *Mind* 97, 343–79.
Bowen, K. A. 1979. *Model Theory for Modal Logic: Kripke Models for Modal Predicate Calculi*. Dodrecht: Reidel.
Boyd, R. 1980. "Materialism Without Reductionism: What Physicalism does not Entail". In *Readings in the Philosophy of Psychology*, vol. 1, N. Block (ed.), 67–107. Cambridge, MA: Harvard University Press.
Bradley, R. D. 1984. "Essentialism and the New Theory of Reference", *Dialogue* 23, 59–77.
Bradley, R. & N. Swartz 1979. *Possible Worlds*. Indianapolis, IN: Hackett.
Braun, D. 1991. "Proper Names, Cognitive Contents, and Beliefs", *Philosophical Studies* 62, 289–305.
Braun, D. 1995. "Katz on Names Without Bearers", *Philosophical Review* 104(4), 553–76.
Braun, D. 1996. "Demonstratives and their Linguistic Meanings", *Noûs* 30, 145–73.
Brennan, A. 1988. *Conditions of Identity*. Oxford: Clarendon Press.
Brody, B. 1973. "Why Settle for Anything Less than Good Old-Fashioned Aristotelian Essentialism?", *Noûs* 7, 351–65.
Brody, B. 1977. "Kripke on Proper Names", *Midwest Studies in Philosophy* 2, 64–9.
Brody, B. 1980. *Identity and Essence*. Princeton, NJ: Princeton University Press.
Brown, C. 1984. "The Necessary A Posteriori: A Response to Tichy", *Philosophical Studies* 45, 379–97.
Brown, C. 1986. "What is a Belief State?", *Midwest Studies in Philosophy* 10, 357–78.
Budd, M. 1984. "Wittgenstein on Meaning, Interpretation and Rules", *Synthese* 58, 303–24.
Burdick, H. 1993. "Non-Essentialistic Modal Logic, or Meaning and Necessity Revisited", *Philosophia* 22(1–2), 87–92.
Burge, T. 1973. "Reference and Proper Names", *Journal of Philosophy* 70, 425–39.
Burge, T. 1979a. "Semantical Paradox", *Journal of Philosophy* 76, 169–98.
Burge, T. 1979b. "Individualism and the Mental", *Midwest Studies in Philosophy* 4, 73–121.
Burgess, J. 1996. "Marcus, Kripke, and Names", *Philosophical Studies* 84, 1–47.

Burke, M. 1994. "Dion and Theon: An Essentialist Solution to an Ancient Puzzle", *Journal of Philosophy* **91**(3), 129–39.

Byrne, A. 1996. "On Misinterpreting Kripke's Wittgenstein", *Philosophy and Phenomenological Research* **56**, 339–43.

Byrne, A. 1998. "Chalmers' Two-Dimensional Argument against Physicalism", *Working Papers in Linguistics and Philosophy* **1**, 1–20.

Canfield, J. 1979. "Names and Causes", *Philosophical Studies* **35**, 71–80.

Canfield, J. 1996. "The Community View", *The Philosophical Review* **105**(4) (October), 469–88.

Carnap, R. 1946. "Modalities and Quantification", *Journal of Symbolic Logic* **11**, 33–43.

Carnap, R. 1947. *Meaning and Necessity*. Chicago, IL: University of Chicago Press.

Carney, J. D. 1975. "Kripke and Materialism", *Philosophical Studies* **27**, 279–82.

Carney, J. D. 1980. "The Hesperus and Phosphorous Puzzle", *Mind* **89**, 577–81.

Carril, D. 1978. "Designation and Identity", *Critica* **10**, 33–55.

Carter, W. 1976. "On A Priori Contingent Truths", *Analysis* **36**, 105–6.

Carter, W. 1982. "On Contingent Identity and Temporal Worms", *Philosophical Studies* **41**, 213–30.

Carter, W. 1987. "Contingent Identity and Rigid Designation", *Mind* **96**, 250–55.

Cartwright, R. L. 1968. "Some Remarks on Essentialism", *Journal of Philosophy* **65**, 615–26.

Cartwright, R. L. 1979. "Indiscernibility Principles", *Midwest Studies in Philosophy* **4**, 293–306. Also published in *Philosophical Essays*, 201–15 (Cambridge, MA: MIT Press, 1987).

Cassam, Q. 1986. "Science and Essence", *Philosophy* **61**, 95–107.

Casullo, A. 1974. "Kripke on the Identity Theory", *The Journal of Philosophy* **71** (October), 665–76.

Casullo, A. 1977. "Kripke on the A Priori and the Necessary", *Analysis* **37**, 152–9.

Casullo, A. 1988a. "Actuality and the A Priori", *Australasian Journal of Philosophy* **66**, 390–402.

Casullo, A. 1988b. "Necessity, Certainty, and the A Priori", *Canadian Journal of Philosophy* **18**, 43–66.

Casullo, A. 1988c. "Revisability, Reliabilism, and A Priori Knowledge", *Philosophy and Phenomenological Research* **44**, 187–213.

Chalmers, D. 1996. *The Conscious Mind: In Search of a Fundamental Theory*. New York: Oxford University Press.

Chalmers, D. 1999. "Materialism and the Metaphysics of Modality", *Philosophy and Phenomenological Research* **59**, 473–93.

Chandler, H. 1975. "Rigid Designation", *The Journal of Philosophy* **72**(9), 363–8.

Chandler, H. 1976. "Plantinga and the Contingently Possible", *Analysis* **36**, 106–9.

Chastain, C. 1975. "Reference and Context". In *Language, Mind, and Knowledge*, K. Gunderson (ed.), 194–269. Minneapolis, MN: University of Minnesota Press.

Chisholm, R. 1968. "Identity Through Possible Worlds: Some Questions", *Noûs* **1**, 1–8.

Chisholm, R. 1970. "Identity Through Time". In *Language, Belief and Metaphysics*, H. E. Kiefer & M. Munitz (eds), 163–82. New York: SUNY Press.

Chomsky, N. 1986. *Knowledge of Language: Its Nature, Origin, and Use*. New York: Praeger.

Christensen, C. 2001. "Escape from Twin Earth – Putnam's 'Logic' of Natural Kind Terms", *International Journal of Philosophical Studies* **9**(2), 123–50.

Cleve, J. V. 1986. "Mereological Essentialism, Mereological Conjunctivism, and Identity Through Time", *Midwest Studies in Philosophy* **11**, 141–56.

Coates, P. 1986–87. "Kripke's Sceptical Paradox: Normativeness and Meaning", *Mind* **95**, 77–80.

Coburn, R. 1986. "Individual Essences and Possible Worlds", *Midwest Studies in Philosophy* **9**, 165–83.

Cohen, S. 1978. "Essentialism in Aristotle", *Review of Metaphysics* **31**, 387–405.

Cole, D. J. & F. Foelber 1984. "Contingent Materialism", *Pacific Philosophical Quarterly* **65**, 74–85.

Collins, A. 1992. "On the Paradox Kripke Finds in Wittgenstein", *Midwest Studies in Philosophy* **14**, 74–88.

Cook, J. 1995. *Wittgenstein's Metaphysics*. Cambridge: Cambridge University Press.

Cook, M. 1979. "Singular Terms and Rigid Designators", *Southern Journal of Philosophy* **10**, 157–62.

Cover, J. A. & J. Hawthorne 1992. "Leibnizian Essentialism, Transworld Identity, and Counterparts", *History of Philosophy Quarterly* **9**, 425–44.

Cowles, D. 1994. "The Contingent A Priori: An Example Free of Existential Worry", *Philosophical Studies* **74**, 137–41.

Crary, A. & R. Read (eds) 2000. *The New Wittgenstein*. London: Routledge.

Crawford, E. 1994. "Laws, Natures, and Contingent Necessities", *Philosophy and Phenomenological Research* **54**(3), 649–67.

Crawford, E. 1998. "Essential Properties and Coinciding Objects", *Philosophy and Phenomenological Research* **53**(2), 649–67.

Crimmins, M. 1992. *Talk About Beliefs*. Cambridge, MA: MIT Press.

Crimmins, M. & J. Perry 1989. "The Prince and the Phone Booth: Reporting Puzzling Beliefs", *Journal of Philosophy* **86**(12), 685–711.

Dale, A. J. 1980. "Numerals and Number Designations", *Philosophical Studies*, **38**(4), 427–34.

Davies, M. K. 1981. *Meaning, Quantification, Necessity*. London: Routledge & Kegan Paul.

Davies, S. 1988. "Kripke, Crusoe and Wittgenstein", *Australasian Journal of Philosophy* **66**, 52–66.

Davis, L. 1979. "An Alternative Formulation of Kripke's Theory of Truth", *Journal of Philosophical Logic* **8**, 289–96.

De Sousa, R. B. 1974. "Kripke on Naming and Necessity", *Canadian Journal of Philosophy* **3**, 447–64.

Denkel, A. 1995. "Artifacts and Constituents", *Philosophy and Phenomenological Research* **55**(2), 311–22.

Devitt, M. 1975–76. "Semantics and the Ambiguity of Proper Names", *The Monist* **59**, 404–23.

Devitt, M. 1981a. "Donnellan's Distinction", *Midwest Studies in Philosophy* **6**, 511–24.

Devitt, M. 1981b. *Designation*. New York: Columbia University Press.

Devitt, M. 1990. "On Removing Puzzles About Belief Ascription", *Pacific Philosophical Quarterly* **71**, 165–81.

Diamond, C. 1991. *Realism and the Realistic Spirit*. Cambridge, MA: MIT Press.

Doepke, F. 1992. "Identity and Natural Kinds", *Philosophical Quarterly* **42**, 89–94.

Donnellan, K. 1966. "Reference and Definite Descriptions", *The Philosophical Review* **75**, 281–304.

Donnellan, K. 1972. "Proper Names and Identifying Descriptions". In *Semantics for Natural Languages*, D. Davidson & G. Harman (eds), 356–79. Dordrecht: Reidel.

Donnellan, K. 1973. "Substances as Individuals", *Journal of Philosophy* **70**, 711–12.

Donnellan, K. 1977. "The Contingent A Priori and Rigid Designators", *Midwest Studies in Philosophy* **2**, 12–27.

Donnellan, K. 1983. "Kripke and Shoemaker on Natural Kind Terms". In *Knowledge and Mind*, C. Ginet & S. Shoemaker (eds), 84–104. New York: Oxford University Press.

Double, R. 1976. "The Inconclusiveness of Kripke's Argument Against the Identity Theory", *Ausstellung* **3**, 156–65.

Dretske, F. 1970. "Epistemic Operators", *Journal of Philosophy* **67**, 1007–23.

Dummett, M. 1991. *The Logical Basis of Metaphysics*. Cambridge, MA: Harvard University Press.

Dummett, M. 1994. "Wittgenstein on Necessity: Some Reflections". In *Reading Putnam*, P. Clark & B. Hale (eds). Oxford: Blackwell.

Ebbs, G. 1997. *Rule Following and Realism*. Cambridge, MA: Harvard University Press.

Elder, C. 1994. "Laws, Natures, and Contingent Necessities", *Philosophy and Phenomenological Research* **54**(3), 649–67.

Eldridge, R. 1985–86. "The Normal and the Normative: Wittgenstein's Legacy, Kripke, and Cavell", *Philosophy and Phenomenological Research* **46**, 555–76.

Elga, A. 1998. *A Conceivability Argument*. Cambridge, MA: Department of Linguistics and Philosophy, MIT.

Ellis, B. D. & C. Lierse 1994. "Dispositional Essentialism", *Australasian Journal of Philosophy* **72**, 27–45.

Enc, B. 1975. "Necessary Properties and Linnaean Essentialism", *Canadian Journal of Philosophy* **5**, 83–102.

Erwin, E. 1974. "Are the Notions of 'A Priori Truth' and 'Necessary Truth' Extensionally Equivalent?", *Canadian Journal of Philosophy* **3**, 591–602.

Evans, G. 1973. "The Causal Theory of Names", *Aristotelian Society Supplementary Volume* **47**, 187–208.

Evans, G. 1979. "Reference and Contingency", *Monist* **62**, 161–89.

Evans, G. 1982. *The Varieties of Reference*. Oxford: Oxford University Press.

Fagin, R. 1994. "A Quantitative Analysis of Modal Logic", *Journal of Symbolic Logic* **59**, 209–52.

Fales, E. 1986. "Essentialism and the Elementary Constituents of Matter", *Midwest Studies in Philosophy* **11**, 391–402.

Farrell, R. 1981. "Metaphysical Necessity is Not Logical Necessity", *Philosophical Studies* **39**, 141–53.

Feit, N. 2001. "Rationality and Puzzling Beliefs", *Philosophy and Phenomenological Research* **63**(1) (July), 29–55.

Feldman, F. 1973. "Kripke's Argument Against Materialism", *Philosophical Studies* **24**, 416–19.

Feldman, F. 1974. "Kripke on the Identity Theory", *The Journal of Philosophy*, **71**, 665–76.

Feldman, F. 1980. "Identity, Necessity, and Events". In *Readings in the Philosophy of Psychology*, vol. 1, N. Block (ed.), 148–56. Cambridge, MA: Harvard University Press.

Feldman, F. 1985. "Wittgenstein on Rules and Private Language: An Elementary Exposition by Saul Kripke" (critical notices), *Philosophy and Phenomenological Research* **49**, 683–87.

Field, H. 1986. "Stalnaker on Intentionality", *Pacific Philosophical Quarterly* **67**, 98–112.

Fine, K. 1977. "Postscript". In *Worlds, Times and Selves*, A. N. Prior & K. Fine, 116–68. London: Duckworth.

Fine, K. 1978a. "Model Theory for Modal Logic Part I: The *De Re / De Dicto* Distinction", *Journal of Philosophical Logic* **7**, 125–56.

Fine, K. 1978b. "Model Theory for Modal Logic Part II: The Elimination of *De Re* Modality", *Journal of Philosophical Logic* **7**, 277–306.

Fine, K. 1981a. "Model Theory for Modal Logic Part III: Existence and Predication", *Journal of Philosophical Logic* **10**, 293–307.

Fine, K. 1981b. "First-Order Modal Theories I – Sets", *Noûs* **15**, 177–205.

Fine, K. 1991. "A Study of Ontology", *Noûs* **25**, 263–94.

Fine, K. 1994a. "Essence and Modality", *Philosophical Perspectives* **8**: *Logic and Language*, 1–16.

Fine, K. 1994b. "Senses of Essence". In *Modality, Morality, and Belief: Essays in Honor of Ruth Barcan Marcus*, W. Sinnott-Armstrong (ed.), 53–74. Cambridge: Cambridge University Press.

Fine, K. 1994–95. "Ontological Dependence", *Aristotelian Society Proceedings* **95**, 269–90.

Fine, K. 1995a. "Senses of Essence". In *Modality, Morality and Belief*, W. Sinnott-Armstrong (ed.), 53–77. Cambridge: Cambridge University Press.

Fine, K. 1995b. "The Logic of Essence", *Journal of Philosophical Logic* **24**, 241–73.

Fine, K. 2000. "Semantics for the Logic of Essence", *Journal of Philosophical Logic* **29**(5), 543–84.

Fitch, G. 1976. "Are There Necessary *A Posteriori* Truths?", *Philosophical Studies* **30**, 243–7.

Fitch, G. 1981. "Names and the '*De Re–De Dicto*' Distinction", *Philosophical Studies* **39**, 25–34.

Fitch, G. 1984. "Indeterminate Descriptions", *Canadian Journal of Philosophy* **14**, 257–76.

Fitch, G. 1987. *Naming and Believing*. Dordrecht: Reidel.

Fitch, G. 1988. "The Nature of Singular Propositions". In *Philosophical Analysis: A Defense by Example*, D. Austin (ed.), 281–97. Dordrecht: Kluwer.

Fitch, G. 1993. "Non Denoting", *Philosophical Perspectives* **7**, 461–86.

Fitch, G. 2001. "On Theoretical Identifications", *Philosophical Perspectives* **15**, 379–92.

Fitch, G. 2004. "On Kripke and Statements", *Midwest Studies in Philosophy* (forthcoming).

Fitting, M. 1985. "A Kripke–Kleene Semantics for Logic Programs", *Journal of Logic Programming* **4**, 295–312.

Fitting, M. 1986. "Notes on the Mathematical Aspects of Kripke's Theory of Truth", *Notre Dame Journal of Formal Logic* **27**, 75–88.

Follesdal, D. 1986. "Essentialism and Reference". In *The Philosophy of W.V. Quine*, L. E. Hahn & P. A. Schilpp (eds), 97–114. La Salle, IL: Open Court.

Fogelin, R. 1995. "Pierre, Saul, Ruth, and Bob and a Puzzle About Belief". In *Modality, Morality, and Belief: Essays in Honor of Ruth Barcan Marcus*, W. Sinnott-Armstrong (ed.), 201–14. Cambridge: Cambridge University Press.

Forbes, G. 1980. "Origin and Identity", *Philosophical Studies* **37**(4) (May), 353–62.

Forbes, G. 1981a. "An Anti-Essentialist Note on Substances", *Analysis* **41**, 32–7.

Forbes, G. 1981b. "On the Philosophical Basis of Essentialist Theories", *Journal of Philosophical Logic* **10**, 73–99.

Forbes, G. 1983. "Actuality and Context-Dependence I", *Analysis* **43**, 123–8.

Forbes, G. 1985. *The Metaphysics of Modality*. Oxford: Oxford University Press.

Forbes, G. 1989. *Languages of Possibility*. Oxford: Blackwell.

Forbes, G. 1991. "States of Affairs, Bedeutung and the Contingent A Priori", I *New Inquiries*

Saul Kripke

into *Meaning and Truth*, N. Cooper & P. Engel (eds), 111–13. Hemel Hempstead: Harvester Wheatsheaf.

Forbes, G. 1994. "Donnellan on a Puzzle about Belief", *Philosophical Studies* **73**, 169–80.

Forbes, G. 1997. "Essentialism". In *A Companion to the Philosophy of Language*, B. Hale & C. Wright (eds), 515–33. Oxford: Blackwell.

Gallois, A. 1986–87. "Rigid Designation and the Contingency of Identity", *Mind* **95**, 57–76.

Gallois, A. 1988. "Carter on Contingent Identity and Rigid Designation", *Mind* **97**, 273–8.

Gallois, A. 1993a. "Ramachandran on Restricting Rigidity", *Mind* **102**, 151–5.

Gallois, A. 1993b. "Reply to Ramachandran" *Mind* **102**, 159–62.

Gallois, A. 1998. *Occasions of Identity*. Oxford: Oxford University Press.

Garcia-Carpintero, M. 1998a. "Fregean versus Kripkean Reference", *Teorema* **17**, 21–44.

Garcia-Carpintero, M. 1998b. "Indexicals as Token-reflexives", *Mind* **107**, 529–63.

Garrett, R. 1991. "Putnam on Kripke's Puzzle", *Erkenntnis* **34**(3), 271–85.

Gibbard, A. 1975. "Contingent Identity", *Journal of Philosophical Logic* **4**, 187–221.

Ginet, C. 1992. "The Dispositionalist Solution to Wittgenstein's Problem about Understanding a Rule: Answering Kripke's Objections". In *The Wittgenstein Legacy*, Midwest Studies in Philosophy 12, P. A. French, T. E. Uehling Jr & H. K. Wettstein (eds), 53–73. Notre Dame, IN: University of Notre Dame Press.

Gjelsvik, O. 1987. "A Kripkean Objection to Kripke's Argument against Identity Theories", *Inquiry* **30**, 435–50.

Goble, L. F. 1972. "Necessity and Identity", *Canadian Journal of Philosophy* **2**, 55–72.

Goldfarb, W. 1985. "Kripke on Wittgenstein on Rules", *The Journal of Philosophy* **82**, 471–88.

Graham, P. 1999. "Defending Millianism", *Mind* **108**(431) (July), 555–61.

Gumb, R. 1984. "Conservative Kripke Closures", *Synthese* **60**, 39–49.

Gupta, A. 1982. "Truth and Paradox", *Journal of Symbolic Logic* **11**, 1–60.

Hacking, I. 1993. "On Kripke's and Goodman's Uses of 'Grue'", *Philosophy* **68**, 269–95.

Halbach, V. 1977. "Tarskian and Kripkean Truth", *Journal of Philosophical Logic* **26**(1), 69–80.

Hale, B. 1997. "Rule-Following, Objectivity and Meaning". In *A Companion to the Philosophy of Language*, B. Hale & C. Wright (eds), 369–96. Oxford: Blackwell.

Hall, R. 1984. "Pierre and the New World Makers", *Australasian Journal of Philosophy* **62**(3), 283–8.

Handfield, T. 2001. "Dispositional Essentialism and the Possibility of a Law-abiding Miracle", *Philosophical Quarterly* **51**(205), 484–94.

Hanna, R. 1998. "A Kantian Critique of Scientific Essentialism", *Philosophy and Phenomenological Research* **58**(3), 497–528.

Hawthorne, J. & T. Gendler 2000. "Origin Essentialism: The Arguments Reconsidered", *Mind* **109**, 285–98.

Hazen, A. 1981. "Davis' Formulation of Kripke's Theory of Truth: A Correction", *Journal of Philosophical Logic* **10**(2), 309–11.

Heimir, G. 1991. "The Contingent A Priori, Kripke's Two Types of Examples", *Australasian Journal of Philosophy* **69**, 195–205.

Heimir, G. 1994. "Necessity, A Priority, and True Identity Statements", *Erkenntnis* **40**, 227–42.

Heimir, G. 1999. "Justification and Relative A Priority", *Ratio* **12**, 148–61.

Herzberger, H. G. 1982. "Notes on Naive Semantics", *Journal of Symbolic Logic* **11**, 61–102.

Hill, C. S. 1981. "Why Cartesian Intuitions are Compatible with the Identity Thesis", *Philosophy and Phenomenological Research* **42**, 254–65.

Hill, C. S. 1997. "Imaginability, Conceivability, Possibility and the Mind–Body Problem", *Philosophical Studies* **87**, 61–85.

Hill, C. S. 1998. "Chalmers on the Apriority of Modal Knowledge", *Analysis* **58**, 20–26.

Hintikka, J. 1961. "Modality and Quantification", *Theoria* **27**, 119–28.

Hintikka, J. 1967. "Individuals, Possible Worlds, and Epistemic Logic" *Noûs* **1**, 33–62.

Hintikka, J. & G. Sandu 1995. "The Fallacies of the New Theory of Reference", *Synthese* **104**, 245–83.

Hoffman, P. 1985. "Kripke on Private Language", *Philosophical Studies* **47**, 23–8.

Hollinger, R. 1976. "A Defense of Essentialism", *Personalist* **57**, 327–44.

Holman, E. 1979. "Is the Physical World Colourless?", *Australasian Journal of Philosophy* **57**, 295–304.

Holman, E. 1988. "Qualia, Kripkean Arguments, and Subjectivity", *Philosophy Research Archives* **13**, 411–29.

Hooker, J. 1976. "Brody on Essentialism", *Philosophical Studies* **29**(5), 263–71.

Horgan, T. 1983. "Supervenience and Cosmic Hermeneutics", *Southern Journal of Philosophy* **22**, 19–38.

Horwich, P. 1984. "Critical Notice of Kripke's *Wittgenstein on Rules and Private Language*", *Philosophy of Science* **51**, 163–71.

Horwich, P. 1990. "Wittgenstein and Kripke on the Nature of Meaning", *Mind and Language* **5**, 105–21.

Hudson, J. & M. Tye 1980. "Proper Names and Definite Descriptions with Widest Possible Scope", *Analysis* **40**, 63–4.

Humphrey, J. 1996. "Kripke's Wittgenstein and the Impossibility of Private Language: The Same Old Story?", *Journal of Philosophical Research* **21**, 197–207.

Humphreys P. W. & J. H. Fetzer (eds) 1998. *The New Theory of Reference: Kripke, Marcus, and its Origins*. Dordrecht: Kluwer.

Inwagen, P. 1992. "There Is No Such Thing As Addition", *Midwest Studies in Philosophy* **17**, 138–59.

Ishiguro, H. 1979. "Contingent Truths and Possible Worlds", *Midwest Studies in Philosophy* **4**, 352–67.

Jackson, F. 1998. *From Metaphysics to Ethics: A Defense of Conceptual Analysis*. Oxford: Oxford University Press.

Jacquette, D. 1987. "Kripke and the Mind–Body Problem", *Dialectica* **41**, 293–300.

Jeshion, R. 2000. "Ways of Taking a Meter", *Philosophical Studies* **99**(3) (June), 297–318.

Jeshion, R. 2002. "Acquaintanceless *DE RE* Belief". In *Meaning and Truth: Investigations in Philosophical Semantics*, J. Campbell, M. O'Rourke & D. Shier (eds), 53–78. New York: Seven Bridges Press.

Johnston, M. 1997. "Manifest Kinds", *The Journal of Philosophy* **94**, 564–83.

Johnston, P. 1977. "Origin and Necessity", *Philosophical Studies* **32**, 413–18.

Jubien, M. 1988. "Problems with Possible Worlds". In *Philosophical Analysis: A Defense by Example*, D. Austin (ed.), 299–322. Dordrecht: Kluwer.

Jubien, M. 1993a. *Ontology, Modality, and the Fallacy of Reference*. Cambridge: Cambridge University Press.

Jubien, M. 1993b. "Proper Names", *Philosophical Perspectives* **7**, 487–504.

Kaplan, D. 1973. "Bob and Carol and Ted and Alice". In *Approaches to Natural Language*, J. Hintikka (ed.), 490–518. Dordrecht: Reidel.

Kaplan, D. 1989a. "Demonstratives". In *Themes from Kaplan*, J. Almog, J. Perry & H. Wettstein (eds), 481–563. Oxford: Oxford University Press. Originally published 1977.

Kaplan, D. 1989b. "Afterthoughts". In *Themes from Kaplan*, J. Almog, J. Perry & H. Wettstein (eds), 565–614. Oxford: Oxford University Press.

Karmo, T. 1983. "Contingent Non-Identity", *Australasian Journal of Philosophy* **61**, 185–7.

Katz, J. 1994. "Names Without Bearers", *Philosophical Review* **103**(1), 1–39.

Keefe, R. 1995. "Contingent Identity and Vague Identity", *Analysis* **55**, 183–90.

Kirk, R. 1982. "Physicalism, Identity, and Strict Implication", *Ratio* **24**, 131–41.

Kirwan, C. 1970. "How Strong are the Objections to Essence?", *Proceedings of the Aristotelian Society* **71**, 43–59.

Kitcher, P. 1980. "Apriority and Necessity", *Australian Journal of Philosophy*, **58**(2) (June), 89–101.

Kleene, S. C. 1952. *Introduction to Metamathematics*. New York: Van Nostrand.

Kober, M. 1998. "Kripkenstein Meets the Chinese Room: Looking for the Place of Meaning from a Natural Point of View", *Inquiry* **41**, 317–32.

Kreisel, G. 1983. "Review of *Wittgenstein on Rules and Private Language*", *Canadian Philosophical Reviews* **3**, 287–89.

Kremer, M. 1988. "Kripke and the Logic of Truth", *Journal of Philosophical Logic* **17**, 225–78.

Kremer, M. 2000. "Wilson on Kripke's Wittgenstein", *Philosophy and Phenomenological Research* **60**(3) (May), 571–84.

Kroon, F. 1981. "Kant and Kripke on the Identifiability of Modal and Epistemic Notions", *Southern Journal of Philosophy* **19**, 49–60.

Kroon, F. 1982. "Contingency and the A Posteriori", *Australasian Journal of Philosophy* **60**, 40–45.

Kroon, F. 1987. "Kant, Kripke, and Gold", *Kant-Studien* **78**, 442–58.

Kroon, F. 1989. "Circles and Fixed Points in Description Theories of Reference", *Noûs* **23**, 373–82.

Kvart, I. 1986. "Kripke's Belief Puzzle", *Midwest Studies in Philosophy* **10**, 287–325.

Langford, S. & M. Ramachandran 2000. "Rigidity, Occasional Identity and Leibniz' Law", *Philosophical Quarterly* **50**, 518–26.

LaPorte, J. 1996. "Chemical Kind Term Reference and the Discovery of Essence", *Noûs* **30**(1), 112–32.

LaPorte, J. 2000. "Rigidity and Kind", *Philosophical Studies* **97**, 293–316.

Lehmann, S. K. 1978. "The Hintikka–Kripke Problem", *Philosophia* **8**(1), 59–70.

Leplin, J. 1979. "Theoretical Identification and the Mind–Body Problem", *Philosophia* **8**, 673–88.

Leplin, J. 1988. "Is Essentialism Unscientific?", *Philosophy of Science* **55**, 493–510.

Levin, M. 1975. "Kripke's Argument Against the Identity Thesis", *The Journal of Philosophy* **72**, 149–67.

Levine, J. 1998. "Conceivability and the Metaphysics of Mind", *Noûs* **32**(4), 449–80.

Lewis, C. I. & C. H. Langford 1932. *Symbolic Logic*. New York: Dover Publications. Second edition 1959.

Lewis, D. K. 1968. "Counterpart Theory and Quantified Modal Logic", *Journal of Philosophy* **65**, 113–26. Republished in D. K. Lewis, *Philosophical Papers*, vol. 1 (Oxford: Oxford University Press, 1983), 26–46.

Lewis, D. K. 1979a. "Scorekeeping in a Language Game", *Journal of Philosophical Logic* **8**, 339–59

Lewis, D. K. 1979b. "Attitudes *de dicto* and *de se*", *Philosophical Review* **88**, 513–43.

Lewis, D. K. 1981a. "Index, Content, and Context". In *Philosophy and Grammar*, S. Kanger & S. Ohman (eds), 79–100. London: Reidel.

Lewis, D. K. 1981b. "What Puzzling Pierre Does Not Believe", *Australasian Journal of Philosophy* **59**, 3–32.

Lewis, D. K. 1983. *Philosophical Papers*, vol. 1. Oxford: Oxford University Press.

Lewis, D. K. 1986. *On the Plurality of Worlds*. Oxford: Basil Blackwell.

Lewis, D. K. 1999. *Papers in Metaphysics and Epistemology*. Cambridge: Cambridge University Press.

Linsky, L. 1969. "Reference, Essentialism, and Modality", *Journal of Philosophy* **66**, 287–300.

Linsky, L. (ed.) 1971. *Reference and Modality*. Oxford: Oxford University Press.

Linsky, L. 1977. *Names and Descriptions*. Chicago, IL: University of Chicago Press.

Linsky, B. & E. Zalta 1994. "In Defense of the Simplest Quantified Modal Logic", *Philosophical Perspectives* **8**, 431–58.

Loar, B. 1976. "The Semantics of Singular Terms", *Philosophical Studies* **30**, 53–377.

Loar, B. 1985. "Review of Kripke's Book", *Noûs* **19**.

Loar, B. 1987. "Names in Thought", *Philosophical Studies* **51**(2), 169–85.

Loar, B. 1988a. "Social Content and Psychological Content". In *Contents of Thought*, R. Grimm & D. Merrill (eds), 99–110. Tucson, AZ: University of Arizona Press.

Loar, B. 1988b. "Reply: A New Kind of Content". In *Contents of Thought*, R. Grimm & D. Merrill (eds), 121–39. Tucson, AZ: University of Arizona Press.

Lourdes, V. 1995. "Can Peter Be Rational?". In *Philosophical Issues 6: Content*, E. Villanueva (ed.), 311–24. Atascadero, CA: Ridgeview.

Lowe, E. J. 1982. "On the Alleged Necessity of True Identity Statements", *Mind* **91**, 579–84.

Lycan, W. 1974. "Kripke and the Materialists", *The Journal of Philosophy* **71** (October), 677–98.

Lycan, W. 1994. *Modality and Meaning*. Dordrecht: Kluwer.

Lycan, W. & S. Shapiro 1986. "Actuality and Essence", *Midwest Studies in Philosophy* **11**, 343–77.

MacBeth, D. 1995. "Pragmatism and the Philosophy of Language", *Philosophy and Phenomenological Research* **50**(3) (September), 501–24.

Mackie, J. 1974. "De *What* Re *Is* De Re *Modality*?", *The Journal of Philosophy* **71**(16), 551–61.

Mackie, J. 1974. "Locke's Anticipation of Kripke", *Analysis* **34**(16), 177–80.

Mackie, P. 1987. "Essence, Origin, and Bare Identity", *Mind* **96**, 173–201.

Mackie, P. 1994. "Sortal Concepts and Essential Properties", *Philosophical Quarterly* **44**, 311–33.

Marcus, R. 1946. "A Functional of First Order Based on Strict Implication", *Journal of Symbolic Logic* **11**, 1–16.

Marcus, R. 1947. "The Identity of Individuals in a Strict Functional Calculus of First Order", *Journal of Symbolic Logic* **12**, 12–15.

Marcus, R. 1961. "Modalities and Intentional Languages", *Synthese* **13**, 303–22.

Marcus, R. 1962. "Discussion on the Paper of Ruth B. Marcus" (panel discussion includes R. Marcus, W. Quine, S. Kripke, J. McCarty, and D. Follesdal), *Synthese* **14**, 132–43.

Marcus, R. 1967. "Essentialism in Quantified Modal Logic", *Noûs* **1**, **91–6**.

Marcus, R. 1981. "A Proposed Solution to a Puzzle About Belief", *Midwest Studies in Philosophy* **6**, 501–10.

Martin, C. B. & J. Heil 1998. "Rules and Powers", *Philosophical Perspectives* **12**, 283–312.

Martin, R. L. & P. W. Woodruff 1975. "On Representing 'True-in-*L*' in *L*", *Philosophia* **5**, 213–17.

Matthen, M. 1984. "Ostension, Names and Natural Kind Terms", *Dialogue* **23**, 43–58.

Maxwell, G. 1978. "Rigid Designators and Mind–Brain Identity", *Minnesota Studies in the Philosophy of Science* **9**, 365–405.

McClure, G. 1978. "Contingent A Priori Truths", *Philosophy and Phenomenological Research* **38**, 399–409.

McDowell, J. 1980. "Quotation and Saying That". In *Reference, Truth and Reality*, M. Platts (ed.), 206–37. London: Routledge & Kegan Paul.

McDowell, J. 1981. "Review of Naming and Necessity", *The Times Literary Supplement*, 16 January, 61–2.

McGee, V. 1989. "Symposium: Kripke's Theory of Truth: Applying Kripke's Theory of Truth", *Journal of Philosophy* **86**(10), 530–39.

McGee, V. 1991. *Truth, Vagueness, and Paradox: An Essay on the Logic of Truth*. Indianapolis, IN: Hackett.

McGinn, C. 1976a. "'A Priori' and 'A Posteriori' Knowledge", *Proceedings of the Aristotelian Society* **76**, 195–208.

McGinn, C. 1976b. "On the Necessity of Origin", *The Journal of Philosophy* **73** (Mar.), 127–35.

McGinn, C. 1977. "Anomalous Monism and Kripke's Cartesian Intuitions", *Analysis* **37**, 78–80.

McGinn, C. 1975. "A Note on the Essence of Natural Kinds", *Analysis* **35**(6), 177–83.

McGinn, C. 1982. "Rigid Designation and Semantic Value", *Philosophical Quarterly* **32**(127), 97–115.

McGinn, C. 1984. *Wittgenstein on Meaning: An Interpretation and Evaluation*. Oxford: Basil Blackwell.

McGinn, M. 1984. "Kripke on Wittgenstein's Sceptical Problem", *Ratio* **26**, 19–32.

McKinsey, M. 1976. "Divided Reference in Causal Theories of Names", *Philosophical Studies* **30**, 235–42.

McKinsey, M. 1978. "Names and Intentionality", *Philosophical Review* **87**, 171–200.

McKinsey, M. 1980. "Against a Defence of Cluster Theories", *Analysis* **40**(1), 1–5.

McKinsey, M. 1984. "Causality and the Paradox of Names", *Midwest Studies* **9**, 491–515.

McKinsey, M. 1986. "Mental Anaphora", *Synthese* **66**, 159–75.

McKinsey, M. 1994. "Individuating Beliefs", *Philosophical Perspectives* **8**, 303–30.

McKinsey, M. 2002. "The Semantic Basis of Externalism". In *Meaning and Truth: Investigations in Philosophical Semantics*, J. Campbell, M. O'Rourke & D. Shier (eds), 34–52. New York: Seven Bridges Press.

Mendelsohn, R. 1979. "Rigid Designation and Informative Identity Sentences", *Midwest Studies in Philosophy* **4**, 307–20.

Miller, A. 1998. *Philosophy of Language*, London: UCL Press.

Miller, A. 2000. "Horwich, Meaning and Kripke's Wittgenstein", *Philosophical Quarterly* **50**(199), 161–74.

Millikan, R. 1990. "Truth Rules, Hoverflies, and the Kripke–Wittgenstein Paradox", *Philosophical Review* **99**, 323–53.

Minar, E. 1994. "Paradox and Privacy: On sec. 201–202 of Wittgenstein's *Philosophical Investigations*", *Philosophy and Phenomenological Research* **54**, 43–75.

Minar, E. 1991. 1991. "Wittgenstein and the 'Contingency' of Community", *Pacific Philosophical Quarterly* **72**, 203–34.

Miscevic, N. 1996. "Computationalism and the Kripke–Wittgenstein Paradox", *Aristotelian Society Proceedings* **96**, 215–30.

Moore, M. J. 1982–83. "Rigidity and Identity Across Possible Worlds", *Analysis* **42**, 83–4.

Moser, P. & K. Flannery 1985. "Kripke and Wittgenstein: Intention Without Paradox", *The Heythrop Journal* **26**, 311–16.

Mucciolo, L. 1975. "On Kripke's Argument against the Identity Thesis", *Philosophia* **5**, 499–506.

Myro, G. 1985. "Time and Essence", *Midwest Studies in Philosophy* **11**, 331–41.

Neale, S. 1990. *Descriptions*. Cambridge, MA: MIT Press.

Noonan, H. 1979. "Rigid Designation", *Analysis* **39**, 174–82.

Noonan, H. 1981. *Objects and Identity*. The Hague: Martinus Nijhoff.

Noonan, H. 1980–81. "Names and Belief", *Proceedings of the Aristotelian Society* **81**, 93–108.

Noonan, H. 1983. "The Necessity of Origin", *Mind* **92**, 1–20.

Noonan, H. 1991. "Indeterminate Identity, Contingent Identity and Abelaidian Predicates", *Philosophical Quarterly* **41**, 183–93.

Nute, D. 1978a. "Do Proper Names Always Rigidly Designate?", *Canadian Journal of Philosophy* **8**, 475–84.

Nute, D. 1978b. "Proper Names: How to Become a Causal Theorist While Remaining a Sense Theorist", *Philosophia* **8**, 43–57.

Oderberg, D. 1976. "On A Priori Contingency", *Analysis* **36**, 201–3.

Oderberg, D. 1987. "Kripke and 'Quus'", *Theoria* **53**, 115–20.

Oderberg, D. 1993. *The Metaphysics of Identity Over Time*. New York: St Martin's Press.

O'Leary-Hawthorne, J. & J. McDonough 1998. "Numbers, Minds, and Bodies: A Fresh Look at Mind–Body Dualism", *Philosophical Perspectives* **12**, 356–9.

Oppy, G. 1987. "Williamson and the Contingent A Priori", *Analysis* **47**, 188–93.

Oppy, G. 1995. "On An Argument About Reference to Future Individuals", *Philosophical Quarterly* **45**(178), 84–7.

Over, D. 1983. "On Kripke's Puzzle", *Mind* **92**, 253–6.

Parsons, T. 1967. "Grades of Essentialism in Quantified Modal Logic", *Noûs* **1**, 181–91.

Parsons, T. 1969. "Essentialism and Quantified Modal Logic", *Philosophical Review* **78**, 35–52.

Peacocke, C. 1975. "Proper Names, Reference and Rigid Designation". In *Meaning, Reference and Necessity: New Studies in Semantics*, S. Blackburn (ed.), 109–32. Cambridge: Cambridge University Press.

Peacocke, C. 1978. "Necessity and Truth Theories", *Journal of Philosophical Logic* **7**, 473–500.

Perrick, M. 1985. "Kant and Kripke on Necessary Empirical Truths", *Mind* **94**, 596–8.

Perry, J. 1979. "The Problem of the Essential Indexical", *Noûs* **13**, 3–21.

Perry, J. 2001. "Of Knowledge, Possibility and Consciousness", the 1999 Jean Nicod Lectures, May, Massachusetts Institute of Technology.

Peterson, P. 1986. "Revealing Designators and Acquaintance with Universals", *Noûs* **20**, 291–311.

Peterson, P. 1995. "Are Some Propositions Empirically Necessary?", *Philosophy and Phenomenological Research* **55**, 251–77.

Pineau, L. 1990. "Russell on Ordinary Names and Synonymy", *History of Philosophy Quarterly* **7**, 93–108.

Plantinga, A. 1970. "World and Essence", *Philosophical Review* **79**, 461–92.

Plantinga, A. 1974. *The Nature of Necessity*. Oxford: Oxford University Press.

Plantinga, A. 1976. "Actualism and Possible Worlds", *Theoria* **42**, 139–60.

Plantinga, A. 1978. "The Boethian Compromise", *American Philosophical Quarterly* **15**, 129–38.

Plantinga, A. 1983. "On Existentialism", *Philosophical Studies* **44**, 1–20.

Plantinga, A. 1987. "Two Concepts of Modality: Modal Realism and Modal Reductionism", *Philosophical Perspectives* **1**, *Metaphysics*, 189–231.

Price, M. 1982. "On the Non-Necessity of Origin", *Canadian Journal of Philosophy* **12**, 33–45.

Prior, A. 1956. "Modality and Quantification in S5", *Journal of Symbolic Logic* **21**, 60–62.

Prior, A. 1957. *Time and Modality*. Oxford, Oxford University Press.

Prior, A. 1963. "Is the Concept of Referential Opacity Really Necessary?", *Acta Philosophica Fennica* **16**, 189–99.

Putnam, H. 1962. "It Ain't Necessarily So", *Journal of Philosophy* **59**, 658–71.

Putnam, H. 1973. "Meaning and Reference", *Journal of Philosophy* **70**, 699–711.

Putnam, H. 1977. "Is Semantics Possible?". In *Naming, Necessity, and Natural Kinds*, S. Schwartz (ed.), 102–18. Ithaca, NY: Cornell University Press.

Putnam, H. 1979. "Comments". In *Meaning and Use*, A. Margolis (ed.), 284–8. Dordrecht: Reidel.

Putnam, H. 1983. "Analyticity and Apriority: Beyond Wittgenstein and Quine". In *Realism and Reason, Philosophical Papers, Volume 3*, 115–39. Cambridge: Cambridge University Press.

Putnam, H. 1990. "Is Water Necessarily H_2O?". In *Realism with a Human Face*, J. B. Conant (ed.), 54–79. Cambridge, MA: Harvard University Press.

Quine, W. V. 1943. "Notes on Existence and Necessity", *Journal of Philosophy* **40**, 113–27.

Quine, W. V. 1960. *Word and Object*. Cambridge, MA: MIT Press.

Quine, W. V. 1966a. "Three Grades of Modal Involvement". In *The Ways of Paradox*, 156–74. New York: Random House.

Quine, W. V. 1966b. "Reply to Professor Marcus". In *The Ways of Paradox*, 175–83. New York: Random House. Originally published 1961.

Ramachandran, M. 1989. "Sense and Schmidentity (Discussions)", *Philosophical Quarterly* **39**(157) (October), 463–71.

Ramachandran, M. 1994–95. "Methodological Reflections on Two Kripkean Strategies", *Aristotelian Society Proceedings* **95**, 67–81.

Ray, R. 1980. "Transparent and Opaque Reference", *Philosophical Studies* **38**(4) (November), 435–45.

Ray, G. 1994. "Kripke and The Existential Complaint", *Philosophical Studies* **74**, 121–35.

Read, R. 1995. "The Unstatability of Kripkean Scepticisms", *Philosophical Papers* **24**(1), 67–74.

Reimer, M. 1998. "Donnellan's Distinction/Kripke's Test", *Analysis* **58**, 89–100.

Richard, M. 1983. "Direct Reference and Ascription of Belief", *Journal of Philosophical Logic* **12**, 425–52.

Richard, M. 1990. *Propositional Attitudes*. Cambridge, Cambridge University Press.

Richard, M. 1993a. "Articulated Terms", *Philosophical Perspectives* **7**, 207–30.

Richard, M. 1993b. "Sense, Necessity, and Belief", *Philosophical Studies* **69**, 243–63.

Richard, M. 1998. "Commitment", *Philosophical Perspectives* **12**, 255–81.

Roberts, L. 1985. "Problems about the Material and Formal Modes in the Necessity of Identity Statements", *Journal of Philosophy* **82**, 562–72.

Robertson, T. 1998. "Possibilities and the Argument for Origin Essentialism", *Mind* **107**, 729–49.

Robertson, T. 2000. "Essentialism: Origin and Order", *Mind* **109**(434) (April), 299–307.

Rocca, M. 1993. "Kripke's Essentialist Argument Against the Identity Theory", *Philosophical Studies* **69**, 101–12.

Rocca, M. 1996. "Essentialists and Essentialism", *Journal of Philosophy* **93**(4), 186–202.

Rosenberg, J. F. 1993. "Another Look at Proper Names", *Philosophical Perspectives* **7**, 505–30.

Rosenberg, J. F. 1994. *Beyond Formalism: Naming and Necessity for Human Beings*. Philadelphia, PA: Temple University Press.

Roy, T. 2000. "Things and De Re Modality", *Noûs* **34**(1), 56–84.

Rudebusch, G. 1986–87. "Hoffman on Kripke's Wittgenstein", *Philosophical Research Archives* **12**, 177–82.

Russell, B. 1905. "On Denoting", *Mind* **14**, 479–93.

Russell, B. 1956. "The Philosophy of Logical Atomism". In *Logic and Knowledge*, R. Marsh (ed.), 177–281. New York: Macmillan. Originally published 1918.

Russell, B. 1959. *The Problems of Philosophy*. Oxford: Oxford University Press. Originally published 1912.

Russell, B. & A. Whitehead 1910–13. *Principia Mathematica*, 3 vols. Cambridge: Cambridge University Press.

Ryckman, T. 1988. "The Millian Theory of Names and the Problems of Negative Existentials and Non-Referring Names". In *Philosophical Analysis: A Defense by Example*, D. Austin (ed.), 241–9. Dordrecht: Kluwer.

Ryckman, T. 1993. "Contingency, A Prioricity and Acquaintance", *Philosophy and Phenomenological Research* **53**, 323–43.

Saarinen, E. 1982. "How to Frege a Russell–Kaplan", *Noûs* **16**, 253–76.

Salmon, N. 1979. "How Not to Derive Essentialism from the Theory of Reference", *The Journal of Philosophy* **76**, 703–25.

Salmon, N. 1982. *Reference and Essence*. New York: Blackwell.

Salmon, N. 1986a. *Frege's Puzzle*. Cambridge, MA: MIT Press.

Salmon, N. 1986b. "Modal Paradox: Parts and Counterparts, Points and Counterpoints", *Midwest Studies in Philosophy* **9**, 75–120.

Salmon, N. 1987. "Existence", *Philosophical Perspectives* **1**, *Metaphysics*, 49–108.

Salmon, N. 1989. "The Logic of What Might Have Been", *Philosophical Review* **98**, 3–38.

Salmon, N. 1991. "How Not to Become a Millian Heir", *Philosophical Studies* **62**, 165–77.

Salmon, N. 1993a. "Analyticity and Apriority", *Philosophical Perspectives* **7**, *Language & Logic*, 125–33.

Salmon, N. 1993b. "Relative and Absolute Apriority", *Philosophical Studies* **69**, 83–100.

Salmon, N. 1995. "Being of Two Minds: Belief with Doubt", *Noûs* **29**, 1–20.

Salmon, N. 1998. "Nonexistence", *Noûs* **32**, 277–319.

Salmon, N. 2002. "Mythical Objects". In *Meaning and Truth: Investigations in Philosophical Semantics*, J. Campbell, M. O'Rourke & D. Shier (eds), 105–23. New York: Seven Bridges Press.

Salmon, N. & S. Soames 1988. *Propositions and Attitudes*. New York: Oxford University Press.

Sartorelli, J. 1991. "McGinn on Concept Scepticism and Kripke's Sceptical Argument", *Analysis* **51**(2) (March), 79–84.

Schiffer, S. 1977. "Naming and Knowing", *Midwest Studies in Philosophy* **2**, 28–41.

Schiffer, S. 1978. "The Basis of Reference", *Erkenntnis* **13**, 171–206.

Schiffer, S. 1981. "Indexicals and the Theory of Reference", *Synthese* **49**, 43–100.

Schiffer, S. 1987. *Remnants of Meaning*. Cambridge, MA: MIT Press.

Schiffer, S. 1996. "Belief Ascription", *Journal of Philosophy* **92**, 102–7.

Schwartz, S. (ed.) 1977. *Naming, Necessity, and Natural Kinds*. Ithaca, NY: Cornell University Press.

Scruton, R. 1984. *"Wittgenstein on Rules and Private Language* by S. A. Kripke", *Mind* **93**, 592–602.

Searle, J. 1958. "Proper Names", *Mind* **67**, 166–73.

Searle, J. 1979. "Referential and Attributive", *Monist* **62**, 190–208.

Searle, J. 1983. *Intentionality*. Cambridge: Cambridge University Press.

Searle, J. 1987. "Indeterminacy, Empiricism, and the First Person", *The Journal of Philosophy* **84**, 123–46.

Segerberg, K. 1973. "Two-dimensional Modal Logic", *Journal of Philosophical Logic* **2**, 77–96.

Sharvy, R. 1983. "Individuation, Essence and Plentitude", *Philosophical Studies* **44**, 61–70.

Sher, G. 1977. "Kripke, Cartesian Intuitions and Materialism", *Canadian Journal of Philosophy* **7**, 227–38.

Sidelle, A. 1989. *Necessity, Essence and Individuation*. Ithaca, NY: Cornell University Press.

Sidelle, A. 1992a. "Identity and the Identity-like", *Philosophical Topics* **20**(1), 269–92.

Sidelle, A. 1992b. "Rigidity, Ontology, and Semantic Structure", *The Journal of Philosophy* **89**, 410–30.

Sidelle, A. 1995. "A Semantic Account of Rigidity", *Philosophical Studies* **80**, 69–105.

Skvortsov, D. 1995. "On the Predicate Logic of Finite Kripke Frames", *Studia Logica* **54**, 79–88.

Skvortsov, D. 1998. "On some Kripke Complete and Kripke Incomplete Intermediate Predicate Logics", *Studia Logica* **61**, 281–92.

Slote, M. 1974. *Metaphysics and Essence*. Oxford: Oxford University Press.

Smith, A. D. 1984. "Rigidity and Scope", *Mind* **93**, 177–93.

Smith, A. D. 1987. "Semantical Considerations on Rigid Designators", *Mind* **96**, 83–92.

Smith, P. 1985. "Names, Identity, and Necessity". In *Exercises in Analysis*, I. Hacking (ed.), 147–69. Cambridge: Cambridge University Press.

Soames, S. 1987. "Direct Reference, Propositional Attitudes, and Semantic Content", *Philosophical Topics* **15**, 47–87.

Soames, S. 1998a. "Facts, Truth Conditions, and the Skeptical Solution to the Rule-Following Paradox", *Philosophical Perspectives* **12**, 313–48.

Soames, S. 1998b. "Skepticism about Meaning: Indeterminacy, Normativity, and the Rule-Following Paradox". In *Meaning and Reference*, A. Kazmi (ed.), 211–49. Calgary: University of Calgary Press.

Soames, S. 1998c. "The Modal Argument: Wide Scope and Rigidified Descriptions", *Noûs* **32**, 1–23.

Soames, S. 1999. *Understanding Truth*. Oxford: Oxford University Press.

Soames, S. 2002. *Beyond Rigidity: The Unfinished Semantic Agenda of* Naming and Necessity. Oxford: Oxford University Press.

Sosa, D. 1996. "The Import of the Puzzle about Belief", *The Philosophical Review* **105**, 373–402.

Splitter, L. 1980. "McGinn and Essential Properties of Natural Kinds", *Australian Journal of Philosophy* **58**, 19–25.

Stalnaker, R. 1976. "Possible Worlds", *Noûs* **10**, 65–75.

Stalnaker, R. 1978. "Assertion". In *Syntax and Semantics: Pragmatics*, vol. 9, P. Cole (ed.), 315–32. New York: Academic Press.

Stalnaker, R. 1986. "Counterparts and Identity", *Midwest Studies in Philosophy* **11**, 121–40.

Stalnaker, R. 1987. "Semantics for Belief", *Philosophical Topics* **15**, 177–90.

Stalnaker, R. 1997. "Reference and Necessity". In *A Companion to the Philosophy of Language*, B. Hale & C. Wright (eds), 534–54. Oxford: Blackwell.

Stalnaker, R. 1999. *Context and Content: Essays on Intentionality in Speech and Thought*. New York: Oxford University Press.

Stanford, K. & P. Kitcher 2000. "Refining the Causal Theory of Reference for Natural Kind Terms", *Philosophical Studies* **97**, 99–129.

Stanley, J. 1997. "Names and Rigid Designation". In *A Companion to the Philosophy of Language*, B. Hale & C. Wright (eds), 555–85. Oxford: Blackwell.

Stebbins, S. 1980. "Necessity and Natural Language", *Philosophical Studies* **37**(1) (January), 1–13.

Steinman, R. 1985. "Kripke Rigidity versus Kaplan Rigidity", *Mind* **94**, 431–42.

Stern, D. 1995. *Wittgenstein On Mind and Language*. Oxford: Oxford University Press.

Steward, H. 1990. "Identity Statements and the Necessary A Posteriori", *Journal of Philosophy* **87**, 385–98.

Stine, G. 1973. "Essentialism, Possible Worlds, and Propositional Attitudes", *Philosophical Review* **82**, 471–82.

Stock, G. 1988. "Leibniz and Kripke's Sceptical Paradox", *Philosophical Quarterly* **38**, 326–9.

Stroud, B. 2000. *Meaning, Understanding, and Practice*. Oxford: Oxford University Press.

Summerfield, D. 1990. "*Philosophical Investigations 201*: A Wittgensteinian Reply to Kripke", *Journal of the History of Philosophy* **28** (July), 417–38.

Sussman, A. 1981. "Counterfactuals and Non-Trivial 'De Re' Modalities", *Ratio* **23**, 139–40.

Suter, R. 1992. *Interpreting Wittgenstein: A Cloud of Philosophy, a Drop of Grammar*. Philadelphia, PA: Temple University Press.

Sutton, J. 2001. "The Contingent *A Priori* and Implicit Knowledge", *Philosophy and Phenomenological Research* **63**, 251–77.

Suzuki, Nobu-Yuki, 1997. "Kripke Frame with Graded Accessibility and Fuzzy Possible World Semantics", *Studia Logica* **59**, 249–69.

Swinburne, R. G. 1975. "Analyticity, Necessity and Apriority", *Mind* **84**, 225–43.

Tarski, A. 1944. "The Semantic Conception of Truth", *Philosophy and Phenomenological Research* **4**, 341–76.

Tarski, A. 1956. "The Concept of Truth in Formalized Languages". In *Logic, Semantics, and Metamathematics*, J. H. Woodger (trans.), 152–278. Oxford: Oxford University Press. Originally published 1933.

Taschek, W. 1988. "Would a Fregean be Puzzled by Pierre? (Discussions)" *Mind* **97**, 99–104.

Teghrarian, S. 1994. "Wittgenstein, Kripke, and the 'Paradox' of Meaning". In *Wittgenstein and Contemporary Philosophy*, S. Teghrarian (ed.). Bristol: Thoemmes.

Teller, P. 1975. "Essential Properties: Some Problems and Conjectures", *The Journal of Philosophy* **72**, 233–48.

Tienson, J. 1984. "Hesperus and Phosphorous I", *Australasian Journal of Philosophy* **62**(2), 169–73.

Tomberlin, J. 1990. "Essentialism and Possible Worlds", *Philosophy and Phenomenological Research* **50**, supplement, 251–62.

Tye, M. 1978. "The Puzzle of Hesperus and Phosphorous", *Australasian Journal of Philosophy* **56**, 219–24.

Vision, G. 1980. "Linsky on Rigid Designation and Sense", *Australian Journal of Philosophy* **58**, 291–7.

Von Morstein, P. 1980. "Kripke, Wittgenstein and the Private Language Argument", *Grazer Philosophische Studien* **11**, 61–74.

Wettstein, H. 1981. "Demonstrative Reference and Definite Descriptions", *Philosophical Studies* **40**, 241–57.

Wettstein, H. 1989. "Turning the Tables on Frege or How is it That 'Hesperus is Hesperus' is Trivial?", *Philosophical Perspectives* **3**, 316–39.

Wettstein, H. 1991. *Has Semantics Rested on a Mistake? And Other Essays*. Stanford, CA: Stanford University Press.

White, S. 1982. Partial Character and the Language of Thought", *Pacific Philosophical Quarterly* **63**, 347–65.

White, S. 1991. *The Unity of the Self*. Cambridge, MA: MIT Press.

Wiggins, D. 1974. "Essentialism, Continuity and Identity", *Synthese* **28**, 321–59.

Wiggins, D. 1975. "Identity, Designation, Essentialism and Physicalism", *Philosophia* **5**(1–2), 1–30.

Saul Kripke

Wiggins, D. 1976. "The *De Re* 'Must'; a Note on the Logical Form of Essentialist Claims". In *Truth and Meaning: Essays in Semantics*, G. Evans & J. McDowell (eds), 285–312. Oxford: Oxford University Press.

Wiggins, D. 1976. "Identity, Necessity and Physicalism". In *Philosophy of Logic: Papers and Discussions*, S. Körner (ed.). Berkeley, CA: University of California Press.

Wiggins, D. 1979. "Mereological Essentialism: Asymmetrical Essential Dependence and the Nature of Continuants", *Grazer Philosophischer Studien* **718**, 297–315.

Wiggins, D. 1980. *Sameness and Substance*. Cambridge, MA: Harvard University Press.

Wilkerson, T. E. 1993. "Species, Essences and the Names of Natural Kinds", *Philosophical Quarterly* **43**, 1–19.

Williamson, T. 1986. "The Contingent A Priori: Has it Anything to do with Indexicals?", *Analysis* **46**, 113–17.

Wilson, G. 1983. "Why Contingent Identity is Necessary", *Philosophical Studies* **43**, 301–27.

Wilson, G. 1998. "Semantic Realism and Kripke's Wittgenstein", *Philosophy and Phenomenological Research* **58**, 99–122.

Winch, P. 1984. "Facts and Super-facts (Saul A. Kripke, *Wittgenstein on Rules and Private Language*", *The Philosophical Quarterly* **33**, 398–404.

Wong, K. 1996a. "Sentence-Relativity and the Necessary A Posteriori", *Philosophical Studies* **81**, 53–91.

Wong, K. 1996b. "Singular Propositions and the 'A Priori'", *Journal of Philosophical Research* **21**, 107–16.

Woodfield, A. 1978. "Identity Theories and the Argument from Epistemic Counterparts", *Analysis* **38**, 140–43.

Woods, J. 1971. "Essentialism, Self-Identity, and Quantifying In". In *Identity and Individuation*, M. K. Munitz (ed.), 165–98. New York: New York University Press.

Wreen, M. 1983. "Kripke's Contingent A Priori", *International Studies in Philosophy* **15**, 55–9.

Wreen, M. 1998. "Proper Names and the Necessity of Identity Statements", *Synthese* **114**, 319–35.

Wright, C. 1984. "Kripke's Account of the Argument Against Private Language", *The Journal of Philosophy* **81**, 759–78.

Wright, C. 1989. "Critical Notice of Colin McGinn, *Wittgenstein on Meaning*", *Mind* **98**, 289–305.

Yablo, S. 1987. "Identity, Essence, and Indiscernibility", *The Journal of Philosophy* **84**, 293–314.

Yablo, S. 1989. "Symposium: Kripke's Theory of Truth: Truth, Definite Truth, and Paradox", *Journal of Philosophy* **86**, 530–39.

Yablo, S. 1992. "Cause and Essence", *Synthese* **93**, 403–49.

Yablo, S. 1993. "Is Conceivability a Guide to Possibility?", *Philosophy and Phenomenological Research* **53**, 1–42.

Yoshida, R. M. 1975. "De Sousa on Kripke and the Theoretical Identities", *Canadian Journal of Philosophy* **5**, 137–41.

Yu, P. 1980. "The Modal Argument Against Description Theories of Names", *Analysis* **40**, 208–9.

Zalabardo, J. 1989. "Rules, Communities and Judgement", *Critica* **21**, 33–58.

Zalabardo, J. 1997. "Kripke's Normativity Argument", *Canadian Journal of Philosophy* **27**, 467–88.

Zalta, E. 1988a. "Logical and Analytic Truths that are Not Necessary", *Journal of Philosophy* **85**, 57–74.

Zalta, E. 1988b. *Intensional Logic and the Metaphysics of Intentionality*. Cambridge, MA: MIT Press.

Zemach, E. M. 1994. "Identity and Epistemic Counterparts", *Philosophia* **23**, 265–70.

Index